# Mastering Dart

Master the art of programming high-performance applications with Dart

**Sergey Akopkokhyants**

[PACKT] open source
community experience distilled
PUBLISHING

BIRMINGHAM - MUMBAI

# Mastering Dart

First published: November 2014

Production reference: 1131114

Published by Packt Publishing Ltd.
Livery Place
35 Livery Street
Birmingham B3 2PB, UK.

ISBN 978-1-78398-956-0

www.packtpub.com

Cover image by Pratyush Mohanta (tysoncinematics@gmail.com)

# Credits

**Author**
Sergey Akopkokhyants

**Reviewers**
Yan Cui

Predrag Končar

Jana Moudrá

Martin Sikora

**Acquisition Editor**
Sonali Vernekar

**Content Development Editor**
Govindan K

**Technical Editor**
Shashank Desai

**Copy Editor**
Roshni Banerjee

**Project Coordinator**
Sageer Parkar

**Proofreaders**
Simran Bhogal

Maria Gould

Ameesha Green

Paul Hindle

**Indexers**
Monica Ajmera Mehta

Priya Sane

**Graphics**
Disha Haria

Abhinash Sahu

**Production Coordinator**
Shantanu N. Zagade

**Cover Work**
Shantanu N. Zagade

# About the Author

**Sergey Akopkokhyants** is a software architect with more than 20 years of professional experience in designing and developing client- and server-side applications. He is also a certified Java developer and a project manager. He has general knowledge of many tools, languages, and platforms.

For the past 5 years, Sergey has been responsible for customizing and producing web-oriented applications for wholesale business management solutions projects for several worldwide mobile communication companies. His responsibilities have been architecture design and guidance of client software development using Flex, ActionScript, HTML, JavaScript, TypeScript, Dart, and client-server integration with Java. He is also a founder and active contributor in several open source projects on GitHub, such as Dart Web Toolkit (DWT) and Angular Dart UI.

Sergey is passionate about web design and development and likes sharing his expertise with others, helping them develop their skills and increase their productivity. He has also reviewed the books *Learning Dart* and *Dart Cookbook*, both by Packt Publishing.

I would like to thank my wife, Lada, and my parents, Alexander and Tamara, for their constant and invaluable support.

I also wish to express my deep gratitude and appreciation to Jeffrey Johnson for his valuable feedback.

# About the Reviewers

**Yan Cui** is a lead server developer at the award-winning, London-based gaming company, Gamesys. He focuses on building highly distributed and scalable server solutions for Gamesys's social and mobiles games. He is a regular speaker at conferences on topics such as F#, AOP, and NoSQL and is active on his blog at http://theburningmonk.com.

He is the co-author of *F# Deep Dives*, *Manning Publications*, and the author of an upcoming book on cross-platform mobile development with F# by Packt Publishing. His Twitter handle is @theburningmonk.

**Predrag Končar** is a game developer and multimedia researcher. His primary areas of interest are games and combining technology and art. He is also into image and audio processing and interactive design, and he likes to spend his free time painting. In the past 12 years, he has worked as a technical and creative director for many online projects, published over 40 online games, participated in the production of several iOS apps, and also reviewed the books *Corona SDK Mobile Game Development Beginner's Guide* and *Corona SDK Application Design*, both by Packt Publishing. He has a strong background in Unity, C#, ActionScript, Lua, MEL script, Maya, and Python. He is a member of Mensa and ACM SIGGRAPH.

**Jana Moudrá** is a passionate developer and modern web and mobile technologies evangelist. She created her first web page at the age of 10. At that time, she had no idea what her future field of expertise would be. Later, she became interested in technologies such as JavaScript and jQuery, but finally ended up with the Dart programming language. She has been exploring it since Milestone 2 (M2). She is also interested in the area of user experience, design, and Android app development. She cofounded the company Juicymo, where she works on juicy apps and products. When she is not working, she organizes developer-related events on her favorite technologies for the Czech developers' community. You can visit her company's website at `http://www.juicymo.cz/en`.

**Martin Sikora** has been professionally programming since 2006 for companies such as Miton CZ and SYMBIO Digital in various languages, mostly PHP. Since 2012, he has been freelancing, working on projects in Python, PHP, Dart, Objective-C, and AngularJS. He is a Zend Certified Engineer and was member of the winning team of Google Dart Hackathon 2012, Prague. Occasionally, Martin writes tutorials at `http://www.binpress.com/`.

# www.PacktPub.com

## Support files, eBooks, discount offers, and more

For support files and downloads related to your book, please visit www.PacktPub.com.

Did you know that Packt offers eBook versions of every book published, with PDF and ePub files available? You can upgrade to the eBook version at www.PacktPub.com and as a print book customer, you are entitled to a discount on the eBook copy. Get in touch with us at service@packtpub.com for more details.

At www.PacktPub.com, you can also read a collection of free technical articles, sign up for a range of free newsletters and receive exclusive discounts and offers on Packt books and eBooks.

http://PacktLib.PacktPub.com

Do you need instant solutions to your IT questions? PacktLib is Packt's online digital book library. Here, you can search, access, and read Packt's entire library of books.

## Why subscribe?

- Fully searchable across every book published by Packt
- Copy and paste, print, and bookmark content
- On demand and accessible via a web browser

## Free access for Packt account holders

If you have an account with Packt at www.PacktPub.com, you can use this to access PacktLib today and view 9 entirely free books. Simply use your login credentials for immediate access.

# Table of Contents

# Preface

It's only been a few years since the Dart programming language was born and it has become eminent and well-known not only within Google, but also in the wider community of developers. It has grown into a powerful tool to help developers produce efficient and consistent source code for web clients and standalone and server-side programs. The Dart development team and independent contributors have created some good documentation, so getting started with programming using Dart isn't that hard. You can program within different development environments such as the Eclipse-based Dart Editor; IDE plugins for IntelliJ IDEA and WebStorm; and text editor plugins for Sublime Text 3, Emacs, and Vim.

Actual development on Dart is quite similar to Java, C#, or any other object-oriented languages, so you can have your first short application up and running in a short amount of time. To go further, you can use the tutorials, code labs, and examples on the official Dart website (`https://www.dartlang.org/`). If you want to improve your level of expertise, you can read through the set of books on Dart that have been published in the last couple of years. You should always bear in mind that creating high-level, secure, and internationally compliant code is more complex than the application created in the beginning.

This book is designed to help you make the most effective use of the Dart programming language, its SDK libraries, and a rich set of publicly available packages. Feel free to refer to any chapter that you need to get more in-depth knowledge about. If you feel you have missed something major, go back and read the earlier chapters. The chapters in the book are arranged in such a way that you can easily learn more in a step by step manner.

I enjoy working with the Dart programming language and am really happy to share my enthusiasm and expertise with you to help you make use of the language in a more effective and comfortable manner.

# What this book covers

*Chapter 1, Beyond Dart's Basics,* helps you take a step further to understand the concept of programming in the Dart language. It shows the best practices to use functions and closures and dives into the world of classes and mixins.

*Chapter 2, Advanced Techniques and Reflection,* lets you get a firm grasp on how to use generics, errors and exceptions, and annotations, and it takes you through Mirrors of reflection.

*Chapter 3, Object Creation,* helps you understand how objects can be created and will help you make a right choice that will be useful in different business cases.

*Chapter 4, Asynchronous Programming,* explores advanced technologies to organize asynchronous code execution. It shows you the best practices of Future, zones, and isolates.

*Chapter 5, The Stream Framework,* shows you how Dart manages streams. It teaches you how the single-subscription and broadcast streams can be used in different cases and scenarios.

*Chapter 6, The Collection Framework,* introduces you to the Dart collection frameworks. It shows which data structure of a collection is appropriate in specific cases based on patterns and performance consideration.

*Chapter 7, Dart and JavaScript Interoperation,* shows you how to use Dart and JavaScript together to build web applications. It lists problems and shows solutions you can use to communicate between Dart and JavaScript and the existing JavaScript program.

*Chapter 8, Internalization and Localization,* explains you how the i18n and l10n access can be embedded into your code to help you design and develop web applications that enable easy localization for different cultures, regions, and languages.

*Chapter 9, Client-to-server Communication,* helps you organize and create client-to-server communications. It has the answer on presumably the most important questions about the right choice of libraries and packages in specific scenarios.

*Chapter 10, Advanced Storage,* explains how can store data locally on a client, break the storage limits, and prevent security issues in your web applications. It will again touch upon cookies and demonstrate how to use Web Storage and the elaborate, more powerful, and more useful IndexedDB to store a large amount of data in the web browser.

*Chapter 11, Supporting Other HTML5 Features*, introduces you to different HTML5 features such as notifications, native drag-and-drop, geolocation, and canvas.

*Chapter 12, Security Aspects*, helps you understand the different aspects of security in web applications.

# What you need for this book

Any modern PC installed with Windows, Linux, or Mac OS should be sufficient to run the code samples in the book. All the software used in the book is open source and freely available on the Web. The following are the links to the software:

- Java (https://java.com/en/download)
- Dart (https://www.dartlang.org)
- wrk—a HTTP benchmarking tool (https://github.com/wg/wrk)

# Who this book is for

If you are a software engineer who has basic or intermediate knowledge of the Dart programming language and have possibly used this language to develop applications earlier, this is the book for you. The book reveals the different ways of developing client- and server-side applications on Dart and includes enough examples for both. For beginners, it will serve as a guide to rapidly accelerate from a novice level to the master level; for intermediate to advanced developers, it will quickly fill in the gaps on Dart.

# Conventions

In this book, you will find a number of styles of text that distinguish between different kinds of information. Here are some examples of these styles, and an explanation of their meaning.

Code words in text, database table names, folder names, filenames, file extensions, pathnames, dummy URLs, user input, and Twitter handles are shown as follows: "The inst variable holds a reference to the original object in the reflectee property."

A block of code is set as follows:

```
// AssemblyLine.
class AssemblyLine {
  // List of items on line.
```

```
List _items = [];

// Add [item] to line.
add(item) {
  _items.add(item);
}

// Make operation on all items in line.
make(operation) {
  _items.forEach((item) {
    operation(item);
  });
}
}
```

Any command-line input or output is written as follows:

```
sudo apt-get install libnss3-tools
```

**New terms** and **important words** are shown in bold. Words that you see on the screen, in menus or dialog boxes for example, appear in the text like this: "Expand the **Web SQL** tree item from the **Resources** tab to see the Web SQL storage data."

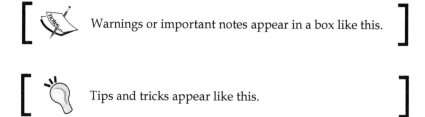

Warnings or important notes appear in a box like this.

Tips and tricks appear like this.

# Reader feedback

Feedback from our readers is always welcome. Let us know what you think about this book—what you liked or may have disliked. Reader feedback is important for us to develop titles that you really get the most out of.

To send us general feedback, simply send an e-mail to feedback@packtpub.com, and mention the book title via the subject of your message.

If there is a topic that you have expertise in and you are interested in either writing or contributing to a book, see our author guide on www.packtpub.com/authors.

# Customer support

Now that you are the proud owner of a Packt book, we have a number of things to help you to get the most from your purchase.

# Downloading the example code

You can download the example code files for all Packt books you have purchased from your account at `http://www.packtpub.com`. If you purchased this book elsewhere, you can visit `http://www.packtpub.com/support` and register to have the files e-mailed directly to you.

# Errata

Although we have taken every care to ensure the accuracy of our content, mistakes do happen. If you find a mistake in one of our books—maybe a mistake in the text or the code—we would be grateful if you could report this to us. By doing so, you can save other readers from frustration and help us improve subsequent versions of this book. If you find any errata, please report them by visiting `http://www.packtpub.com/submit-errata`, selecting your book, clicking on the **Errata Submission Form** link, and entering the details of your errata. Once your errata are verified, your submission will be accepted and the errata will be uploaded to our website or added to any list of existing errata under the Errata section of that title.

To view the previously submitted errata, go to `https://www.packtpub.com/books/content/support` and enter the name of the book in the search field. The required information will appear under the **Errata** section.

# Piracy

Piracy of copyright material on the Internet is an ongoing problem across all media. At Packt, we take the protection of our copyright and licenses very seriously. If you come across any illegal copies of our works, in any form, on the Internet, please provide us with the location address or website name immediately so that we can pursue a remedy.

Please contact us at copyright@packtpub.com with a link to the suspected pirated material.

We appreciate your help in protecting our authors, and our ability to bring you valuable content.

# Questions

You can contact us at questions@packtpub.com if you are having a problem with any aspect of the book, and we will do our best to address it.

# 1
# Beyond Dart's Basics

Dart is a very young computer language with many interesting features. Dart is a class-based, object-oriented language with optional types, and it can help you write very powerful programs. In this chapter, we will cover the following topics:

- Modularity and a namespace
- Functions and closures in different scopes
- Classes and mixins
- Methods and operators

## Modularity and a namespace

Complex things are the foundation of our world. To understand the complexity of the things around us, it is necessary to understand the parts that make them up. The evolution of complex things is due to functional and behavioral modularity. Functional modularity is the composition of smaller independent components with clear boundaries and functions. Behavioral modularity is mainly about traits and attributes that can evolve independently.

*Modularity* is nothing new. Earlier, product manufacturers figured out ways to increase the output and quality of the product, while still managing to reduce the cost pressures. They accomplished this through modularity. Modular design can be seen in automotive industry, buildings, and many other industries. Henry Ford introduced the notion of modularity in his assembly line with standardized and interchangeable parts. As a result, he reduced the production cycles and costs to achieve the mass production of his automobiles. A lot of these concepts are still used by many companies today.

# Modularity in software development

Representation of complex things as a set of parts is called decomposition. By analogy, the real-world complex software may be broken into functional parts called *modules*. Each module can be created, changed, tested, used, and replaced separately.

Let's take a look at the benefits of modularity. For the sake of simplicity, we divide them into development and postproduction phases. Each of these phases has its own specific tasks to be solved in the scope of that phase.

The development phase has the following benefits:

- Each module requires less code.
- New features or changes can be introduced to modules in isolation, separate from the other modules.
- Errors can be easily identified and fixed in a module.
- Modules can be built and tested independently.
- Programmers writing the modules can collaborate on the same application.
- The same modules can be reused in many applications.
- Applications have a main module and many auxiliary modules. Each module encapsulates a specific functionality and each one is integrated through loosely coupled communication channels provided by the main module.

The postproduction phase has the following benefits:

- Modules kept in a versioning system can be easily maintained and tested
- Fixed and noninfrastructural changes in a module can be done without affecting other modules

One significant disadvantage of modularity is that it increases complexity when managing many modules, especially when each one is individually versioned, updated, and has dependencies on the other modules.

# Modularity in Dart

The Dart language was designed by keeping the modules in mind. Modularity in Dart is realized through packages, libraries, and classes.

A **library** exposes functionality as a set of interfaces and hides the implementation from the rest of the world. As a concept, it's very similar to the separation of concern between objects in **object-oriented programming (OOP)**. Separating an application into libraries helps minimize tight coupling and makes it easier to maintain the code. A library can be implemented as a simple function, a single class, several classes, or a collection of parts representing the entire API of a library. The Dart application is a library as well.

A **package** is simply a directory that contains a `pubspec.yaml` file and may include any number of libraries and resources. The `pubspec.yaml` file contains significant information about the package, its authors, and its dependencies on other packages. Here is a sample `pubspec.yaml` file:

```
name: animation_library
version: 0.1.0
author: Sergey Akopkokhyants
description: Animation library for Web application
dependencies:
  browser: any
```

The real `pubspec.yaml` file can have more fields as specified at `https://www.dartlang.org/tools/pub/pubspec.html`. Before a package can be used, it must be published to a package management system, which is available as an online resource called *pub* at `https://pub.dartlang.org/`. To publish and retrieve packages from pub, we use a utility application of the same name. The pub utility uses information about dependencies from the `pubspec.yaml` file to retrieve all the necessary packages from the following locations:

- The recently updated packages at `https://pub.dartlang.org/`
- The Git repository
- The directory in the local filesystem

Dart Editor manages dependencies automatically for you. You can publish your packages right in Dart Editor.

# Libraries

A **namespace** is a container for all the members of a library. A namespace is defined by the library name. A library that is implicitly named has an empty namespace. This results in a conflict when trying to import libraries with the same namespaces. Import library namespace conflicts can be easily avoided with a prefix clause (`as`) and a name prefix.

The following is an implicitly named library in which all the resources from
dart:html are made available within the scope of our library with the prefix dom:

```
/**
 * Implicitly named library.
 * The dart:core library is automatically imported.
 */
import 'dart:html' as dom;

/**
 * Get [Element] by [id].
 */
dom.Element getById(String id) => dom.querySelector('#$id');
```

The library namespace make sense only in the Dart environment.

 The code that is compiled in JavaScript loses all the
library information.

Dart implements encapsulation through privacy. Each member or identifier of a
library has one of the two levels of access: private or public. Private members are
visible only inside the library in which they are declared. Conversely, members
with a public access are visible everywhere. The difference between them is the
underscore prefix (_), as shown in the following code:

```
// Animation library.
library animation;

// Class publicly available everywhere.
class Animation {
  // ...
}

// Class visible only inside library.
class _AnimationLibrary {
  // ...
}

// Variable publicly available everywhere.
var animationSpeed;
```

The preceding code shows an animation library with two classes and one variable.
The Animation class and the animationSpeed variable are public, and therefore
visible outside the library. The _AnimationLibrary class is private and it can be
used only in the library.

Public access can be managed with the show and hide extensions of the import statement. Use the following show extension with a specific class, which will then be available inside the library in which it is imported:

```
import 'animation.dart' as animation show Animation;

// Main entry into Dart Web application.
main() {
  // Animate
  new animation.Animation();
}
```

The animation prefix in the import statement defines the namespace to import the animation.dart library. All members of the animation.dart library are available in the global namespace via this prefix. We are referring to an Animation class with the animation prefix, as shown here:

```
1  import 'animation.dart' as animation show Animation;
2
3  // Main entry into Dart Web application.
4  main() {
5    // Animate
6    new animation.Animation();
7  }
            Animation - animation.dart
```

Use the hide extension with a specific class, which will then be unavailable inside the library in which it is imported; everything else from the library will be available, as shown in the following code:

```
import 'animation.dart' as animation hide Animation;

// Main entry into Dart Web application.
main() {
  // Animate
  var speed = animation.animationSpeed;
}
```

Now we hide the `Animation` class, but all the other public members in the namespace animation are still available, as seen in the following screenshot:

```
1   import 'animation.dart' as animation hide Animation;
2
3   // Main entry into Dart Web application.
4 ⊖ main() {
5     // Animate
6     var speed = animation.animationSpeed;
7   }                          ┌─────────────────────────────┐
8                              │ ○ animationSpeed — dynamic  │
                               └─────────────────────────────┘
```

As you can see, the members of the imported library become invisible. This happens because the library exports members from the public namespace. It can be possible to re-export the imported library with the `export` statement if this necessary `export` statement can be managed with `show` and `hide` as it was for the `import` statement, as shown in the following code:

```
library animation.css;

import 'animation.dart' as animation;
export 'animation.dart' show Animation;


class CssAnimation extends animation.Animation {
  // ...
}
```

The preceding code shows the `animation.css` library. We export the `Animation` class as part of the library namespace. Let's take a look at how we can use them:

```
1   import 'animation_library_with_export.dart' as animation;
2
3   // Main entry into Dart Web application.
4 ⊖ main() {
5     // Animate
6     new animation.Animation();
7   }                  ┌──────────────────────────────────────────────────┐
                       │ Ⓒ Animation - animation.dart                     │
                       │ Ⓒ CssAnimation - animation_library_with_export.dart │
                       └──────────────────────────────────────────────────┘
```

There are the exported `Animation` and original `CssAnimation` classes available for use in our main code. Without the export, the `Animation` class would be inaccessible in the main code.

# Functions and closures in different scopes

I like Dart because everything is an object. Functions are first-class citizens because they support all the operations that are generally available to other types. This means each function have the following properties:

- They can be named by a variable
- They can be passed as an argument to a function
- They can be returned as the result of a function
- They can be stored in data structures
- They can be created in any scope

Let's see where and how can we use functions as usual or as first-class citizens.

## Naming functions with a variable

Naming functions by variable means that we can create a reference to a function and assign it to a variable, as shown in the following code:

```
library function_var;

// Returns sum of [a] and [b]
add(a, b) {
  return a + b;
}

// Operation
var operation;

void main() {
  // Assign reference to function [add]
  operation = add;
  // Execute operation
  var result = operation(2, 1);
  print("Result is ${result}");}");
}
```

Here is the result of the preceding code:

```
Result is 3
```

We have the add function and the operation variable. We assign the reference of the add function to a variable and call the variable as a function later.

# Passing a function as an argument to another function

Passing functions as arguments to other functions can be very useful in cases when we need to implement the strategy design pattern to enable the program code to be selected and executed at runtime, as shown in the following code:

```
library function_param;

// Returns sum of [a] and [b]
add(a, b) {
  return a + b;
}

// Operation executor
executor(operation, x, y) {
  return operation(x, y);
}

void main() {
  // Execute operation
  var result = executor(add, 2, 1);
  print("Result is ${result}");
}
```

Here is the result of the preceding code:

```
Result is 3
```

The global `executor` function from the preceding example can call any function that accepts two arguments. You can see the implementation of the strategy design pattern in the form of anonymous functions passed as parameters of methods in collections.

# Returning a function as a result of another function

Sometimes, a function can be returned as a result of another function, as shown in the following code:

```
library function_return;

// Returns sum of [a] and [b]
```

```
add(a, b) => a + b;

// Returns difference between [a] and [b]
sub(a, b) => a - b;

// Choose the function depends on [type]
chooser(bool operation) =>operation ? add : sub;

void main() {
  // Choose function depends on operation type
  var operation = chooser(true);
  // Execute it
  var result = operation(2, 1);
  // Result
  print("Result is ${result}");
}
```

Here is the result of the preceding code:

```
Result is 3
```

This option can be very useful in implementing closures.

# Storing a function in data structures

We can store a function in data structures in any collection, as shown in the following code:

```
library function_store;

// Returns sum of [a] and [b]
add(a, b) => a + b;

// Returns difference between [a] and [b]
sub(a, b) => a - b;

// Choose the function depends on [type]
var operations = [add, sub];

void main() {
  // Choose function from list
  var operation = operations[0];
  // Execute it
  var result = operation(2, 1);
  // Result
  print("Result is ${result}");
}
```

Here is the result of the preceding code:

```
Result is 3
```

We have two functions and the array **operations** in our example that stores references to them.

# Closures

A function can be created in the global scope or within the scope of another function. A function that can be referenced with an access to the variables in its lexical scope is called a closure, as shown in the following code:

```
library function_closure;

// Function returns closure function.
calculate(base) {
  // Counter store
  var count = 1;
  // Inner function - closure
  return () => print("Value is ${base + count++}");
}

void main() {
  // The outer function returns inner
  var f = calculate(2);
  // Now we call closure
  f();
  f();
}
```

Here is the result of the preceding code:

```
Value is 3
Value is 4
```

We have the `calculate` function, which contains the `count` variable and returns a an inner function. The inner function has an access to the `count` variable because both are defined in the same scope. The `count` variable exists only within the scope of `calculate` and would normally disappear when the function exits. This does not happen in this case because the inner function returned by `calculate` holds a reference to `count`. The variable has been closed covered, meaning it's within a closure.

Finally, we know what a **first-class function** is, where we can use them, and how important it is to use closures. Let's move ahead to classes and mixins.

# Classes and mixins

We all know its wasteful trying to reinvent the wheel. It's even more wasteful trying to do it each time we want to build a car. So how can a program code be written more efficiently and made reusable to help us develop more powerful applications? In most cases, we turn to the OOP paradigm when trying to answer this question. OOP represents the concept of objects with data fields and methods that act on that data. Programs are designed to use objects as instances of classes that interact with each other to organize functionality.

# Types

The Dart language is dynamically typed, so we can write programs with or without the type annotations in our code. It's better to use the type annotations for the following reasons:

- The type annotations enable early error detection. The static analyzer can warn us about the potential problems at the points where you've made the mistakes.

- Dart automatically converts the type annotations into runtime assertion checks. In the checked mode, the dynamic type assertions are enabled and it can catch some errors when types do not match.

- The type annotations can improve the performance of the code compiled in JavaScript.

- They can improve the documentation making it much easier to read the code.

- They can be useful in special tools and IDE such as the name completion.

The fact that the type annotations were not included in our code does not prevent our program from running. The variables without the type annotations have a dynamic type and are marked with **var** or **dynamic**. Here are several recommendations where the type annotations are appropriate:

- You should add types to public and private variables

- You can add types to parameters of methods and functions

- You should avoid adding types to the bodies of methods or functions

# Classes

In the real world, we find many individual objects, all of the same kind. There are many cars with the same make and model. Each car was built from the same set of blueprints. All of them contain the same components and each one is an instance of the class of objects known as Car, as shown in the following code:

```
library car;

// Abstract class [Car] can't be instantiated.
abstract class Car {
  // Color of the car.
String color;
  // Speed of the car.
  double speed;
  // Carrying capacity
  double carrying;

  // Create new [Car] with [color] and [carrying] info.
  Car(this.color, this.carrying);

  // Move car with [speed]
  void move(double speed) {
    this.speed = speed;
  }

  // Stop car.
  void stop() {
    speed = 0.0;
  }
}
```

Objects have methods and instance variables. The color, speed, and carrying are instance variables. All of them have the value null as they were not initialized. The instance methods move and stop provide the behavior for an object and have access to instance variables and the this keyword. An object may have getters and setters — special methods with the get and set keywords that provide read and write access to the instance variables. The Car class is marked with the abstract modifier, so we can't create an instance of this class, but we can use it to define common characteristics and behaviors for all the subclasses.

# Inheritance

Different kinds of objects can have different characteristics that are common with others. Passenger cars, trucks, and buses share the characteristics and behaviors of a car. This means that different kinds of cars inherit the commonly used characteristics and behaviors from the Car class. So, the Car class becomes the superclass for all the different kinds of cars. We allow passenger cars, trucks, and buses to have only one direct superclass. A Car class can have unlimited number of subclasses. In Dart, it is possible to extend from only one class. Every object extends by default from an Object class:

```dart
library passenger_car;

import 'car.dart';

// Passenger car with trailer.
class PassengerCar extends Car {
  // Max number of passengers.
  int maxPassengers;

  // Create [PassengerCar] with [color], [carrying] and
[maxPassengers].
  PassengerCar(String color, double carrying, this.maxPassengers) :
    super(color, carrying);
}
```

The PassengerCar class is not an abstract and can be instantiated. It extends the characteristics of the abstract Car class and adds the maxPassengers variable.

# Interface

Each Car class defines a set of characteristics and behaviors. All the characteristics and behaviors of a car define its interface — the way it interacts with the outside world. Acceleration pedal, steering wheel, and other things help us interact with the car through its interface. From our perspective, we don't know what really happens when we push the accelerator pedal, we only see the results of our interaction. Classes in Dart implicitly define an interface with the same name as the class. Therefore, you don't need interfaces in Dart as the abstract class serves the same purpose. The Car class implicitly defines an interface as a set of characteristics and behaviors.

If we define a racing car, then we must implement all the characteristics and behaviors of the Car class, but with substantial changes to the engine, suspension, breaks, and so on:

```dart
import 'car.dart';
import 'passenger_car.dart';

void main() {
  // Create an instance of passenger car of white color,
  // carrying 750 kg and max passengers 5.
  Car car = new PassengerCar('white', 750.0, 5);
  // Move it
  car.move(100.0);
}
```

Here, we just created an instance of PassengerCar and assigned it to the car variable without defining any special interfaces.

# Mixins

Dart has a mixin-based inheritance, so the class body can be reused in multiple class hierarchies, as shown in the following code:

```dart
library trailer;

// The trailer
class Trailer {
  // Access to car's [carrying] info
  double carrying = 0.0;

  // Trailer can carry [weight]
  void carry(double weight) {
    // Car's carrying increases on extra weight.
    carrying += weight;
  }
}
```

The Trailer class is independent of the Car class, but can increase the carrying weight capacity of the car. We use the with keyword followed by the Trailer class to add mixin to the PassengerCar class in the following code:

```dart
library passenger_car;

import 'car.dart';
```

```
import 'trailer.dart';

// Passenger car with trailer.
class PassengerCar extends Car with Trailer {
  // Max number of passengers.
  int maxPassengers = 4;

  /**
   * Create [PassengerCar] with [color], [carrying] and
[maxPassengers].
   * We can use [Trailer] to carry [extraWeight].
   */
  PassengerCar(String color, double carrying, this.maxPassengers,
      {double extraWeight:0.0}) : super(color, carrying) {
    // We can carry extra weight with [Trailer]
    carry(extraWeight);
  }
}
```

We added `Trailer` as a mixin to `PassengerCar` and, as a result, `PassengerCar` can now carry more weight. Note that we haven't changed `PassengerCar` itself, we've only extended its functionality. At the same time, `Trailer` can be used in conjunction with the `Truck` or `Bus` classes. A mixin looks like an interface and is implicitly defined via a class declaration, but has the following restrictions:

- It has no declared constructor
- The superclass of a mixin can only be an Object
- They do not contain calls to `super`

# Well-designed classes

What is the difference between well-designed and poorly-designed classes? Here are the features of a well-designed class:

- It hides all its implementation details
- It separates its interface from its implementation through the use of abstract classes
- It communicates with other classes only through their interfaces

All the preceding properties lead to encapsulation. It plays a significant role in OOP. Encapsulation has the following benefits:

- Classes can be developed, tested, modified, and used independently
- Programs can be quickly developed because classes can be developed in parallel
- Class optimization can be done without affecting other classes
- Classes can be reused more often because they aren't tightly coupled
- Success in the development of each class leads to the success of the application

All our preceding examples include public members. Is that right? So what is the rule that we must follow to create well-designed classes?

# To be private or not

Let's follow the simple principles to create a well-designed class:

- Define a minimal public API for the class. Private members of a class are always accessible inside the library scope so don't hesitate to use them.
- It is not acceptable to change the level of privacy of the member variables from private to public to facilitate testing.
- Nonfinal instance variables should never be public; otherwise, we give up the ability to limit the values that can be stored in the variable and enforce invariants involving the variable.
- The final instance variable or static constant should never be public when referring to a mutable object; otherwise, we restrict the ability to take any action when the final variable is modified.
- It is not acceptable to have the public, static final instance of a collection or else, the getter method returns it; otherwise, we restrict the ability to modify the content of the collection.

The last two principles can be seen in the following example. Let's assume we have a Car class with defined final static list of parts. We can initialize them with Pedal and Wheel, as shown in the following code:

```
class Car {
  // Be careful with that code !!!
  static final List PARTS = ['Pedal', 'Wheel'];
}
void main() {
  print('${Car.PARTS}'); // Print: [Pedal, Wheel]
```

```
    // Change part
    Car.PARTS.remove('Wheel');
    print('${Car.PARTS}'); // Print: [Pedal]
}
```

However, there's a problem here. While we can't change the actual collection variable because it's marked as final, we can still change its contents. To prevent anyone from changing the contents of the collection, we change it from final to constant, as shown in the following code:

```
class Car {
    // This code is safe
    static const List PARTS = const ['Pedal', 'Wheel'];
}

void main() {
    print('${Car.PARTS}'); // Print: [Pedal, Wheel]

    // Change part
    Car.PARTS.remove('Wheel');
    print('${Car.PARTS}');
}
```

This code will generate the following exception if we try to change the contents of PARTS:

```
Unhandled exception:
Unsupported operation: Cannot modify an immutable array
#0 List.remove (dart:core-patch/array.dart:327)
...
```

# Variables versus the accessor methods

In the previous section, we mentioned that nonfinal instance variables should never be public, but is this always right? Here's a situation where a class in our package has a public variable. In our Car class, we have a color field and it is deliberately kept as public, as shown in the following code:

```
// Is that class correct?
class Car {
    // Color of the car.
    String color;
}
```

If the Car class is accessible only inside the library, then there is nothing wrong with it having public fields, because they don't break the encapsulation concept of the library.

# Inheritance versus composition

We defined the main rules to follow and create a well-designed class. Everything is perfect and we didn't break any rules. Now, it's time to use a well-designed class in our project. First, we will create a new class that extends the current one. However, that could be a problem as inheritance can break encapsulation.

It is always best to use inheritance in the following cases:

- Inside the library, because we control the implementation and relationship between classes
- If the class was specifically designed and documented to be extended

It's better not to use inheritance from ordinary classes because it's dangerous. Let's discuss why. For instance, someone developed the following `Engine` class to start and stop the general purpose engine:

```
// General purpose Engine
class Engine {
  // Start engine
  void start() {
    // ...
  }

  // Stop engine
  void stop() {
    // ...
  }
}
```

We inherited the `DieselEngine` class from the `Engine` class and defined when to start the engine that we need to initialize inside the `init` method, as shown in the following code:

```
import 'engine.dart';

// Diesel Engine
class DieselEngine extends Engine {
  DieselEngine();

  // Initialize engine before start
  void init() {
    // ...
  }
  void start() {
    // Engine must be initialized before use
```

```
    init();
    // Start engine
    super.start();
  }
}
```

Then, suppose someone changed their mind and decided that the implementation
Engine must be initialized and added the init method to the Engine class,
as follows:

```
// General purpose Engine
class Engine {
  // Initialize engine before start
  void init() {
    // ...
  }

  // Start engine
  void start() {
    init();
  }

  // Stop engine
  void stop() {
    // ...
  }
}
```

As a result, the init method in DieselEngine overrides the same method from
the Engine superclass. The init method in the superclass is an implementation
detail. The implementation details can be changed many times in future from release
to release. The DieselEngine class is tightly-coupled with and depends on the
implementation details of the Engine superclass. To fix this problem, we can use
a different approach, as follows:

```
import 'engine.dart';

// Diesel Engine
class DieselEngine implements Engine {
  Engine _engine;

  DieselEngine() {
    _engine = new Engine();
  }

  // Initialize engine before start
  void init() {
```

```
    // ...
  }

  void start() {
    // Engine must be initialized before use
    init();
    // Start engine
    _engine.start();
  }

  void stop() {
    _engine.stop();
  }
}
```

We created the private `engine` variable in our `DieselEngine` class that references an instance of the `Engine` class. `Engine` now becomes a component of `DieselEngine`. This is called a composition. Each method in `DieselEngine` calls the corresponding method in the `Engine` instance. This technique is called forwarding, because we forward the method's call to the instance of the `Engine` class. As a result, our solution is safe and solid. If a new method is added to `Engine`, it doesn't break our implementation.

The disadvantages of this approach are associated performance issues and increased memory usage.

# Methods and operators

Now that we've introduced well-designed classes, we need to discuss methods.

# Checking the values of the parameters before using them

The class constructors, methods, mutators (setters), and operators remove some restrictions on the values that must be passed into their parameters .What will happen if an invalid parameter value is passed to a method? One possibility is that the method will fail with a confusing exception or worse it will succeed but with a wrong result. In any case, it's dangerous not check the parameters of a method before using them. The rule here is to check whether the parameter value is valid as soon as possible. The best place to do that is at the beginning of the method.

The Dart VM can work in a developer-friendly checked mode and a speed-obsessed production mode. We usually use the checked mode when developing our applications. One of the benefits of this mode is the dynamic assertion. We should use the `assert` statement to check whether the parameters of the method are valid before using it. The Dart VM continues the program execution if the Boolean result of the dynamic assertion is `true`, otherwise stops it. This is shown in the following code:

```
/**
 * Return sum of [a] and [b].
 * It throws [AssertionError] if any of [a] or [b] equals null
 */
sum(int a, int b) {
  assert(a != null);
  assert(b != null);
  return a + b;
}
```

 The `assert` statement has no effect when the program executes in the production mode or is compiled with the JavaScript code.

We must check the validity of the parameters stored in the method for later use. Ignoring this can lead to problems later because an error associated with the parameter can be thrown in a completely different place, making it harder to trace its source. This has serious implications, especially in constructors.

Sometimes, it is important to validate the internal state of a class in the method and generate a special error, as shown in the following code. The typical errors are `StateError`, `RangeError`, and `ArgumentError`.

```
class Car {
  double petrol;

  /**
   * Start engine.
   * That method throws [StateError] if petrol is null
   * or less than 5 liters.
   */
  void startEngine() {
    if (petrol == null || petrol <= 5.0) {
      throw new StateError('Not enough petrol');
    }
  }
}
```

Here, we have a `Car` class with the `petrol` variable and the `startEngine` method. The `startEngine` method checks whether there is enough petrol to start the engine; otherwise, it throws an error.

 Each time you create a method, think about the restrictions that apply to its parameters.

# Well-designed methods

So, now that we've defined well-designed classes, it's time to define well-designed methods. We must remember that methods are part of a class' interface and the following simple rules can make them easier to use and also less error-prone:

- Choose the right method name. Remember, Dart doesn't support method overloading. Instead, we can have different method names or optional parameters.

- Use optional named parameters. This helps programmers to use your methods without the need to remember the position of each parameter.

- Refer to objects in terms of their interfaces over classes as the type of parameters. For example, we have an interface and the class implements that interface. Use the interface as the parameter type of the method instead of a solid one. Don't restrict the solution to a particular implementation.

A car may have the following different types of engines:

```
// Engine interface
abstract class Engine {
  void start();
}

// Diesel engine
class DieselEngine implements Engine {
  void start() {
    // ...
  }
}

// Carburetor engine
class CarburetorEngine implements Engine {
  void start() {
    // ...
  }
```

```
}

// Car
class Car {
  var engine;

  // Car may have any engine
  Car(Engine this.engine);
}
```

It's better to pass the abstract `Engine` class as a parameter of the constructor for the car to prevent any problems in future.

> **Downloading the example code**
> You can download the example code files for all Packt books you have purchased from your account at http://www.packtpub.com. If you purchased this book elsewhere, you can visit http://www.packtpub.com/support and register to have the files e-mailed directly to you.

# Summary

This chapter covered some of the most useful advanced features of the Dart language. The Dart language was designed with the modules in mind. Modularity in Dart is realized through packages, libraries, and classes. The code compiled in JavaScript loses all the library information.

Functions are first-class citizens because they support all the operations generally available to other types. A function that can be referenced with an access to the variables in its lexical scope is called a closure.

Programs are designed to use objects as instances of classes that interact with each other to organize functionality. The Dart language is dynamically typed, so we can write programs with or without the type annotations in our code.

In the next chapter, we will talk about generics, errors and exceptions, and annotations and reflection.

# 2
# Advanced Techniques and Reflection

In this chapter, we will discuss the flexibility and reusability of your code with the help of advanced techniques in Dart. Generic programming is widely useful and is about making your code type-unaware. Using types and generics makes your code safer and allows you to detect bugs early. The debate over errors versus exceptions splits developers into two sides. Which side to choose? It doesn't matter if you know the secret of using both. Annotation is another advanced technique used to decorate existing classes at runtime to change their behavior. Annotations can help reduce the amount of boilerplate code to write your applications. And last but not least, we will open Pandora's box through Mirrors of reflection. In this chapter, we will cover the following topics:

- Generics
- Errors versus exceptions
- Annotations
- Reflection

## Generics

Dart originally came with **generics** — a facility of generic programming. We have to tell the static analyzer the permitted type of a collection so it can inform us at compile time if we insert a wrong type of object. As a result, programs become clearer and safer to use. We will discuss how to effectively use generics and minimize the complications associated with them.

# Raw types

Dart supports arrays in the form of the `List` class. Let's say you use a list to store data. The data that you put in the list depends on the context of your code. The list may contain different types of data at the same time, as shown in the following code:

```
// List of data
List raw = [1, "Letter", {'test':'wrong'}];
// Ordinary item
double item = 1.23;

void main() {
  // Add the item to array
  raw.add(item);
  print(raw);
}
```

In the preceding code, we assigned data of different types to the `raw` list. When the code executes, we get the following result:

```
[1, Letter, {test: wrong}, 1.23]
```

So what's the problem with this code? There is no problem. In our code, we intentionally used the default `raw` list class in order to store items of different types. But such situations are very rare. Usually, we keep data of a specific type in a list. How can we prevent inserting the wrong data type into the list? One way is to check the data type each time we read or write data to the list, as shown in the following code:

```
// Array of String data
List parts = ['wheel', 'bumper', 'engine'];
// Ordinary item
double item = 1.23;

void main() {
  if (item is String) {
    // Add the item to array
    parts.add(item);
  }
  print(parts);
}
```

Now, from the following result, we can see that the code is safer and works as expected:

```
[wheel, bumper, engine]
```

The code becomes more complicated with those extra conditional statements. What should you do when you add the wrong type in the list and it throws exceptions? What if you forget to insert an extra conditional statement? This is where generics come to the fore.

Instead of writing a lot of type checks and class casts when manipulating a collection, we tell the static analyzer what type of object the list is allowed to contain. Here is the modified code, where we specify that parts can only contain strings:

```
// Array of String data
List<String> parts = ['wheel', 'bumper', 'engine'];
// Ordinary item
double item = 1.23;

void main() {
  // Add the item to array
  parts.add(item);
  print(parts);
}
```

Now, List is a generic class with the String parameter. Dart Editor invokes the static analyzer to check the types in the code for potential problems at compile time and alert us if we try to insert a wrong type of object in our collection, as shown in the following screenshot:

```
1  // Array of String data
2  List<String> parts = ['wheel', 'bumper', 'engine'];
3  // Ordinary item
4  double item = 1.23;
5
6  void main() {
```
The argument type 'double' cannot be assigned to the parameter type 'String'
```
8      parts.add(item);
9      print(parts);
10 }
```

This helps us make the code clearer and safer because the static analyzer checks the type of the collection at compile time. The important point is that you shouldn't use raw types. As a bonus, we can use a whole bunch of shorthand methods to organize iteration through the list of items to cast safer. Bear in mind that the static analyzer only warns about potential problems and doesn't generate any errors.

 Dart checks the types of generic classes only in the check mode. Execution in the production mode or code compiled to JavaScript loses all the type information.

# Using generics

Let's discuss how to make the transition to using generics in our code with some real-world examples. Assume that we have the following `AssemblyLine` class:

```
part of assembly.room;

// AssemblyLine.
class AssemblyLine {
  // List of items on line.
  List _items = [];

  // Add [item] to line.
  add(item) {
    _items.add(item);
  }

  // Make operation on all items in line.
  make(operation) {
    _items.forEach((item) {
      operation(item);
    });
  }
}
```

Also, we have a set of different kinds of cars, as shown in the following code:

```
part of assembly.room;

// Car
abstract class Car {
  // Color
```

```
    String color;
}

// Passenger car
class PassengerCar extends Car {
    String toString() => "Passenger Car";
}

// Truck
class Truck extends Car {
    String toString() => "Truck";
}
```

Finally, we have the following `assembly.room` library with a `main` method:

```
library assembly.room;

part 'assembly_line.dart';
part 'car.dart';

operation(car) {
    print('Operate ${car}');
}

main() {
    // Create passenger assembly line
    AssemblyLine passengerCarAssembly = new AssemblyLine();
    // We can add passenger car
    passengerCarAssembly.add(new PassengerCar());
    // We can occasionally add Truck as well
    passengerCarAssembly.add(new Truck());
    // Operate
    passengerCarAssembly.make(operation);
}
```

In the preceding example, we were able to add the occasional truck in the assembly line for passenger cars without any problem to get the following result:

```
Operate Passenger Car
Operate Truck
```

This seems a bit far fetched since in real life, we can't assemble passenger cars and trucks in the same assembly line. So to make your solution safer, you need to make the `AssemblyLine` type generic.

# Generic types

In general, it's not difficult to make a type generic. Consider the following example of the AssemblyLine class:

```
part of assembly.room;

// AssemblyLine.
class AssemblyLine <E extends Car> {
  // List of items on line.
  List<E> _items = [];

  // Add [item] to line.
  add(E item) {
    _items.insert(0, item);
  }

  // Make operation on all items in line.
  make(operation) {
    _items.forEach((E item) {
      operation(item);
    });
  }
}
```

In the preceding code, we added one type parameter, E, in the declaration of the AssemblyLine class. In this case, the type parameter requires the original one to be a subtype of Car. This allows the AssemblyLine implementation to take advantage of Car without the need for casting a class. The type parameter E is known as a bounded type parameter. Any changes to the assembly.room library will look like this:

```
library assembly.room;

part 'assembly_line.dart';
part 'car.dart';

operation(car) {
  print('Operate ${car}');
}

main() {
  // Create passenger assembly line
```

```
AssemblyLine<PassengerCar> passengerCarAssembly =
    new AssemblyLine<PassengerCar>();
// We can add passenger car
passengerCarAssembly.add(new PassengerCar());
// We can occasionally add truck as well
passengerCarAssembly.add(new Truck());
// Operate
passengerCarAssembly.make(operation);
}
```

The static analyzer alerts us at compile time if we try to insert the Truck argument in the assembly line for passenger cars, as shown in the following screenshot:

```
1  library assembly.room;
2
3  part 'generics_assembly_line.dart';
4  part 'cars.dart';
5
6  operation(car) {
7    print('Operate ${car}');
8  }
9
10 main() {
11   // Create passenger assembly line
12   AssemblyLine<PassengerCar> passengerCarAssembly =
13       new AssemblyLine<PassengerCar>();
14   // We can add passenger car
15   passengerCarAssembly.add(new PassengerCar());
```
The argument type 'Truck' cannot be assigned to the parameter type 'PassengerCar'
```
17   passengerCarAssembly.add(new Truck());
18   // Operate
19   passengerCarAssembly.make(operation);
20 }
```

After we fix the code in line **17**, all looks good. Our assembly line is now safe. But if you look at the operation function, it is totally different for passenger cars than it is for trucks; this means that we must make the operation generic as well. The static analyzer doesn't show any warnings and, even worse, we cannot make the operation generic directly because Dart doesn't support generics for functions. But there is a solution.

# Generic functions

Functions, like all other data types in Dart, are objects, and they have the data type `Function`. In the following code, we will create an `Operation` class as an implementation of `Function` and then apply generics to it as usual:

```
part of assembly.room;

// Operation for specific type of car
class Operation<E extends Car> implements Function {
  // Operation name
  final String name;
  // Create new operation with [name]
  Operation(this.name);
  // We call our function here
  call(E car) {
    print('Make ${name} on ${car}');
  }
}
```

The gem in our class is the `call` method. As `Operation` implements `Function` and has a `call` method, we can pass an instance of our class as a function in the `make` method of the `assembly` line, as shown in the following code:

```
library assembly.room;

part 'assembly.dart';
part 'car.dart';
part 'operation.dart';

main() {
  // Paint operation for passenger car
  Operation<PassengerCar> paint = new
    Operation<PassengerCar>("paint");
  // Paint operation for Trucks
  Operation<Truck> paintTruck = new Operation<Truck>("paint");
  // Create passenger assembly line
  Assembly<PassengerCar> passengerCarAssembly =
    new Assembly<PassengerCar>();
  // We can add passenger car
  passengerCarAssembly.add(new PassengerCar());
  // Operate only with passenger car
  passengerCarAssembly.make(paint);
  // Operate with mistake
  passengerCarAssembly.make(paintTruck);
}
```

In the preceding code, we created the `paint` operation to paint the passenger cars and the `paintTruck` operation to paint trucks. Later, we created the `passengerCarAssembly` line and added a new passenger car to the line via the `add` method. We can run the `paint` operation on the passenger car by calling the `make` method of the `passengerCarAssembly` line. Next, we intentionally made a mistake and tried to paint the truck on the assembly line for passenger cars, which resulted in the following runtime exception:

```
Make paint on Passenger Car
Unhandled exception:
type 'PassengerCar' is not a subtype of type 'Truck' of 'car'.
#0 Operation.call (…/generics_operation.dart:10:10)
#1 Assembly.make.<anonymous
   closure>(…/generics_assembly.dart:16:15)
#2 List.forEach (dart:core-patch/growable_array.dart:240)
#3 Assembly.make (…/generics_assembly.dart:15:18)
#4 main (…/generics_assembly_and_operation_room.dart:20:28)
...
```

This trick with the `call` method of the `Function` type helps you make all the aspects of your assembly line generic. We've seen how to make a class generic and function to make the code of our application safer and cleaner.

 The documentation generator automatically adds information about generics in the generated documentation pages.

To understand the differences between errors and exceptions, let's move on to the next topic.

# Errors versus exceptions

Runtime faults can and do occur during the execution of a Dart program. We can split all faults into two types:

- Errors
- Exceptions

There is always some confusion on deciding when to use each kind of fault, but you will be given several general rules to make your life a bit easier. All your decisions will be based on the simple principle of recoverability. If your code generates a fault that can reasonably be recovered from, use exceptions. Conversely, if the code generates a fault that cannot be recovered from, or where continuing the execution would do more harm, use errors.

Let's take a look at each of them in detail.

# Errors

An **error** occurs if your code has programming errors that should be fixed by the programmer. Let's take a look at the following `main` function:

```
main() {
  // Fixed length list
  List list = new List(5);
  // Fill list with values
  for (int i = 0; i < 10; i++) {
    list[i] = i;
  }
  print('Result is ${list}');
}
```

We created an instance of the `List` class with a fixed length and then tried to fill it with values in a loop with more items than the fixed size of the `List` class. Executing the preceding code generates `RangeError`, as shown in the following screenshot:

```
Unhandled exception:
RangeError: 5
#0      List.[]= (dart:core-patch/array.dart:13)
#1      main (file:///C:/Users/sergey/errors_vs_exceptions/bin/range_error.dart:6:9)
#2      _startIsolate.isolateStartHandler (dart:isolate-patch/isolate_patch.dart:214)
#3      _RawReceivePortImpl._handleMessage (dart:isolate-patch/isolate_patch.dart:122)
```

This error occurred because we performed a precondition violation in our code when we tried to insert a value in the list at an index outside the valid range. Mostly, these types of failures occur when the contract between the code and the calling API is broken. In our case, `RangeError` indicates that the precondition was violated. There are a whole bunch of errors in the Dart SDK such as `CastError`, `RangeError`, `NoSuchMethodError`, `UnsupportedError`, `OutOfMemoryError`, and `StackOverflowError`. Also, there are many others that you will find in the `errors.dart` file as a part of the `dart.core` library. All error classes inherit from the `Error` class and can return stack trace information to help find the bug quickly. In the preceding example, the error happened in line **6** of the `main` method in the `range_error.dart` file.

We can catch errors in our code, but because the code was badly implemented, we should rather fix it. Errors are not designed to be caught, but we can throw them if a critical situation occurs. A Dart program should usually terminate when an error occurs.

# Exceptions

**Exceptions**, unlike errors, are meant to be caught and usually carry information about the failure, but they don't include the stack trace information. Exceptions happen in recoverable situations and don't stop the execution of a program. You can throw any non-null object as an exception, but it is better to create a new exception class that implements the abstract class Exception and overrides the toString method of the Object class in order to deliver additional information. An exception should be handled in a catch clause or made to propagate outwards. The following is an example of code without the use of exceptions:

```dart
import 'dart:io';

main() {
  // File URI
  Uri uri = new Uri.file("test.json");
  // Check uri
  if (uri != null) {
    // Create the file
    File file = new File.fromUri(uri);
    // Check whether file exists
    if (file.existsSync()) {
      // Open file
      RandomAccessFile random = file.openSync();
      // Check random
      if (random != null) {
        // Read file
        List<int> notReadyContent =
          random.readSync(random.lengthSync());
        // Check not ready content
        if (notReadyContent != null) {
          // Convert to String
          String content = new
            String.fromCharCodes(notReadyContent);
          // Print results
          print('File content: ${content}');
        }
        // Close file
        random.closeSync();
      }
```

```
        } else {
          print ("File doesn't exist");
        }
    }
}
```

Here is the result of this code execution:

```
File content: [{ name: Test, length: 100 }]
```

As you can see, the error detection and handling leads to a confusing spaghetti code. Worse yet, the logical flow of the code has been lost, making it difficult to read and understand it. So, we transform our code to use exceptions as follows:

```
import 'dart:io';

main() {
  RandomAccessFile random;
  try {
    // File URI
    Uri uri = new Uri.file("test.json");
    // Create the file
    File file = new File.fromUri(uri);
    // Open file
    random = file.openSync();
    // Read file
    List<int> notReadyContent =
      random.readSync(random.lengthSync());
    // Convert to String
    String content = new String.fromCharCodes(notReadyContent);
    // Print results
    print('File content: ${content}');
  } on ArgumentError catch(ex) {
    print('Argument error exception');
  } on UnsupportedError catch(ex) {
    print('URI cannot reference a file');
  } on FileSystemException catch(ex) {
    print ("File doesn't exist or accessible");
  } finally {
    try {
      random.closeSync();
    } on FileSystemException catch(ex) {
      print("File can't be close");
    }
  }
}
```

The code in the `finally` statement will always be executed independent of whether the exception happened or not to close the `random` file. Finally, we have a clear separation of exception handling from the working code and we can now propagate uncaught exceptions outwards in the call stack.

The suggestions based on recoverability after exceptions are fragile. In our example, we caught `ArgumentError` and `UnsupportError` in common with `FileSystemException`. This was only done to show that errors and exceptions have the same nature and can be caught any time. So, what is the truth? While developing my own framework, I used the following principle:

*If I believe the code cannot recover, I use an error, and if I think it can recover, I use an exception.*

Let's discuss another advanced technique that has become very popular and that helps you change the behavior of the code without making any changes to it.

# Annotations

An **annotation** is metadata—data about data. An annotation is a way to keep additional information about the code in the code itself. An annotation can have parameter values to pass specific information about an annotated member. An annotation without parameters is called a marker annotation. The purpose of a marker annotation is just to mark the annotated member.

Dart annotations are constant expressions beginning with the @ character. We can apply annotations to all the members of the Dart language, excluding comments and annotations themselves. Annotations can be:

- Interpreted statically by parsing the program and evaluating the constants via a suitable interpreter
- Retrieved via reflection at runtime by a framework

 The documentation generator does not add annotations to the generated documentation pages automatically, so the information about annotations must be specified separately in comments.

# Built-in annotations

There are several built-in annotations defined in the Dart SDK interpreted by the static analyzer. Let's take a look at them.

## Deprecated

The first built-in annotation is deprecated, which is very useful when you need to mark a function, variable, a method of a class, or even a whole class as deprecated and that it should no longer be used. The static analyzer generates a warning whenever a marked statement is used in code, as shown in the following screenshot:

```
 1   part of annotations;
 2
 3   // Sum [ab] and [b]
 4⊖ @deprecated
 5   sum(a, b) {
 6     return a + b;
 7   }
'KindOfPrice' is deprecated
 9     * The [KindOfPrice] of product.
10     */
11⊖ @deprecated
12   class KindOfPrice {
13     // Kind of price
14⊖   @deprecated
15     String kind;
16
17     // Calculate
18⊖   @deprecated
19     void calculate() {
20       // ...
21     }
22   }
```

## Override

Another built-in annotation is override. This annotation informs the static analyzer that any instance member, such as a method, getter, or setter, is meant to override the member of a superclass with the same name. The class instance variables as well as static members never override each other. If an instance member marked with override fails to correctly override a member in one of its superclasses, the static analyzer generates the following warning:

```
 1  part of annotations;
 2
 3  /**
 4   * Type of price.
 5   */
 6  class PriceType extends KindOfPrice {
 7    // Calculate the Price.
 8    @override
 9    void calculate() {
10      // ...
11    }
12
13    // Try override not exists method
14    @override
```
Method does not override an inherited method
```
16    void sum() {
17      // ...
18    }
19  }
```

# Proxy

The last annotation is `proxy`. Proxy is a well-known pattern used when we need to call a real class's methods through the instance of another class. Let's assume that we have the following `Car` class:

```
part of cars;

// Class Car
class Car {
  int _speed = 0;
  // The car speed
  int get speed => _speed;

  // Accelerate car
  accelerate(acc) {
    _speed += acc;
  }
}
```

To drive the car instance, we must accelerate it as follows:

```dart
library cars;

part 'car.dart';

main() {
  Car car = new Car();
  car.accelerate(10);
  print('Car speed is ${car.speed}');
}
```

We now run our example to get the following result:

```
Car speed is 10
```

In practice, we may have a lot of different car types and would want to test all of them. To help us with this, we created the `CarProxy` class by passing an instance of `Car` in the proxy's constructor. From now on, we can invoke the car's methods through the proxy and save the results in a log as follows:

```dart
part of cars;

// Proxy to [Car]
class CarProxy {

  final Car _car;
  // Create new proxy to [car]
  CarProxy(this._car);

  @override
  noSuchMethod(Invocation invocation) {
    if (invocation.isMethod &&
        invocation.memberName == const Symbol('accelerate')) {
      // Get acceleration value
      var acc = invocation.positionalArguments[0];
      // Log info
      print("LOG: Accelerate car with ${acc}");
      // Call original method
      _car.accelerate(acc);
    } else if (invocation.isGetter &&
               invocation.memberName == const Symbol('speed')) {
      var speed = _car.speed;
      // Log info
```

```
        print("LOG: The car speed ${speed}");
        return speed;
    }
    return super.noSuchMethod(invocation);
  }
}
```

As you can see, CarProxy does not implement the Car interface. All the magic happens inside noSuchMethod, which is overridden from the Object class. In this method, we compare the invoked member name with accelerate and speed. If the comparison results match one of our conditions, we log the information and then call the original method on the real object. Now let's make changes to the main method, as shown in the following screenshot:

```
1  library cars;
2
3  part 'car.dart';
4  part 'car_proxy.dart';
5
6  main() {
7      Car car = new Car();
8      car.accelerate(10);
9      print('Car speed is ${car.speed}');
10     //
11     CarProxy proxy = new CarProxy(car);
   The method 'accelerate' is not defined for the class 'CarProxy'
13     proxy.accelerate(10);
14     // Get car speed through proxy
15     print('Car speed through proxy is ${proxy.speed}');
16  }
```

Here, the static analyzer alerts you with a warning because the CarProxy class doesn't have the accelerate method and the speed getter. You must add the proxy annotation to the definition of the CarProxy class to suppress the static analyzer warning, as shown in the following screenshot:

```
3  // Proxy to [Car]
4  @proxy
5  class CarProxy {
```

Now with all the warnings gone, we can run our example to get the following successful result:

```
Car speed is 10
LOG: Accelerate car with 10
LOG: The car speed 20
Car speed through proxy is 20
```

# Custom annotations

Let's say we want to create a test framework. For this, we will need several custom annotations to mark methods in a testable class to be included in a test case. The following code has two custom annotations. In the case, where we need only marker annotation, we use a constant string test. In the event that we need to pass parameters to an annotation, we will use a `Test` class with a constant constructor, as shown in the following code:

```
library test;

// Marker annotation test
const String test = "test";

// Test annotation
class Test {
  // Should test be ignored?
  final bool include;
  // Default constant constructor
  const Test({this.include:true});

  String toString() => 'test';
}
```

The `Test` class has the final `include` variable initialized with a default value of `true`. To exclude a method from tests, we should pass `false` as a parameter for the annotation, as shown in the following code:

```
library test.case;

import 'test.dart';
import 'engine.dart';

// Test case of Engine
class TestCase {
  Engine engine = new Engine();

  // Start engine
  @test
  testStart() {
    engine.start();
    if (!engine.started) throw new Exception("Engine must start");
  }

  // Stop engine
  @Test()
```

```
testStop() {
  engine.stop();
  if (engine.started) throw new Exception("Engine must stop");
}

// Warm up engine
@Test(include:false)
testWarmUp() {
  // ...
}
}
```

In this scenario, we test the Engine class via the invocation of the testStart and testStop methods of TestCase, while avoiding the invocation of the testWarmUp method.

So what's next? How can we really use annotations? Annotations are useful with reflection at runtime, so now it's time to discuss how to make annotations available through reflection.

# Reflection

Introspection is the ability of a program to discover and use its own structure. Reflection is the ability of a program to use introspection to examine and modify the structure and behavior of the program at runtime. You can use reflection to dynamically create an instance of a type or get the type from an existing object and invoke its methods or access its fields and properties. This makes your code more dynamic and can be written against known interfaces so that the actual classes can be instantiated using reflection. Another purpose of reflection is to create development and debugging tools, and it is also used for meta-programming.

There are two different approaches to implementing reflection:

- The first approach is that the information about reflection is tightly integrated with the language and exists as part of the program's structure. Access to program-based reflection is available by a property or method.
- The second approach is based on the separation of reflection information and program structure. Reflection information is separated inside a distinct Mirror object that binds to the real program member.

Dart reflection follows the second approach with Mirrors. You can find more information about the concept of **Mirrors** in the original paper written by Gilad Bracha at `http://bracha.org/mirrors.pdf`. Let's discuss the advantages of Mirrors:

- Mirrors are separate from the main code and cannot be exploited for malicious purposes
- As reflection is not part of the code, the resulting code is smaller
- There are no method-naming conflicts between the reflection API and inspected classes
- It is possible to implement many different Mirrors with different levels of reflection privileges
- It is possible to use Mirrors in command-line and web applications

Let's try Mirrors and see what we can do with them. We will continue to create a library to run our tests.

# Introspection in action

We will demonstrate the use of Mirrors with something simple such as introspection. We will need a universal code that can retrieve the information about any object or class in our program to discover its structure and possibly manipulate it with properties and call methods. For this, we've prepared the `TypeInspector` class. Let's take a look at the code. We've imported the `dart:mirrors` library here to add the introspection ability to our code:

```
library inspector;

import 'dart:mirrors';
import 'test.dart';

class TypeInspector {
  ClassMirror _classMirror;
  // Create type inspector for [type].
  TypeInspector(Type type) {
    _classMirror = reflectClass(type);
  }
```

The `ClassMirror` class contains all the information about the observing type. We perform the actual introspection with the `reflectClass` function of Mirrors and return a distinct Mirror object as the result. Then, we call the `getAnnotatedMethods` method and specify the name of the `annotation` that we are interested in. This will return a list of `MethodMirror` that will contain methods annotated with specified parameters. One by one, we step through all the instance members and call the private `_isMethodAnnotated` method. If the result of the execution of the `_isMethodAnnotated` method is successful, then we add the discovering method to the `result` list of found `MethodMirror`'s, as shown in the following code:

```
// Return list of method mirrors assigned by [annotation].
List<MethodMirror> getAnnotatedMethods(String annotation) {
  List<MethodMirror> result = [];
  // Get all methods
  _classMirror.instanceMembers.forEach(
    (Symbol name, MethodMirror method) {
    if (_isMethodAnnotated(method, annotation)) {
      result.add(method);
    }
  });
  return result;
}
```

The first argument of `_isMethodAnnotated` has the `metadata` property that keeps a list of annotations. The second argument of this method is the `annotation` name that we would like to find. The `inst` variable holds a reference to the original object in the `reflectee` property. We pass through all the method's metadata to exclude some of them annotated with the `Test` class and marked with include equals `false`. All other method's annotations should be compared to the annotation name, as follows:

```
// Check is [method] annotated with [annotation].
bool _isMethodAnnotated(MethodMirror method, String annotation) {
  return method.metadata.any(
    (InstanceMirror inst) {
    // For [Test] class we check include condition
    if (inst.reflectee is Test &&
      !(inst.reflectee as Test).include) {
      // Test must be exclude
      return false;
    }
    // Literal compare of reflectee and annotation
    return inst.reflectee.toString() == annotation;
  });
}
}
```

Dart Mirrors have the following three main functions for introspection:

- `reflect`: This function is used to introspect an instance that is passed as a parameter and saves the result in `InstanceMirror` or `ClosureMirror`. For the first one, we can call methods, functions, or get and set fields of the `reflectee` property. For the second one, we can execute the closure.

- `reflectClass`: This function reflects the class declaration and returns `ClassMirror`. It holds full information about the type passed as a parameter.

- `reflectType`: This function returns `TypeMirror` and reflects a class, `typedef`, function type, or type variable.

Let's take a look at the main code:

```
library test.framework;

import 'type_inspector.dart';
import 'test_case.dart';

main() {
  TypeInspector inspector = new TypeInspector(TestCase);
  List methods = inspector.getAnnotatedMethods('test');
  print(methods);
}
```

Firstly, we created an instance of our `TypeInspector` class and passed the testable class, in our case, `TestCase`. Then, we called `getAnnotatedMethods` from `inspector` with the name of the annotation, `test`. Here is the result of the execution:

```
[MethodMirror on 'testStart', MethodMirror on 'testStop']
```

The `inspector` method found the methods `testStart` and `testStop` and ignored `testWarmUp` of the `TestCase` class as per our requirements.

# Reflection in action

We have seen how introspection helps us find methods marked with annotations. Now we need to call each marked method to run the actual tests. We will do that using reflection. Let's make a `MethodInvoker` class to show reflection in action:

```
library executor;

import 'dart:mirrors';

class MethodInvoker implements Function {
  // Invoke the method
```

```
    call(MethodMirror method) {
      ClassMirror classMirror = method.owner as ClassMirror;
      // Create an instance of class
      InstanceMirror inst =
        classMirror.newInstance(new Symbol(''), []);
      // Invoke method of instance
      inst.invoke(method.simpleName, []);
    }
  }
```

As the `MethodInvoker` class implements the `Function` interface and has the `call` method, we can call instance it as if it was a function. In order to call the method, we must first instantiate a class. Each `MethodMirror` method has the `owner` property, which points to the owner object in the hierarchy. The owner of `MethodMirror` in our case is `ClassMirror`. In the preceding code, we created a new instance of the class with an empty constructor and then we invoked the method of `inst` by name. In both cases, the second parameter was an empty list of method parameters.

Now, we introduce `MethodInvoker` to the main code. In addition to `TypeInspector`, we create the instance of `MethodInvoker`. One by one, we step through the methods and send each of them to `invoker`. We print `Success` only if no exceptions occur. To prevent the program from terminating if any of the tests failed, we wrap `invoker` in the try-catch block, as shown in the following code:

```
library test.framework;

import 'type_inspector.dart';
import 'method_invoker.dart';
import 'engine_case.dart';

main() {
  TypeInspector inspector = new TypeInspector(TestCase);
  List methods = inspector.getAnnotatedMethods(test);
  MethodInvoker invoker = new MethodInvoker();
  methods.forEach((method) {
    try {
      invoker(method);
      print('Success ${method.simpleName}');
    } on Exception catch(ex) {
      print(ex);
    } on Error catch(ex) {
      print("$ex : ${ex.stackTrace}");
    }
  });
}
```

As a result, we will get the following code:

```
Success Symbol("testStart")
Success Symbol("testStop")
```

To prove that the program will not terminate in the case of an exception in the tests, we will change the code in `TestCase` to break it, as follows:

```
// Start engine
@test
testStart() {
  engine.start();
  // !!! Broken for reason
  if (engine.started)  throw new Exception("Engine must start");
}
```

When we run the program, the code for `testStart` fails, but the program continues executing until all the tests are finished, as shown in the following code:

```
Exception: Engine must start
Success Symbol("testStop")
```

And now our test library is ready for use. It uses introspection and reflection to observe and invoke marked methods of any class.

# Summary

This concludes mastering of the advanced techniques in Dart. You now know that generics produce safer and clearer code, annotation with reflection helps execute code dynamically, and errors and exceptions play an important role in finding bugs that are detected at runtime.

In the next chapter, we will talk about the creation of objects and how and when to create them using best practices from the programming world.

# 3
# Object Creation

In this chapter, we will talk about the creation of objects. We will see how and when to create them using best practices from the programming world, and then find a place for them to be accommodated in Dart. The different techniques covered here will help us to make correct choices that will be useful in different business cases. In this chapter, we will cover the following topics:

- A generative constructor
- A constructor with optional parameters
- A named constructor
- A redirecting constructor
- A private constructor
- A factory constructor
- A constant constructor
- Initialization of variables
- Syntactic sugar

## Creating an object

A **class** is a blueprint for objects. The process of creating objects from a class is called instantiation. An object can be instantiated with a new statement from a class or through reflection. It must be instantiated before it is used.

A class contains a constructor method that is invoked to create objects from the class. It always has the same name as the class. Dart defines two types of constructors: generative and factory constructors.

# A generative constructor

A **generative** constructor consists of a constructor name, a constructor parameter list, either a redirect clause or an initializer list, and an optional body. Dart always calls the generative constructor first when the class is being instantiated, as shown in the following code:

```
class SomeClass {
  // Default constructor
  SomeClass();
}

main() {
  var some = new SomeClass();
}
```

If the constructor is not defined, Dart creates an implicit one for us as follows:

```
class AnyClass {
  // implicit constructor
}

main() {
  var some = new AnyClass();
}
```

The main purpose of a generative constructor is to safely initialize the instance of a class. This initialization takes place inside a class and ensures that the instantiating object is always in a valid state.

# A constructor with optional parameters

A constructor is method of a class and has parameters to specify the initial state or other important information about the class. There are required and optional parameters in a constructor. The optional parameters can either be a set of named parameters or a list of positional parameters. Dart doesn't support method overload; hence, the ability to have optional parameters can be very handy.

 Dart does not allow you to combine named and positional optional parameters.

Let's take a look at the following `Car` class constructor with optional positional parameters:

```
// Class Car
class Car {
  String color;
  int weight;

  Car([this.color = 'white', this.weight = 1000]);
}
```

We can omit one or all the parameters to create an object of the class as follows:

```
import 'car_optional_parameters.dart';

main() {
  var car = new Car('blue');
  var car2 = new Car();
}
```

Let's take a look at the following `Car` class constructor that uses optional named parameters:

```
// Class Car
class Car {
  String color;
  int weight;

  Car({this.color:'white', this.weight:1000});
}
```

In the following main code, I used the named parameters to create an instance of the object:

```
import 'car_named_parameters.dart';

main() {
  var car = new Car(weight:750, color:'blue');
}
```

So, which kind of optional parameters are better? I recommend the use of named parameters due to the following reasons:

- Here, you need not remember the place of the parameters
- It gives you a better explanation of what the parameters do

# A named constructor

Let's say we want to create a `Collection` class to store all our data in one place. We can do it as follows:

```
library collection;

// Collection class
class Collection {
  // We save data here
  List _data;

  // Default constructor
  Collection() {
    _data = new List();
  }

  // Add new item
  add(item) {
    _data.add(item);
  }

  // ...
}
```

Somewhere in the main method, we create the instance of a class and add data to the collection:

```
import 'collection.dart';

var data = [1, 2, 3];

main() {
  var collection = new Collection();
  //
  data.forEach((item) {
    collection.add(item);
  });
}
```

Any chance that my collection will be initialized in this way in the future is high. So, it would be nice to have an initialization method in my `Collection` class to add a list of data. One of the solutions is to create a constructor with named parameters to manage our initialization. The code creates a new collection from the optional parameter value if specified, as shown in the following code:

```
library collection;

// Collection class
class Collection {
  // We save data here
  List _data;

  // Default constructor with optional [values] or [item].
  Collection({Iterable values:null, String item:null}) {
    if (item != null) {
      _data = new List();
      add(item);
    } else {
      _data = values != null ?
              new List.from(values) :
              new List();
    }
  }

  // Add new item
  add(item) {
    _data.add(item);
  }

  // ...
}
```

This solution has a *right to live*, but only if the number of parameters is small. Otherwise, a simple task initialization of variables results in very complicated code. I have specified two options for the named parameters with a really tangled logic. It is difficult to convey the meaning of what values means. A better way is to use named constructors, as shown in the following code:

```
library collection;

// Collection class
class Collection {
  // We save data here
  List _data;
```

```
  // Default constructor
  Collection() {
   _data = new List();
  }

  // Create collection from [values]
  Collection.fromList(Iterable values) {
    _data = values == null ?
        new List() :
        new List.from(values);
  }

  // Create collection from [item]
  Collection.fromItem(String item) {
   _data = new List();
   if (item != null) {
    add(item);
   }
  }
  // ...
}
```

The constructor is referred to as *named* because it has a readable and intuitive way of creating objects of a class. There are constructors named `Collection.fromList` and `Collection.fromItem` in our code. Our class may have a number of named constructors to do the simple task of class instantiation, depending on the type of parameters. However, bear in mind that any superclass named constructor is not inherited by a subclass.

 The named constructors provide intuitive and safer construction operations.

# A redirecting constructor

Constructors with optional parameters and named constructors help us to improve the usability and readability of our code. However, sometimes we need a little bit more. Suppose we want to add values of the map to our collection, we can do this by simply adding the `Collection.fromMap` named constructor as shown in the following code:

```
//...
// Create collection from [values]
Collection.fromList(Iterable values) {
```

```
   _data = values == null ?
       new List() :
       new List.from(values);
}
// Create collection from values of [map]
Collection.fromMap(Map map) {
  _data = map == null ?
          new List() :
          new List.from(map.values);
}
// …
```

The preceding method is not suitable because the two named constructors have similar code. We can correct it by using a special form of a generative constructor (redirecting constructor), as shown in the following code:

```
//…
// Create collection from [values]
Collection.fromList(Iterable values) {
  _data = values == null ?
      new List() :
      new List.from(values);
}
// Create collection from values of [map]
Collection.fromMap(Map map) :
    this.fromList(map == null ? [] : map.values);
```

The redirecting constructor calls another generative constructor and passes values of a map or an empty list. I like this approach as it is compact, less error-prone, and does not contain similar code anymore.

 The redirecting constructor cannot have a body and initialization list.

# A private constructor

I want to mention a couple of things about the private constructor before we continue with our journey. A private constructor is a special generative constructor that prevents a class from being explicitly instantiated by its callers. It is usually used in the following cases:

- For a singleton class
- In the factory method

- When the utility class contains static methods only
- For a constant class

Let's define a Task class as follows:

```
class Task {
    int id;

    Task._();

    Task._internal();
}
```

In the preceding code, there are private named constructors, Task._ and Task._internal, in the Task class. Also, Dart does not allow you to create an instance of Task as no public constructors are available, as shown in the following screenshot:

```
1 main() {
The class 'Task' does not have a default constructor
  3    Task task = new Task();
  4 }
```

 The private constructors are used to prevent creating instances of a class.

# A factory constructor

A **factory** constructor can only create instances of a class or inherited classes. It is a static method of a class that has the same name as the class and is marked with the factory constructor.

 The factory constructor cannot access the class members.

# The factory method design pattern

Let's imagine that we are creating a framework and it's time to log the information about different operations of the class methods. The following simple Log class can work for us:

```
library log;

// Log information
abstract class Log {
  debug(String message);
  // …
}
```

We can print the log information to the console with the ConsoleLog class as follows:

```
library log.console;

import 'log.dart';

// Write log to console
class ConsoleLog implements Log {
  debug(String message) {
    // ...
  }
  // ...
}
```

We can also save the log messages in a file with the FileLog class as follows:

```
library log.file;

import 'log.dart';

// Write log to file
class FileLog implements Log {
  debug(String message) {
    // ...
  }
  // ...
}
```

Now, we can use the `log` variable to print the debug information to the console in the Adventure class, as follows:

```
import 'log.dart';
import 'console_log.dart';

//  Adventure class with log
class  Adventure {
  static Log log = new ConsoleLog();

  walkMethod() {
    log.debug("entering log");
    // ...
  }
}
```

We created an instance of ConsoleLog and used it to print all our messages to the console. There are plenty of classes that will support logging, and we will include code similar to the preceding one in each of them. I can imagine what will happen when we decide to change ConsoleLog to FileLog. A simple operation can turn into a nightmare, because it might take a lot of time and resources to make the changes. At the same time, we must avoid altering our classes.

The solution is to use the factory constructor to replace the type of code with subclasses, as shown in the following code:

```
library log;

part 'factory_console_log.dart';

// Log information
abstract class Log {

  factory Log() {
    return new ConsoleLog();
  }

  debug(String message);
  // ...
}
```

The factory constructor of the `Log` class is a static method and every time it creates a new instance of `ConsoleLog`. The updated version of the `Adventure` class looks like the following code:

```
import 'factory_log.dart';

//  Adventure class with log
class  Adventure {
  static Log log = new Log();

  walkMethod() {
    log.debug("entering log");
    // ...
  }
}
```

Now, we are not referring to `ConsoleLog` as an implementation of `Log`, but only using the factory constructor. All the changes from `ConsoleLog` to `FileLog` will happen in one place, that is, inside the factory constructor. However, it would be nice to use different implementations that are appropriate in specific scenarios without altering the `Log` class as well. This can be done by adding a conditional statement in the factory constructor and instantiating different subclasses, as follows:

```
library log;

part 'factory_console_log.dart';
part 'factory_file_log.dart';

// Log information
abstract class Log {

  static bool useConsoleLog = false;

  factory Log() {
    return useConsoleLog ?
        new ConsoleLog() :
        new FileLog();
  }

  debug(String message);
  // ...
}
```

The `useConsoleLog` static variable can be changed programmatically at any point of time to give us a chance to change the logging direction. As a result, we don't change the `Log` class at all.

In our example, the factory constructor is an implementation of the factory method design pattern. It makes a design more customizable and only a little more complicated.

It is always better to use a factory constructor instead of a generative constructor in the following cases:

- It is not required to always return a new instance of a class
- It is required to instantiate any subtype of the return type
- It is essential to reduce the verbosity of creating parameterized type instances of a class

# The singleton design pattern

If we want to keep unique information about a user somewhere in our imaginable framework, then we would have to create a `Configuration` class for that purpose, as shown in the following code:

```
library configuration;

// Class configuration
class Configuration {
  // It always keep our [Configuration]
  static final Configuration configuration = new Configuration._();

  // Database name
  String dbName;

  // Private default constructor
  Configuration._();
}
```

The `Configuration` class has a `dbName` variable to keep the database's name and probably a number of other properties and methods as well. It has a private default constructor, so the class cannot be instantiated from other classes. A static variable configuration is final and will be initialized only once. All looks good and the standards of implementing the **singleton** design pattern are followed.

We have only one instance of a `Configuration` class at a point of time and that's the main purpose of the singleton pattern. One disadvantage here is the time of initialization of the configuration variable. This only happens when our program starts. It is better to use the Lazy initialization when it calls the `configuration` variable for the first time. The following factory constructor comes in handy here:

```
library configuration;

// Class configuration
class Configuration {
  // It always keep our [Configuration]
  static Configuration _configuration;

  // Factory constructor
  factory Configuration() {
    if (_configuration == null) {
      _configuration = new Configuration._();
    }
    return _configuration;
  }

  // Database name
  String dbName;

  // Private default constructor
  Configuration._();
}
```

For now, when we refer to the `Configuration` class for the first time, Dart will call the factory constructor. It will check whether the private variable configuration was initialized before, create a new instance of the `Configuration` class if necessary, and only then return an instance of our class. The following are the changes in the framework of the code:

```
import 'factory_configuration.dart';

main() {
  // Access to database name
  new Configuration().dbName = 'Oracle';
  // ...
  print('Database name is ${new Configuration().dbName}');
}
```

We always get the same instance of a `Configuration` class when we call the factory method in this solution. Factory constructors can be widely used in the implementation of the flyweight pattern and object pooling.

# A constant constructor

Let's assume we have the following `Request` class in our imaginary framework:

```
library request;

// Request class
class Request {
  static const int AWAIT = 0;
  static const int IN_PROGRESS = 1;
  static const int SUCCESS = 2;
  static const int FAULT = 3;

  // Result of request
  int result = AWAIT;

  // Send request with optional [status]
  void send({status:IN_PROGRESS}) {
    // ...
  }
  // ...
}
```

The `result` variable keeps the status of the last request as an integer value. The `Result` class has constants to keep all the possible values of the status in one place so that we can always refer to them. This makes the code better in readability and safer too. This technique is called the *enumerated pattern* and is widely used. However, it has a problem when it comes to safety as any other integer value could be assigned to the `result` variable. This problem makes a class very fragile. Enumerated types would help us to solve this problem, but unfortunately they do not exist in Dart. The solution to this is that we create an enumerated type ourselves with the help of constant constructors as it can be used to create a compile-time **constant**.

We can create an abstract `Enum` class with the entered parameter, as follows:

```
library enumerated_type;

// Enum class
abstract class Enum<T> {
  // The value
  final T value;
```

```
  // Create new instance of [T] with [value]
  const Enum(this.value);

  // Print out enum info
  String toString() {
    return "${runtimeType.toString()}." +
        "${value == null ? 'null' : value.toString()}";
  }
}
```

I intentionally used a generic class in the preceding code as I don't know which type of enumeration we will create. For example, to create an enumerated type of `RequestStatus` based on the integer values, we can create a concrete class as follows:

```
import 'enum.dart';

// Enumerated type Status of Request
class RequestStatus<int> extends Enum {

  static const RequestStatus AWAIT = const RequestStatus(0);
  static const RequestStatus IN_PROGRESS = const RequestStatus(1);
  static const RequestStatus SUCCESS = const RequestStatus(2);
  static const RequestStatus FAULT = const RequestStatus(3);

  const RequestStatus(int value) : super(value);
}
```

The `RequestStatus` class extends the `Enum` class and defines the request statuses as static constant members of the class. To instantiate the `RequestStatus` class object, we use `const` instead of the `new` instantiation expression.

 A constant constructor creates compile-time immutable instances of a class.

Let's go back to the `Request` class and modify it with `RequestStatus`, as shown in the following code:

```
library request;

import 'request_status.dart';

// Request class with enum
class Request {
```

```
    // Result of request
    var result = RequestStatus.AWAIT;

    // Send request with optional [status]
    void send({status:RequestStatus.IN_PROGRESS}) {
      // ...
    }
  }
}
```

In the preceding code, we used the enumerated type across the whole class. Finally, here is main method in which we use the Request class:

```
import 'request_with_enum.dart';
import 'request_status.dart';

void main() {
  Request request = new Request();
  // ...
  request.send(status:RequestStatus.SUCCESS);
  // ...
  RequestStatus status = request.result;
  //
  switch (status) {
    case RequestStatus.AWAIT:
      print('Result is $status');
      // ...
      break;
  }
}
```

As you can see, the compile-time constants have a wide variety of uses such as default values of variables and constants, default values in method signatures, switch cases, annotations, and enumerators. Moreover, the code uses them to have a better performance and translates them into optimized JavaScript code.

Use cases of the constant constructor have the following restrictions:

- A constant constructor doesn't have a body to prevent any changes of the class state
- All the variables in a class that have a constant constructor must be final as their binding is fixed upon initialization
- The variables from the initialization list of a constant constructor must be initialized with compile-time constants

# Initializing variables

Variables reflect the state of a class instance. There are two types of variables, namely, class and instance variables. Class variables are static in Dart. The static variables of a class share information between all instances of the same class. A class provides instance variables when each instance of a class should maintain information separately from others. As we mentioned, the main purpose of a constructor is to initialize the instance of a class in a safe manner. In other words, we initialize instance variables. Let's discuss when and how we should initialize them.

Uninitialized variables in Dart have the value `null` so we should initialize them before using them. The initialization of variables may happen in several places. They are as follows:

- We can assign any value to a variable at the place of declaration
- A variable can be initialized in the body of a constructor
- A variable can be initialized over a constructor parameter
- Initialization can happen in the initialization list of a constructor

Where is the best place to initialize the variables? Noninitialized variables generate null reference runtime exceptions when we try to use them, as shown in the following code:

```
class First {
  bool isActive;

  doSomething() {
    if (isActive) {
      // ...
    }
  }
}

void main() {
  First first = new First();
  first.doSomething();
}
```

The runtime exception will terminate the program execution and display the following error because the isActive variable of the First class was not initialized:

```
Unhandled exception:
type 'Null' is not a subtype of type 'bool' of 'boolean expression'.
#0 First.doSomething (file:///… / no_initialized.dart:5:9)
#1 main (file:///…/ no_initialized.dart:13:19)
…
```

 The variable must be initialized during the declaration if we are not planning do it in other places.

Now, let's move ahead. The First and Second classes are similar to each other with only a few differences, as shown in the following code:

```
class First {
   bool isActive;

   First(bool isActive) {
      this.isActive = isActive;
   }
}

class Second {
   bool isActive;

   Second(this.isActive);
}
```

In the First class, we initialize a variable in the body of a constructor; otherwise, the Second class initializes a variable via a constructor parameter. Which one is right? The desire to use the Second class is obvious because it is compact.

 It is always preferred to use the compact code to initialize the variables via constructor parameters than in a body of the constructor.

A variable marked final is a read-only variable that must be initialized during the instantiation of a class. This means all the final variables must be initialized:

- At the place of declaration
- Over a constructor parameter
- In the initialization list of a constructor

In the following code, we initialize the isActive variable at the place of declaration:

```
class First {
  final bool isActive = false;

  First();
}
```

In the Second class, we initialize the isActive variable via a parameter of the constructor, as follows:

```
class Second {
  final bool isActive;

  Second(this.isActive);
}
```

If the isActive final variable is indirectly dependent on the parameter of the constructor, we use the initializer list, as shown in the following code, as Dart does not allow us to initialize the final variable in a body of the constructor:

```
class Third {
  final bool isActive;

  Third(value) :
    this.isActive = value != null;
}
```

 The last place to initialize the final variables is in the constructor initializer list.

# Syntactic sugar

We talked a lot about the usability of the code, but I could not resist the desire to mention a couple of things about **syntactic sugar** – a syntax that is designed to make a code easier to read or express.

# Method call

Dart is an object-oriented programming language by definition. However, sometimes we need a piece of the functional language to be present in our estate. To help us with this, Dart has an interesting feature that may change the behavior of any class instance like a function, as shown in the following code:

```
import 'dart:async';

class Request {
  send() {
    print("Request sent");
  }
}

main() {
  Request request = new Request();
  Duration duration = new Duration(milliseconds: 1000);
  Timer timer = new Timer(duration, (Timer timer) {
    request.send();
  });
}
```

We have a `timer` function that invokes a callback function and sends a request to the server periodically to help organize pull requests, as follows:

```
Request sent
Request sent
...
```

The `call` method added to the class helps Dart to emulate instances of the `Request` class as functions, as shown in the following code:

```
import 'dart:async';

class Request {
  send() {
    print("Request sent");
  }

  call(Timer timer) {
    send();
  }
}

main() {
  Duration duration = new Duration(milliseconds: 1000);
  Timer timer = new Timer.periodic(duration, new Request());
}
```

So now we invoke the `send` method from the `call` method of the `Request` class. The result of the execution is similar to the result from the preceding example:

```
Request sent
Request sent
...
```

 The `call` method allows Dart to execute a class instance as a function.

# Cascade method invocation

Dart has quite a large number of innovations to create an application comfortably, but I will mention the one that can help us to write compact code. It is a cascade method invocation. Let's take a look at the ordinary `SomeClass` class in the following code:

```
library some_class;

class SomeClass {
  String name;
  int id;
}
```

Also, we can see the absolutely ordinary object creation:

```
import 'some_class.dart';

void main() {
  SomeClass some = new SomeClass();
  some.name = 'John';
  some.id = 1;
}
```

We created an instance of a class and initialized the instance variables. The preceding code is very simple. A more elegant and compact version of code uses the cascade method invocation, as follows:

```
import 'some_class.dart';

void main() {
  SomeClass some = new SomeClass()
    ..name = 'John'
    ..id = 1;
}
```

In the first line of the `main` method, we create an instance of the `SomeClass` class. At the same time, Dart creates a scope of the `some` variable and invokes all methods located in that scope. The result would be similar to the one that was in the previous code snippet.

 Use the cascade method invocation to make the code less verbose to do multiple operations on the members of an object.

# Summary

In this chapter, you learned that a constructor is a method that is invoked to create an object from a class. There are generative and factory constructors. The main purpose of a generative constructor is to initialize the instance of a class in a safe manner. The constructor can have required or optional parameters. The optional parameters enable the supply of arguments for only a few parameters from the list of optional parameters.

A constructor can be named. The named constructors provide intuitive and safer construction operations, because named constructors have similar code and some of them can be translated into redirecting constructors. A redirecting constructor calls another constructor that makes the code compact.

Dart supports private constructors. If a class has only private constructors, Dart cannot create an instance of a class. Private constructors are usually used in classes that contain static members, which are only useful in combination with the factory constructor. A factory constructor usually implements the popular factory method and singleton design patterns.

No language can exist without constant variables or constants. Constants play a significant role in programming with Dart and constant constructors can create compile-time constants as instances of a class.

The initialization of variables can happen in several places. Some variables must be initialized during declaration; others can be initialized via constructor parameters. Final variables must be initialized during the instantiation of class. This can happen during a declaration, via constructor parameters or in the constructor initializer list.

This syntax in Dart very often provides a form of syntactic sugar. One of those places is a method call that allows you to execute a class instance as a function. Another one is the cascade method invocation that makes the code less verbose.

In the next chapter, we will discuss advanced technologies to organize asynchronous code execution and learn the best practices to use Futures, Zones, and Isolates in different cases.

# Asynchronous Programming

**4**

In this chapter, we will look at the advanced techniques that help us execute asynchronous code—one of the most important components of Dart. Asynchronous programming is a standard programming paradigm and together with object-oriented principles, it plays an important role in the development of applications. In this chapter, we will cover the following topics:

- Event-driven architecture
- The Dart VM execution model
- Future
- Zone
- Isolates

## Call-stack architectures versus event-driven architectures

For a better understanding of asynchronous programming in Dart, we will discuss call-stack and event-driven architectures.

## Call-stack architectures

Traditionally, programs are built on the concept of a **call stack**. This concept is pretty straightforward because a program is basically a path of execution and invocation of sequential operations. Every operation can invoke another operation. At the time of invocation, a program creates a context for the callee operation. The caller operation will wait for the callee operation to return and the program will restore the context of it. Finally, the caller continues with their next operation. The callee operation might have executed another operation on its own behalf.

The program creates a call stack to coordinate and manage the context of each call. The basic primitives of this concept are calls. All calls in the program are tightly coupled, because the program knows which operation must be called after the current one and can share the same memory. The call-stack architecture is very popular and pervasive because it is very similar to the architecture of processors.

# Event-driven architectures

Event-driven architecture is the exact opposite of the call-stack concept. The basic primitives of this concept are events. The system dispatches events and transmits them among loosely coupled software components and services. The benefits of **event-driven architecture (EDA)** are as follows:

- It helps utilize existing resources efficiently
- It is easy to extend, evolve, and maintain implementation, which reduces the cost of maintenance
- It allows the exchange of events in an asynchronous manner that prevents blocking or waiting in queue
- In event-driven architecture, the producers and consumers are loosely coupled

Interaction between the components is limited to the publisher and one or many consumers. The publisher is free of concurrency issues and synchronization problems. The consumer can be changed at any time as the producers and consumers are loosely coupled.

 Event-driven architecture is the right approach to build loosely coupled asynchronous systems.

# The Dart VM execution model

Dart relies on event-driven architecture, which is based on a single-threaded execution model with a single **event loop** and two queues. Dart still provides a call stack. However, it uses events to transport context between the producers and consumers. The event loop is backed by a single thread, so no synchronization and locks are required at all.

 The event loop blocked with the running operation blocks the entire application.

A combination of the single-threaded execution model and asynchronous operations allows an application to perform more efficiently and is less resource intensive.

The main part of Dart VM is an event loop. Independent pieces of code can register callback functions as event handlers for certain types of events. A callback is the name given to the function that is passed as an argument of another function and is invoked in future after the event occurs in another function. Events from the timer, mouse events, events of input and output, and many others occurring in the system are registered in the event queue. Event loop sequentially processes the queued events by executing the associated callback functions that have been registered.

Callbacks must be short-running functions to prevent blocking of the event loop.

Dart supports anonymous functions and closures to define callbacks. The closure has a state bind to the callback function. Once the callback is executed, the state is available in the event loop. Callbacks are never executed in parallel because of single-threaded execution, so the occurrence of a deadlock is impossible. Once the callback has been executed, the event-loop fetches the next event from the event queue and applies its callback.

Dart introduced a new term for tasks that must be completed later: **microtasks**. As the name implies, a microtask is a short-running function that does something significantly small, such as updating the state of variables or dispatching a new event. Dart VM provides a special queue for microtasks. The microtasks queue and the events queue process in a single event loop. However, the microtasks queue has higher priority than the events queue. An event loop processes all the microtasks at once, until the queue becomes empty. Then, it moves on to the events queue and processes one event per loop. Using the long-running code in the microtasks queue increases the risk of starving an event queue and can result in the reduction of responsiveness of an application.

Make sure that the microtasks are extremely small to prevent blocking of the event loop.

Dart VM doesn't expose the event loop and we can't change or manage it. Bear in mind that the sequence of execution of events is predetermined by the events queue. You should also take into account the fact that the time at which the next event will be processed by the event loop is entirely unknown to you.

# Synchronous versus Asynchronous code

There is a lot of speculation regarding what is better: synchronous or asynchronous programming. These conversations always end up in the architecture design. So, the important question is what is the difference between synchrony and asynchrony in code designs?

Let's discuss the terms that we will use. Operations are executed serially in the synchronous (**sync**) code; no more, no less. This is very popular because it is simple. The logical flow of the sync code is clear, and we can read and understand it without any significant effort. Let's take a look at the following code snippet:

```
import 'dart:io';

main() {
  try {
    File file = new File("data.txt");
    RandomAccessFile handler = file.openSync();
    List<int> content = handler.readSync(handler.lengthSync());
    String contentAsString = new String.fromCharCodes(content);
    print("Content:  $contentAsString");
    handler.closeSync();
  } on FileSystemException catch(e) {
    print(e.message);
  }
}
```

First, we create a `file` reference to `data.txt` on the filesystem. Then, we create a `handler` by opening `file`. Next, the `handler` reads the bytes from the `file` into a `content` variable. Finally, we translate the `content` to a string, print the result, and close the `handler` file. Some operations in this code take more time than others. The file-read operation can be quick because the size of the file is small. If it is bigger, then while reading from the file, our program will wait until it is done. It can take time to translate the content of the file. These operations block the execution of our program; each time-consuming operation has to finish before starting another one. This code is implemented in a sync manner and can be useful while doing simple tasks like this one. However, this approach cannot be applied in complex software. The complex program may have different pieces of code communicating with each other to draw a **User Interface (UI)**, process keyboard input, read information from remote sites, or save information into the files at the same time. So, it's time to discuss the code written in an asynchronous (**async**) fashion. Async code does not wait for each operation to complete; the result of each operation will be handled later when available. Async code uses several important classes from Dart SDK and one of them is `Future`.

# Future

Let's change the code from the previous section into async, as follows:

```
import 'dart:io';

main() {
  File file = new File("data.txt");
  file.open().then(processFile);
}

processFile(RandomAccessFile file) {
  file.length().then((int length) {
    file.read(length).then(readFile).whenComplete(() {
      file.close();
    });
  });
}

readFile(List<int> content) {
  String contentAsString = new String.fromCharCodes(content);
  print("Content:  $contentAsString");
}
```

As you can see, the **Future** class is a proxy for an initially unknown result and returns a value instead of calling a callback function. Future can be created by itself or with Completer. Different ways of creating Future must be used in different cases. The separation of concerns between Future and Completer can be very useful. On one hand, we can give Future to any number of consumers to observe the resolution independently; on the other hand, Completer can be given to any number of producers and Future will be resolved by the one that resolves it first. Future represents the eventual value that is returned from the callback handler, and it can be in one of the following states:

- The incomplete state is an initial state when Future is waiting for the result. The result field holds a single-linked list of Future listeners.

- A completed state with a value as the result.

- A completed state with an error as the result.

- A Future class comes in the pending complete or chained state when it is completed or chained to another Future class with a success or an error. It will display an error if you try to complete it again.

 Future can be completed with a value or an error only once.

A consumer can register callbacks to handle the value or error of the Future class. I slightly changed our example to manage exceptions and deliberately used the wrong filename here to throw an exception:

```
//...
main() {
  File file = new File("data1.txt");
  file.open().then(processFile).catchError((error, stackTrace) {
    print("Catched error is $error\n$stackTrace");
  }, test:(error) {
    return error is FileSystemException;
  }).whenComplete((){
    print("File closed");
  });
}
//...
```

In the preceding code, we added the catchError method to catch errors. Pay attention to the optional test parameter of the catchError method. This parameter is the function that is called first if Future completes with an error, so you have a chance to check if the instance of an error must be handled in the catchError method. If optional test parameter is omitted, it defaults to a function that always returns true. If the optional test parameter returns true, the function, specified as the first parameter of catchError, is called with the error and possibly stack trace, and the returned Future is completed with the result of the call of this function. The resulting exceptions will look like this:

```
Catched error is FileSystemException: Cannot open file, path =
'data1.txt' (OS Error: The system cannot find the file specified.
, errno = 2)
#0      _File.open.<anonymous closure> (dart:io/file_impl.dart:349)
#1      _RootZone.runUnary (dart:async/zone.dart:1082)
//...
File closed
```

If the optional test parameter returns false, the exception is not handled by the catchError method and the returned Future class is completed with the same error and stack trace.

 The catchError method is the asynchronous equivalent of a catch block.

Last but not least, the Future class has the whenComplete method. This method has one parameter that is considered a function, which is always called in the end regardless of the future result (refer to the last statement in the preceding code).

The whenComplete method is the asynchronous equivalent of a finally block.

Now when we are finished with definitions, let's discuss the different factory constructors of Future.

# Future and Timer

Let's create a Future class containing the result of the calling computation asynchronously with the run method of the Timer class, as follows:

```
Future calc = new Future(computation);
calc.then((res) => print(res));
```

This Future class does not complete immediately. The Timer class adds the event to the event queue and executes the computation callback when the event is being processed in the event loop. If the result of the computation function throws an error, the returned Future is completed with an error. If the computation function creates another Future, the current one will wait until the new Future is completed and will then be completed with the same result.

# Future and Microtask

In the following code, the Future class is a scheduled task in the microtasks queue, which does not get completed immediately:

```
Future calc = new Future.microtask(computation);
calc.then((res) => print(res));
```

If the result of computation throws, the returned Future is completed with the error. If computation creates another Future, the current one will wait until the new Future is completed and will then be completed with the same result.

# Sync the Future class

It may sound paradoxical, but we can create a sync version of the Future class, as follows:

```
Future calc = new Future.sync(computation);
calc.then((res) => print(res));
```

The reason for this is that the Future immediately calls the computation function. The result of the computation will be returned in the next event-loop iteration.

# Future with a value

The Future class can be created with a specified value, as follows:

```
Future valueFuture = new Future.value(true);
valueFuture.then((res) => print(res));
```

Here, a Future returns specified value in the next event-loop iteration.

# Future with an error

The Future class can be created with an error, as follows:

```
try {
  throw new Error();
} on Error catch(ex, stackTrace) {
  Future errorFuture = new Future.error(ex, stackTrace);
  errorFuture.catchError((err, stack) => print(err));
}
```

This Future completes with an error in the next event-loop iteration.

# Delaying the Future class

Sometimes, it may be necessary to complete Future after a delay. It can be done as follows:

```
Future calc = new Future.delayed(
      new Duration(seconds:1), computation);
calc.then((res) => print(res));
```

The Future will be completed after the given duration has passed with the result of the computation function. It always creates an event in the event queue, and the event gets completed no sooner than the next event-loop iteration if the duration is zero or less than zero.

 The Future class must not change the completed value or the error to avoid side effects from listeners.

If Future doesn't have a successor, any error could be silently dropped.
In preventing these cases, Dart usually forwards the error to the global error handler.

Let's now look at the benefits of the `Future` class:

- It has a consistent pattern to handle callbacks and exceptions
- It is a more convenient way when compared to chain operations
- It is easy to combine `Futures`
- It provides a single control flow to develop web and command-line applications

Now you know why Dart uses `Future` everywhere in its API. The next stop on our journey is **zones**.

# Zones

Often, a program generates an uncaught exception and terminates the execution. The commonly occurring exceptions in the program means that the code is broken and must be fixed. However, sometimes exceptions may happen due to errors in communication, hardware faults, and so on. The following is an example of the HTTP server, which is used to demonstrate this problem:

```
import 'dart:io';

main() {
  runServer();
}

runServer() {
  HttpServer
  .bind(InternetAddress.ANY_IP_V4, 8080)
  .then((server) {
    server.listen((HttpRequest request) {
      request.response.write('Hello, world!');
      request.response.close();
    });
  });
}
```

The code in the `main` function can be terminated due to uncaught errors that may happen in the `runServer` function. Termination of the program under those circumstances can be undesirable.

So, how can this problem be solved? We wrap our code within a try/catch block to catch all the uncaught exceptions and it works perfectly, as shown in the following code:

```
main() {
  try {
    runServer();
  } on Error catch(e) {
    // ...
  }
}
```

This solution is universal and can be used in similar situations, so we will generalize it via the creation of a separate `wrapper` function:

```
wrapper(Function body, {Function onError}) {
  try {
    body();
  } on Error catch(e) {
    if (onError != null) {
      onError(e);
    }
  }
}

main() {
  wrapper(runServer, onError: (e) {
    // ...
  });
}
```

The `body` argument represents any preserved code and is covered within a try/catch block inside `wrapper`. A `wrapper` function uses the `onError` function to handle all the uncaught exceptions. Using a `wrapper` function is a good practice and its use is advised in other such situations. This is the **zone**.

 A zone is a configurable execution context that handles uncaught exceptions and asynchronous tasks.

Let's take a look at what zones can do:

- In critical situations, it allows you to handle exceptions properly
- It provides a way to handle multiple async operations in a single group
- It can have an unlimited number of nested zones, which behave like the parent one

Each zone creates a context, some kind of protected area, where the executing code exists. In addition to intercepting uncaught exceptions, zones can have local variables and can schedule microtasks, create one-off or repeating timers, print information, and save a stack trace for debugging purposes.

# Simple zone example

Let's transform our code to use a zone instead of the `wrapper` function, as follows:

```
import 'dart:io';
import 'dart:async';

main() {
  runZoned(runServer, onError:(e) {
    // ...
  });
}
```

The `runZoned` function is a code wrapper. By default, the `async` library implicitly creates a root zone and assigns it to a static `current` variable in the `Zone` class. So, we have an active zone that is always available to us inside the `runZoned` function. When the `runZoned` function runs, it forks the new nested zone from root one and executes the `runServer` function inside its context. Use the `fork` method of the current zone to create a new child of this one.

 A zone can be created only through the `fork` method of the current zone.

# Zone nesting

Let's say we have to serve static files in our server. So, we will need to read the file and serve it. To do this properly, we fork the nested zone and protect our code with the `runZoned` function, as follows:

```
runServer() {
  HttpServer
  .bind(InternetAddress.ANY_IP_V4, 8080)
  .then((server) {
    server.listen((HttpRequest request) {
      runZoned(() {
        readFile(request.uri.path).then((String context){
          request.response.write(context);
```

```
            request.response.close();
          });
      }, onError:(e) {
        request.response.statusCode = HttpStatus.NOT_FOUND;
        request.response.write(e.toString());
        request.response.close();
      });
    });
  });
}


Future<String> readFile(String fileName) {
  switch (fileName.trim()) {
    case "/":
    case "/index.html":
    case "/favicon.ico":
      return new Future.sync(() => "Hello, world!");
  }
  return new Future.sync(() =>
      throw new Exception('Resource is not available'));
}
```

Inside the nested zone, we call the readFile function with a resource name and it
returns the content. If the resource is not available, readFile generates an exception
and the program catches it in the onError function, which is registered as the zone's
error handler. If we don't specify the error handler, the exception will be bubbled
up through the zone-nested hierarchy until any parent zone gets caught up in it or
reaches a top-level executable and terminates the program.

## Zone values

Now, it's time to discuss authentication on our server as some resources may not be
available to the general public. We will follow the idea of token-based authentication
that relies on a signed token that is sent to the server on each request. We will create
a map of tokens to remember all the authorized clients, and then fork a new zone for
authentication. We will then read the client token from the header that is to be used
for authentication. When we get a map of tokens from the current zone, we will
inject them into the zone via zoneValues, as shown in the following code:

```
runServer() {
  HttpServer
  .bind(InternetAddress.ANY_IP_V4, 8080)
```

```
  .then((server) {
    Set tokens = new Set.from(['1234567890']);
    server.listen((HttpRequest request) {
      runZoned(() {
        authenticate(request.headers.value('auth-token'));
      }, zoneValues: {'tokens': tokens}, onError:(e){
        request.response.statusCode = HttpStatus.UNAUTHORIZED;
        request.response.write(e.toString());
        request.response.close();
      });
      runZoned(() {
        readFile(request.uri.path).then((String context){
          request.response.write(context);
          request.response.close();
        });
      }, onError:(e) {
        request.response.statusCode = HttpStatus.NOT_FOUND;
        request.response.write(e.toString());
        request.response.close();
      });
    });
  });
}
```

The authentication based on the existence of a token within tokens is as follows:

```
authenticate(String token) {
  Set tokens = Zone.current['tokens'];
  if (!tokens.contains(token)) {
    throw new Exception('Access denied');
  }
}
```

In the preceding code, we used the zone-local variables to track tokens and authenticate clients. Here, the variables were injected into the zone with the zoneValues argument of the runZoned function. Our tokens variable works like a static variable in the asynchronous context.

 The zone-local variables can play the role of static variables that are visible only in the scope of the zone.

Now check whether our server-side code works as expected. We installed the Postman extension from `http://www.getpostman.com/` to send requests from the Dartium web browser. Our first request to `http://localhost:8080` that we send without `auth-token` is shown in the following screenshot:

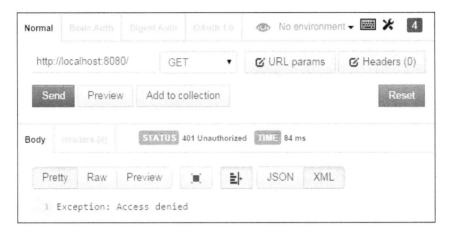

The request was unauthorized because of the absence of `auth-token`. Let's add it to the HTTP headers and see what happens:

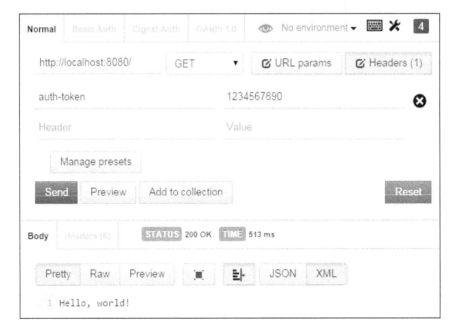

Finally, our request is authorized and returns Hello, world! as a success message.

# Zone specifications

Now, we have decided to log information about each server request and authentication. It is not recommended to inject the `log` function in all the possible places. Zones have `print` functions to print messages as a literal string. The `print` function bubbles up the message with the zone-nested hierarchy until a parent zone intercepts it or reaches up to the root zone to print it. So, we only need to override the `print` function in the `ZoneSpecification` class to intercept the message to the logger. We create a new `zoneSpecification` with the interceptor function to print and call the `log` function inside, as follows:

```
//...
main() {
  runZoned(runServer(),
    zoneSpecification: new ZoneSpecification(
      print:(self, parent, zone, message) {
        log(message);
      }
    ),
    onError:(e) {
    // ...
  });
}
```

Somewhere down the line, our `log` function logs `message` into a standard print, as shown in the following code:

```
log(String message) {
  print(message);
}
```

In the following code, we print the `request` path:

```
runServer() {
  HttpServer
  .bind(InternetAddress.ANY_IP_V4, 8080)
  .then((server) {
    Set tokens = new Set.from(['1234567890']);
    server.listen((HttpRequest request) {
      runZoned(() {
        Zone.current.print('Resource ${request.uri.path}');
        authenticate(request.headers.value('auth-token'));
//...
```

Bear in mind that all the interceptor functions expect the following four arguments:

```
print:(Zone self, ZoneDelegate parent, Zone zone, String message)
```

The first three of them are always the same:

- `self`: This argument represents the zone that's handling the callback
- `parent`: This argument furnishes `ZoneDelegate` to the parent zone and we can use it to communicate with the parent zone
- `zone`: This argument is the first to receive the request (before the request is bubbled up)

The fourth argument always depends on the function. In our example, it is the message that will be printed.

 `ZoneSpecification` is the only way to override the zone-specific functions.

Let's request the `index.html` file via the Postman extension to check this code, as shown in the following screenshot:

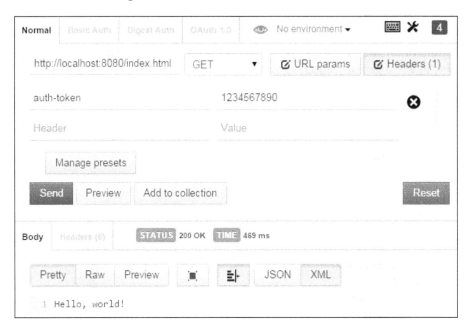

The following result will be displayed in the console log:

```
Resource /index.html
```

Finally, all works as expected.

# Interaction between zones

Let's see how the communication between the parent and the nested zones can be useful in a server example. Suppose you want to have more control on the print content of static pages, you can use the following code:

```
//...
Set tokens = new Set.from(['1234567890']);
bool allowPrintContent = false;
    server.listen((HttpRequest request) {
      runZoned((){
//...
      });
      runZoned(() {
        readFile(request.uri.path).then((String context){
          Zone.current.print(context);
          request.response.write(context);
          request.response.close();
        });
      }, zoneValues: {'allow-print':allowPrintContent},
      zoneSpecification: new ZoneSpecification(
          print: (Zone self, ZoneDelegate parent, Zone zone,
String message) {
            if (zone['allow-print']) {
              parent.print(zone, message);
            }
          }),
      onError:(e) {
//...
```

We add a Boolean variable `allowPrintContent` to manage the `print` operation. We call the `print` function of the zone to print the content of the page when processing `Future` of `readFile`. We inject `allowPrintContent` as a value of the `allow-print` key of `zoneValues`, and finally, inside the overridden `print` function, we add a condition that allows us to print the page content only if `allow-print` is `true`.

We requested the index.html file via the Postman extension again and see the following result in the console:

```
Resource /index.html
Hello, world!
```

As expected, our code prints the information that comes from both the nested zones. Now, we change the value to false and restart the server. The following request only prints the message from the first zone:

```
Resource /index.html
```

Interaction between zones can be easily organized via the zone variables.

# Tracking the zone execution

The server listener contains two zones. The first one is used to authenticate the files and the second one is used to read the content of the static files and send them back to the client. It is quite interesting to know how long each static page takes to load and process. Zones support several run methods to execute a given function in the zone. We can override the run method in ZoneSpecification to count the time spent by the request processing function. We use Stopwatcher as the timer in our example. We are processing each request and print profiling the time just after sending the response back to the client, as shown in the following code:

```
//...
runServer() {
  HttpServer
  .bind(InternetAddress.ANY_IP_V4, 8080)
  .then((server) {
    Set tokens = new Set.from(['1234567890']);
    bool allowPrintContent = true;
    Stopwatch timer = new Stopwatch();
    server.listen((HttpRequest request) {
      runZoned((){
//...
      });
      runZoned(() {
        readFile(request.uri.path).then((String context){
          Zone.current.print(context);
          request.response.write(context);
          request.response.close();
          Zone.current.print(
```

```
             "Process time ${timer.elapsedMilliseconds} ms");
        });
      }, zoneValues: {'allow-print':allowPrintContent},
      zoneSpecification: new ZoneSpecification(
        print: (Zone self, ZoneDelegate parent, Zone zone, String
message) {
          if (zone['allow-print']) {
            parent.print(zone, message);
          }
        },
        run: (Zone self, ZoneDelegate parent, Zone zone, f)
          => run(parent, zone, f, timer)
      ),
      onError:(e) {
        request.response.statusCode = HttpStatus.NOT_FOUND;
        request.response.write(e.toString());
        request.response.close();
      });
    });
  });
}
```

Now, we override the run function in ZoneSpecification to call a global run function with timer, as follows:

```
run(ZoneDelegate parent, Zone zone, Function f, Stopwatch timer) {
  try {
    timer.start();
    return parent.run(zone, f);
  } finally {
    timer.stop();
  }
}
```

In the global run function, we perform a trick when we call the original function from the parent zone delegate. We intend to wrap the function with a try/finally block to stop the timer before returning the result to the zone. Let's request the same resource again, as follows:

```
Resource /index.html
Hello, world!
Process time 54 ms
```

Now, we have the profiling information per request processed on the server. In addition to the standard run function, the zone has the runUnary and runBinary functions to pass one or two extra arguments to execute the given function inside a zone.

# Isolates

Now, it's time to discuss the performance of our server. We use an HTTP benchmarking tool such as **wrk** (`https://github.com/wg/wrk`) by Will Glozer to help us in our investigation. To avoid confusion, we will take the simplest version of our server, as follows:

```
import 'dart:io';

main() {
  HttpServer
    .bind(InternetAddress.ANY_IP_V4, 8080)
    .then((server) {
      server.listen((HttpRequest request) {
        // Response back to client
        request.response.write('Hello, world!');
        request.response.close();
      });
    });
}
```

We use this code with a benchmarking tool and keep the 512 concurrent connections open for 30 seconds, as shown in the following code:

```
./wrk -t1 -c256 -d30s http://127.0.0.1:8080
```

Here is the result of the preceding code:

```
Running 30s test @ http://127.0.0.1:8080
  1 threads and 256 connections
  Thread Stats   Avg      Stdev     Max   +/- Stdev
    Latency    33.89ms   24.51ms 931.37ms   99.76%
    Req/Sec     7.63k    835.29    9.77k    89.93%
  225053 requests in 30.00s, 15.02MB read
Requests/sec:   7501.81
Transfer/sec:    512.82KB
```

The test shows that our server can process close to 7,500 requests per second. Actually, this is not too bad. Can this value be improved? The key issue is that all this work is handled by a single thread:

- A single thread has the code to handle all the clients that appear in one place
- All the work will run sequentially on one thread

If the total work saturates the core, then the additional work will strangle and slow down the responsiveness of the server for all the clients as later requests queue up and wait for the previous work to be completed. **Isolates** can solve this problem and run several instances of the server in different threads. We will continue to improve our server and use the `ServerSockets` feature that came with the Dart 1.4 release. We will use the references of `ServerSocket` to run multiple instances of our server simultaneously. Instead of creating an instance of `HttpServer`, we create `ServerSocket` with the same initial parameters that we used before.

First of all, we need to create `ReceivePort` in the main thread to receive hand-shaking and usual messages from the spawned isolates. We create as many isolates as we can depending on the number of processors we have. The first parameter of the `spawn` static method of the `Isolate` class is a `global` function that helps organize hand-shaking between the main thread and spawned isolate. The second parameter is `port`, which is used as a parameter in the `global` function. The same port is used to send messages from spawned isolates to the main thread. Now, we need to listen to the messages from the spawned isolates. The spawned isolate follows the hand-shaking process and all the sent messages with `SendPort` are listened to in the main thread. On the completion of the hand-shaking procedure, we create and send an instance of `ServerTask`. All other messages will come as a string to be printed out on the console, as shown in the following code:

```dart
import 'dart:isolate';
import 'dart:io';

main() {
  ServerSocket
  .bind(InternetAddress.ANY_IP_V4, 8080)
  .then((ServerSocket server) {
    // Create main ReceivePort
    ReceivePort receivePort = new ReceivePort();
    // Create as much isolates as possible
    for (int i = 0; i < Platform.numberOfProcessors; i++) {
      // Create isolate and run server task
      Isolate.spawn(runTask, receivePort.sendPort);
    }
    // Start listening messages from spawned isolates
    receivePort.listen((msg) {
      // Check what the kind of message we received
      if (msg is SendPort) {
        // There is hand-shaking message.
        // Let's send ServerSocketReference and port
        msg.send(new ServerTask(
          server.reference, receivePort.sendPort));
      } else {
```

```
          // Usual string message from spawned isolates
          print(msg);
      }
    });
  });
}

/**
 * Global function helps organize hand-shaking between main
 * and spawned isolate.
 */
void runTask(SendPort sendPort) {
  // Create ReceivePort for spawned isolate
  ReceivePort receivePort = new ReceivePort();
  // Send own sendPort to main isolate as response on hand-shaking
  sendPort.send(receivePort.sendPort);
  // First message comes from main contains a ServerTask instance
  receivePort.listen((ServerTask task) {
    // Just execute our task
    task.execute();
  });
}

/**
 * Task helps create ServerSocket from ServerSocketReference.
 * We use new instance of ServerSocket to create new HttpServer
 * which starts listen HttpRequests and sends requested path into
 * main's ReceivePort.
 */
class ServerTask {
  ServerSocketReference reference;
  SendPort port;

  ServerTask(this.reference, this.port);

  execute() {
    // Create ServerSocket
    reference.create().then((serverSocket) {
      // Create HttpServer and start listening income HttpRequests
      new HttpServer.listenOn(serverSocket)
      .listen((HttpRequest request) {
        // Send requested path into main's ReceivePort
        port.send(request.uri.path);
        // Response back to client
        request.response.write("Hello, world");
        request.response.close();
      });
    });
  }
}
```

Our code is clear enough and potentially faster with isolates. The program is clearer because the code to handle each request is nicely wrapped up in its own function and is faster because each `SocketServer` instance keeps different connections asynchronous and independent; the work on one connection doesn't have to wait to be processed sequentially behind work on another connection. In general, this gives a better responsiveness even on a single-core server. In practice, it delivers better scalability under the load on servers that do have parallel hardware. Now, run the tests and we will see a significant improvement in our server:

```
./wrk -t1 -c256 -d30s http://127.0.0.1:8080
```

The following is the result of the preceding code:

```
Running 30s test @ http://127.0.0.1:8080
  1 threads and 256 connections
  Thread Stats   Avg      Stdev     Max    +/- Stdev
    Latency    10.31ms   6.11ms  50.81ms   73.78%
    Req/Sec    24.01k    2.00k   28.32k   67.52%
  709163 requests in 30.00s, 46.67MB read
Requests/sec:  23638.95
Transfer/sec:      1.56MB
```

Our server can process close to 24,000 requests per second in a concurrency-enabled environment. Fantastic!

So, after that quick dive into the world of concurrency, let's discuss isolates in general. Just repeat the best practices of the async programming:

- The program is driven by the queued events coming in from different independent sources
- All the pieces of the program must be loosely coupled

Isolate is a process that builds around the model of servicing a simple FIFO messaging queue. It does not share memory with other isolates and all isolates communicate by passing messages, which are copied before they are sent. As you can see, the implementation of isolates follows the same main principles as async programming.

 Always set the receiver port to the main isolate if you need to receive messages from other isolates or send them to each other.

# Summary

You now have a better understanding of event-driven architecture, which is one of the key concepts of Dart VM. Event-driven architecture is the right approach to build loosely coupled asynchronous systems.

Dart relies on event-driven architecture based on a single-threaded execution model with a single event loop and two queues. The event loop is backed by a single thread, so no synchronization or locks are required at all. When the event loop is blocked with an operation, this blocks the entire application. A combination of single-threaded execution models and asynchronous operations allows an application to be more productive and less resource intensive.

Future is a proxy for an initially unknown result that returns as a value instead of calling a callback function. Future almost always adds an event or microtask into the queue that is being processed in the event loop. Future can be completed with a value or error only once.

Zones implement the best practices of a configurable code wrapper to handle the uncaught errors. Zones can have local variables and can schedule microtasks, create one-off or repeating timers, print information, and save a stack trace for debugging purposes.

An isolate is a process built around the model of servicing simple messaging queue. It does not share the memory with other isolates and all isolates communicate by passing messages, which are copied before they are sent.

In the next chapter, we will see the stream framework and show when and how to properly use it.

# 5
# The Stream Framework

In this chapter, we will talk about streams. Streams have existed since the early days of UNIX. They have proven to be a dependable way to compose large systems out of small components, which does one thing well. Streams restrict the implementation of a surface area into a consistent interface that can be reused. You can plug the output of one stream as the input to another and use libraries that operate abstractly on streams to institute high-level flow control. Streams are an important component of small program design and have important abstractions that are worth considering. In this chapter, we will cover the following topics:

- Single-subscription streams versus broadcast streams
- The stream framework API

## Why you should use streams

Just imagine that you need to provide a file on a server in response to a client's request. The following code will do this:

```dart
import 'dart:io';

main() {
  HttpServer
  .bind(InternetAddress.ANY_IP_V4, 8080)
  .then((server) {
    server.listen((HttpRequest request) {
      new File('data.txt').readAsString()
      .then((String contents) {
        request.response.write(contents);
        request.response.close();
      });
    });
  });
}
```

In the preceding code, we read the entire file and buffered it into the memory of every request before sending the result to the clients. This code works perfectly for small files, but what will happen if the data.txt file is very large? The program will consume a lot of memory because it serves a lot of users concurrently, especially on slow connections. One big disadvantage of this code is that we have to wait for an entire file to be buffered in memory before the content can be submitted to the clients.

The HttpServer object listens for the HTTP request, which is a Stream. The HttpServer object then generates an HttpRequest object and adds it to the stream. The body of the request that is delivered by an HttpRequest object is a stream of byte lists. An HttpRequest object provides you with an access to the response property associated with an HttpResponse object. We will write the content of a file into the body of the HttpResponse object. The fact that the HttpRequest and HttpResponse classes are streams means that we can write our example in a better way, as shown in the following code:

```
import 'dart:io';

main() {
  HttpServer
  .bind(InternetAddress.ANY_IP_V4, 8080)
  .then((server) {
    server.listen((HttpRequest request) {
      new File('data.txt')
      .openRead()
      .pipe(request.response);
    });
  });
}
```

The openRead method creates a new independent Stream Instance of byte lists for the content of this file. The pipe method binds this stream as the input of the provided stream consumer and listens for the data, error, or done events. The preceding code has the following benefits:

- The code is cleaner, so you don't need to remember how to push data through the nonstreaming API

- The file streams to clients in chunks, one chunk at a time as soon as they are received from the disk

- The server doesn't need buffer chunks of a file in the memory when the remote clients are on a slow or high-latency connection, because the stream handling backs the pressure automatically

Streams make development simple and elegant.

# Single-subscription streams versus broadcast streams

The Dart stream framework supports the single-subscription and broadcast streams in order to have different approaches depending on the required solution. Let's see the difference between single-subscription and broadcast streams.

## A single-subscription stream

A stream that allows you to have only one listener during the entire lifetime is called a single-subscription stream. You are not allowed to cancel and subscribe to the same stream again. The newly created stream starts generating events only after the subscription starts listening to them. It stops generating events after the subscription is canceled even if the stream can provide more. The single-subscription stream always delivers each event in the correct order to a listener.

 Use single-subscription streams when the event delivery and its order are important for your solution.

A good usage example of a single-subscription stream is getting data from the file or server.

## A broadcast stream

A stream that allows you to have multiple listeners during the entire lifetime is called the broadcast stream. You are allowed to subscribe or cancel the subscription at any time. A broadcast stream starts to generate events immediately after the creation if it ready, independent of whether any subscription is registered or not. This fact means that some portion of the events can be lost in a moment when no listener is registered. There is no guarantee that multiple listeners will get the event in the same order that they were registered. A broadcast stream only guarantees that each listener will get all the events in the correct order.

 Use broadcast streams when delivering events to multiple listeners is important for your solution.

A good example of using the broadcast stream is the eventbus implementation that supports multiple listeners.

# An overview of the stream framework API

You can see the hierarchy of the stream framework classes in the following diagram:

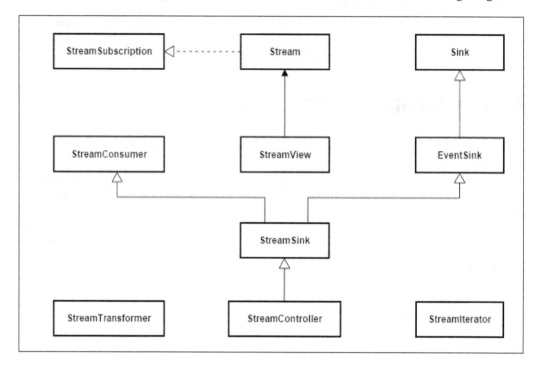

# The Stream class

The stream class is abstract and provides a generic view on the sequence of byte lists. It implements numerous methods to help you manage or republish streams in your application. The sequence of events can be seamlessly provided by stream. The events that are generated by stream store the data to be delivered. In case of a failure, the stream class generates an error event. When all the events have been sent, the stream class generates done event.

# The validation methods of the Stream class

The stream class has the following methods that help you validate data returned from a stream:

- any: This method checks whether the test callback function accepts any element provided by this stream

- every: This method checks whether the test callback function accepts all the elements provided by this stream

- contains: This method checks whether the needle object occurs in the elements provided by this stream

# The search methods of the Stream class

The following methods of the Stream class help you search for specific elements in a stream:

- firstWhere: This method finds the first element of a stream that matches the test callback function

- lastWhere: This method finds the last element of a stream that matches the test callback function

- singleWhere: This method finds the single element in a stream that matches the test callback function

# The subset methods of the Stream class

The Stream class provides the following methods to create a new stream that contains a subset of data from the original one:

- where: This method creates a new stream from the original one with data events that satisfy the test callback function

- skip: This method creates a new stream with data events that are left after skipping the first count of the data events from the original stream

- skipWhere: This method creates a new stream with the data events from the original stream when they are matched by the test callback function

- take: This method creates a new stream with the data events that are provided at most the first count values of this stream

- takeWhere: This method creates a new stream with the data events from the original stream when the test callback function is successful

You will find other methods of the Stream class on the official help page at https://api.dartlang.org/apidocs/channels/stable/dartdoc-viewer/dart-async.Stream.

# Creating a stream

The Stream class has several factory constructors to create single-subscription or broadcast streams. Let's discuss them in detail.

# A new stream from the Future class

The first factory constructor could confuse you because it creates a new single-subscription stream from the Future instance with the following command:

```
factory Stream.fromFuture(Future<T> future)
```

This confusion will be quickly cleared if I remind you about the translation of the Future class into the Stream class via the asStream method from the same class, as shown in the following code:

```
...
Stream<T> asStream() => new Stream.fromFuture(this);
...
```

The resulting stream will fire an data or error event when the Future class is completed, and closes itself with the done event. The following code snippet shows how this factory constructor can be used:

```
import 'dart:async';

main() {
  // single sample data
  var data = new Future<num>.delayed(
      const Duration(milliseconds:500), () {
    // Return single value
    return 2;
  });
  // create the stream
  Stream<num> stream = new Stream<num>.fromFuture(data);
  // Start listening
  var subscriber = stream.listen((data) {
    print(data);
  }, onError:(error){
    print(error);
  }, onDone:() {
    print('done');
  });
}
```

The execution of the preceding code prints the following result on the console:

```
2
done
```

# A new stream from the Iterable class

It's quite obvious that you should have a factory constructor that creates a single-subscription stream from any `Iterable` instance. Iteration over a stream happens only if the stream has a listener and can be interrupted if the listener cancels the subscription. Any error that occurs in the iteration process immediately ends the stream and throws an error. In this case, the `done` event doesn't fire because the iteration was not complete.

In the following code snippet, we create an instance of the `Iterable` class with a factory constructor that generates the sequence of numbers. We intentionally generate an `Exception` at the location of the third element:

```
import 'dart:async';

main() {
  // some sample generated data
  var data = new Iterable<num>.generate(5, (int indx) {
    if (indx < 3) {
      return indx;
    } else {
      throw new Exception('Wrong data');
    }
  });
  // create the stream
  Stream<num> stream = new Stream<num>.fromIterable(data);
  // Start listening
  var subscriber = stream.listen((data) {
    print(data);
  }, onError: (error){
    print(error);
  }, onDone: () {
    print('done');
  });
}
```

The result of the preceding code is as follows:

```
0
1
2
Exception: Wrong data
```

# A new stream with periodically generated events

In the previous topic, we used the `Iterable.generate` factory constructor to emit numeric data into our stream. However, we can do that well via the `Stream.periodic` factory constructor, as follows:

```
factory Stream.periodic(Duration period,
  [T computation(int computationCount)])
```

We can do this in a natural stream and a less verbose way, as follows:

```
import 'dart:async';

main() {
  // some sample generated data
  Stream<num> stream = new Stream
    .periodic(const Duration(milliseconds: 500), (int count) {
    // Return count
    return count;
  });
  // Start listening
  var subscriber = stream.listen((data) {
    print(data);
  }, onError: (error){
    print(error);
  }, onDone: () {
    print('done');
  });
}
```

The first parameter is the duration that gives you the interval between emitting events. The second parameter is the callback function that computes the event values. This function has a single parameter that defines sequential number of iterations.

# A new stream from the transformation pipe

The `Stream.eventTransformed` factory constructor is quite interesting because it creates a new `Stream` from the existing one with the help of a sink transformation, as shown in the following code:

```
factory Stream.eventTransformed(Stream source,
  EventSink mapSink(EventSink<T> sink))
```

The first parameter is the source stream that provides events to the new one. The `mapSink` callback function is the one that is called when a new stream is listening. All the events from the existing stream pass through the sink to reach a new stream. This constructor is widely used to create stream transformers. In the following code, we will create a `DoublingSink` class. It accepts the output stream as an argument of the constructor. We will implement the number-doubling algorithm inside the `add` method. The other `addError` and `close` methods are simple and pass the incoming parameter values to the underlying stream object, as shown in the following code:

```
import 'dart:async';

/**
 * An interface that abstracts creation or handling of
 * Stream events.
 */
class DoublingSink implements EventSink<num> {
  final EventSink<num> _output;

  DoublingSink(this._output);

  /** Send a data event to a stream. */
  void add(num event) {
    _output.add(event * 2);
  }

  /** Send an async error to a stream. */
  void addError(errorEvent, [StackTrace stackTrace])   =>
      _output.addError(errorEvent, stackTrace);

  /** Send a done event to a stream.*/
  void close() => _output.close();
}
```

The `DoublingTransformer` class implements `StreamTransformer` for numbers. In the `bind` method, which is compulsory, we will create a new stream via the `eventTransformer` constructor and return the instance of `DoublingSink` as result of the constructor's callback, as shown in the following code:

```
class DoublingTransformer implements StreamTransformer<num, num> {
  Stream<num> bind(Stream<num> stream) {
    return new Stream<num>.eventTransformed(stream,
        (EventSink sink) => new DoublingSink(sink));
  }
```

```
}

void main() {
  // some sample data
  var data = [1,2,3,4,5];
  // create the stream
  var stream = new Stream<num>.fromIterable(data);
  // Create DoublingTransformer
  var streamTransformer = new DoublingTransformer();
  // Bound streams
  var boundStream = stream.transform(streamTransformer);
  // Because we start listening the 'bound' stream the 'listen'
method
  // invokes the 'doublingTransformer' closure
  boundStream.listen((data) {
    print('$data');
  });
}
```

In the `main` method, we created a simple stream via the `Stream.fromIterable` factory constructor and created a stream transformer as an instance of `DoublingTransformer`. So, we can combine them together in a call of the `transform` method. When we start listening to the bounded stream, events from the source stream will be doubled inside `DoublingSink` and accommodated here. The following result is expected:

```
2
4
6
8
10
```

# A new stream from StreamController

In the previous topics, we saw how a stream can be easily created from another stream with the help of one of the factory constructors. However, you can create a stream from scratch with help of `StreamController`, which gives you more control over generating events of a stream. With `StreamController`, we can create a stream to send the `data`, `error`, and `done` events to the stream directly. A stream can be created via the `StreamController` class through the different factory constructors. If you plan to create a single-subscription stream, use the following factory constructor:

```
factory StreamController( {void onListen(), void onPause(), void
  onResume(), onCancel(),bool sync: false})
```

The controller has a life cycle that presents the following states:

- **Initial state**: This is where the controller has no subscription. The controller buffers all the `data` events in this state.

- **Subscribed state**: In this state, the controller has a subscription. The `onListen` and `onCancel` callback functions are called when the subscriber registers or ends the subscription accordingly. The callback functions `onPause` and `onResume` are called when the controlling stream via a subscriber changes the state to pause or resume. The controller may not call the `onResume` callback function if the new data from the stream was canceled.

- **Canceled state**: In this state, the controller has no subscription.

- **Closed state**: In this state, adding more events is not allowed.

If the `sync` attribute is equal to `true`, it tells the controller that the events might be directly passed into the listening stream by the subscriber when the `add`, `addError`, or `close` methods are called. In this case, the events will be passed only after the code that creates the events has returned.

A stream instance is available via the `stream` property. Use the `add`, `addError`, and `close` methods of `StreamSink` to manage the underlying stream. The controller buffers the data until a subscriber starts listening, but bear in mind that the buffering approach is not optimized to keep a high volume of events. The following code snippet shows you how to create a single-subscription stream with `StreamController`:

```
import 'dart:async';

main() {
  // create the stream
  Stream<num> stream = createStream();
  // Start listening
  StreamSubscription<num> sub = createSubscription(stream);
}

StreamSubscription<num> createSubscription(Stream<num> stream) {
  StreamSubscription subscriber;
  subscriber = stream.listen((num data) {
    print('onData: $data');
    // Pause subscription on 3-th element
    if (data == 3) {
      subscriber.pause(new Future.delayed(
```

```
                const Duration(milliseconds: 500), () => 'ok'));
      }
    },
    onError:(error) => print('onError: $error'),
    onDone:() => print('onDone'));
    return subscriber;
}

Stream<num> createStream() {
    StreamController<num> controller = new
      StreamController<num>(
        onListen:() => print('Listening'),
        onPause: () => print('Paused'),
        onResume: () => print('Resumed'),
        onCancel: () => print('Canceled'), sync: false);
    //
    num i = 0;
    Future.doWhile((){
      controller.add(i++);
      // Throws exception on 5-th element
      if (i == 5) {
        controller.addError('on ${i}-th element');
      }
      // Stop stream at 7-th event
      if (i == 7) {
        controller.close();
        return false;
      }
      return true;
    });
    return controller.stream;
}
```

In the preceding code, we intentionally throw an error at the 5-th element and stop the stream at the 7-th element. The stream subscriber paused listening to the stream at the 3-th element and resumed it after a delay of 500 milliseconds. This will generate the following result:

```
Listening
onData: 0
onData: 1
onData: 2
onData: 3
Paused
```

```
onData: 4
onError: on 5-th element
onData: 5
onData: 6
Canceled
onDone
```

The following factory constructor creates a controller for the broadcast stream, which can be listened to more than once:

```
factory StreamController.broadcast({void onListen(),
  void onCancel(), bool sync: false})
```

The controller created by this constructor delivers the data, error, or done events to all listeners when the add, addError, or close methods are called. The invocation method with the same name is called in an order and is always before a previous call is returned. This controller, as opposed to the single-subscribed one, doesn't have the internal queue of events. This means that the data or error event will be lost if there are no listeners registered at the time, this event is added. Each listener subscription acts independently. If one subscription pauses, then only this one is affected, so all the events buffer internally in the controller until the subscription resumes or cancels. The controller has a life cycle that has the following states:

- **Initial state**: This is where the controller has no subscription. The controller losses all the fired data and error events in this state.
- **Subscribed state**: This is where the first subscription is added to the controller. The onListen and onCancel callback functions are called at the moment when the first subscriber is registered or the last one ends its subscription simultaneously.
- **Canceled state**: In this state, the controller has no subscription.
- **Closed state**: In this state, adding more events is not allowed.

If the sync attribute is equal to true, it tells the controller that events might be passed directly into the listening stream by subscribers when the add, addError, or close methods are called. Hence, the events will be passed after the code that creates the event is returned, but this is not guaranteed when multiple listeners get the events. Independent of the value of the sync attribute, each listener gets all the events in the correct order. The following is a slightly changed version of the previous code with two subscriptions:

```
import 'dart:async';

main() {
```

```dart
    // create the stream
    Stream<num> stream = createStream();
    StreamSubscription<num> sub1 = createSubscription(stream, 1);
    StreamSubscription<num> sub2 = createSubscription(stream, 2);
}

StreamSubscription<num> createSubscription(Stream<num> stream, num
number) {
  // Start listening
  StreamSubscription subscriber;
  subscriber = stream.listen((num data) {
   print('onData ${number}: $data');
   // Pause subscription on 3-th element
   if (data == 3) {
     subscriber.pause(new Future.delayed(
         const Duration(milliseconds: 500), () => 'ok'));
   }
  },
  onError:(error) => print('onError: $error'),
  onDone:() => print('onDone'));
  return subscriber;
}

Stream<num> createStream() {
  StreamController<num> controller = new
    StreamController<num>.broadcast(
      onListen:() => print('Listening'),
      onCancel: () => print('Canceled'), sync: false);
  //
  num i = 0;
  Future.doWhile((){
    controller.add(i++);
    // Throws exception on 5-th element
    if (i == 5) {
      controller.addError('on ${i}-th element');
    }
    // Stop stream at 7-th event
    if (i == 7) {
      controller.close();
      return false;
    }
    return true;
  });
  return controller.stream;
}
```

The preceding code snippet generates the following result:

```
Listening
onData 1: 1
onData 2: 1
onData 1: 2
onData 2: 2
onData 1: 3
onData 2: 3
onData 1: 4
onError: on 5-th element
onData 1: 5
onData 1: 6
onDone
onData 2: 4
onError: on 5-th element
onData 2: 5
onData 2: 6
Canceled
onDone
```

These results reaffirm the fact that the broadcast stream doesn't guarantee the order of the delivery events to different listeners. It only guarantees an order of the delivery events inside each listener.

# What does the StreamSubscription class do?

The `listen` method of the `Stream` class adds the following subscription to the stream:

```
StreamSubscription<T> listen(
    void onData(T event),
        { Function onError, void onDone(), bool cancelOnError});
```

A callback function `onData` is called every time when a new `data` event comes from this stream. Existence of this function is important because without it nothing will happen. The optional `onError` callback is called when an error comes from the stream. This function accepts one or two arguments. The first argument is always an error from the stream. The second argument, if it exists, is a `StackTrace` instance. It can be equal to `null` if the stream received an error without `StackTrace` itself. When the stream closes, it calls the `onDone` callback function. The `cancelOnError` flag informs the subscription to start the cancellation the moment the error occurs.

A result of this method is the instance of the StreamSubscription class. It provides events to the listener and holds the callback functions used in the listen method of the Stream class. You can set or override all the three callback functions via the onData, onError, and onDone methods of the StreamSubscriber class. The listening stream can be paused and resumed with the pause and resume methods. A special flag isPaused returns true if an instance of the StreamSubscription class is paused. The stream subscription can end with the cancel method at any time. It returns a Future instance, which completes with a null value when the stream is done cleaning up. This feature is also useful for tasks such as closing a file after reading it.

# Minimizing access to the Stream class members using StreamView

The StreamView class is wrapper for the Stream class exposes only the isBroadcast getter, the asBroadCastStream and listen methods from original one. So if you need clear Stream interface in your code, you can use it like this:

```
import 'dart:async';

main() {
  // some sample data
  var data = [1,2,3,4,5];
  // create the stream
  var stream = new Stream<num>.fromIterable(data);
  // Create a view
  var streamView = new StreamView(stream);
  // Now listen stream view like stream
  var subscriber = streamView.listen((data) {
    print(data);
  }, onError: (error){
    print(error);
  }, onDone: () {
    print('done');
  });
}
```

You will get the following result:

```
1
2
3
4
5
done
```

# The Sink and EventSink interfaces

A Sink class represents a generic interface for data receivers. It defines the add method that will put the data in the sink and the close method, which tells the sink that no data will be added in future. The EventSink class uses the add method of the Sink class to send a data event to a stream, as well as the close method to send a done event. The addError method belongs to the EventSink class that sends an asynchronous error to a stream.

# Importance of the StreamConsumer interface

We can bind one stream to another via the pipe method of the Stream class. The consumer stream is represented by the StreamConsumer interface. This interface defines the contract between two streams. The addStream method is used to consume the elements of the source stream. The consumer stream will listen on the source stream and do something for each event. It may stop listening after an error or may consume all errors and stop at the done event. The close method tells the consumer that no future streams will be added. This method returns the Future instance that is completed when the source stream has been consumed and the consumer is closed.

# What does the StreamSink class do?

The StreamSink class combines methods from StreamConsumer and EventSink. You should know that methods from both the classes will block each other. We cannot send the data or error events via the methods of the EventSink class while we are adding the source stream via the addStream method from StreamConsumer. We can start using the methods from EventSink only after the Future instance returned by the addStream method is completed with a value. Also, the addStream method will be delayed until the underling system consumes the data added by the EventSink method. The StreamSink class has a done getter that returns the Future instance that is completed when the owned StreamSink class is finished with one of the following conditions:

- It is completed with an error as a result of adding events in one of the add, addError, or close methods of the EventSink class

- It is completed with success when all the events have been processed and the sink has been closed or the sink has been stopped from handling more events

# Transforming streams with the StreamTransformer class

The `StreamTransformer` class helps you create a new consumer stream that is bound to the original one via the `bind` method. The `StreamTransformer` class can be instantiated through two factory constructors that define different strategies on how the transformation will happen. In following factory constructor, we need to specify the following special `transformer` function:

```
const factory StreamTransformer (Function StreamSubscription<T>
    transformer(Stream<S> stream, boolcancelOnError))
```

The `transformer` function receives a bounded stream as an argument and returns an instance of the `StreamSubscription` class. If you are planning to implement your own stream transformer function, it will look like this:

```
import 'dart:async';

void main() {
  // some sample data
  var data = [1,2,3,4,5];
  // create the stream
  var stream = new Stream<num>.fromIterable(data);
  // Create StreamTransformer with transformer closure
  var streamTransformer =
    new StreamTransformer<num, num>(doublingTransformer);
  // Bound streams
  var boundStream = stream.transform(streamTransformer);
  // Because we start listening the 'bound' stream the
  // 'listen' method invokes the 'doublingTransformer'
  // closure
  boundStream.listen((data) {
    print('$data');
  });
}

StreamSubscription doublingTransformer(Stream<num> input,
    bool cancelOnError) {

  StreamController<num> controller;
  StreamSubscription<num> subscription;
  controller = new StreamController<num>(
    onListen: () {
```

```
      subscription = input.listen((data) {
         // Scale the data double.
         controller.add(data * 2);
      },
      onError: controller.addError,
      onDone: controller.close,
      cancelOnError: cancelOnError);
   });
   return controller.stream.listen(null);
}
```

The preceding code generates the following output:

```
2
4
6
8
10
```

The other factory method creates a `StreamTransformer` class that delegates events to the special functions, which handle the `data`, `error`, and `done` events, as shown in the following code:

```
factory StreamTransformer.fromHandlers({
      void handleData(S data, EventSink<T> sink),
      void handleError(Object error, StackTrace stackTrace,
         EventSink<T> sink),
      void handleDone(EventSink<T> sink)})
```

The changed version of the previous example is as follows:

```
import 'dart:async';

void main() {
  // some sample data
  var data = [1,2,3,4,5];
  // create the stream
  var stream = new Stream<num>.fromIterable(data);
  // Create StreamTransformer with transformer closure
  var streamTransformer = new StreamTransformer<num, num>
    .fromHandlers(
      handleData:handleData,
      handleError:handleError,
      handleDone:handleDone);
  // Bound streams
```

```
    var boundStream = stream.transform(streamTransformer);
    // Because we start listening the 'bound' stream the
    // 'listen' method invokes the 'handleData' function
    boundStream.listen((data) {
      print('$data');
    });
}

handleData(num data, EventSink<num> sink) {
  sink.add(data * 2);
}

handleError(Object error, StackTrace stackTrace, EventSink<num> sink)
{
  sink.addError(error, stackTrace);
}

handleDone(EventSink<num> sink) {
  sink.close();
}
```

The following result of this execution looks similar to previous one:

```
2
4
6
8
10
```

# Traverse streams with StreamIterator

The `StreamIterator` class permits a stream to be read using the iterator operations. It has the `moveNext` method that waits for the next stream's value to become available and returns the `Future` value of the `bool` type, as follows:

```
Future<bool> moveNext();
```

If the result of `moveNext` is a success, then the `Future` class completes with the `true` value, else the iteration is done and no new value will be available. The current value of the stream exists in the `current` property of the `StreamIterator` instance, as shown in the following code:

```
T get current;
```

This value is valid when the `Future` class returned by the `moveNext` method completes with the `true` value and only until the next iteration. A `StreamIterator` class is an abstract class and can be instantiated only via the factory constructor, as follows:

```
factory StreamIterator(Stream<T> stream)
```

Let's change the example from the previous topic to use `StreamIterator`. We will create a simple stream from `Iterable` as we did before. Then, we will create an instance of `StreamIterator`. Finally, we will use the `forEach` function to iterate over the stream and call the closure function to print scaled elements of the stream, as shown in the following code:

```
main() {
  // some sample data
  var data = [1,2,3,4,5];
  // create the stream
  var stream = new Stream<num>.fromIterable(data);
  // Create an iterator
  var iterator = new StreamIterator(stream);
  // Iterate over all elements of iterator and print values
  forEach(iterator, (value) {
    // Scale the data double.
    print(value * 2);
  });
}
```

Actually, this code looks similar to the ones where we used iterators. All the magic happens inside the `forEach` method, as shown in the following code:

```
forEach(StreamIterator iterator, f(element)) {
  return Future.doWhile(() {
    Future future = iterator.moveNext();
    future.then((bool hasNext) {
      if (hasNext) {
        f(iterator.current);
      }
    });
    return future;
  });
}
```

As the `moveNext` method returns the `Future` value, we need to use the `doWhile` method of the `Future` class to perform the iteration. The Boolean result of `Future` returns a `hasNext` parameter. We call the closure function until the value of the `hasNext` parameter is `true`.

The code generates the following result:

```
2
4
6
8
10
```

# Summary

Now you have a better understanding of the stream framework, which is one of the key concepts of Dart VM.

Streams have existed since the early days of UNIX. They have proved to be a dependable way to compose large systems out of the small components. The Dart stream framework supports single-subscription and broadcast streams in order to have different approaches depending on the required solution.

In the next chapter, we will see the collection framework and when and how to properly use different types of collection frameworks. You will also learn how to choose the correct data structure based on the usage patterns, concurrency, and performance considerations.

# 6
# The Collection Framework

The collection framework is a set of high-performance classes used to store and manipulate groups of objects. This framework allows different types of collections to work in a similar manner and is designed around a set of standard interfaces. Several standard implementations of interfaces can be extended or adapted very easily.
In this chapter, we will cover the following topics:

- An introduction to the collection framework
- Ordering of elements in collections
- Class hierarchy of the main interfaces
- The Iterable and Iterator interfaces
- The List, Set, Queue, and Map collections implementation
- Immutable collections
- Choosing the right collection

## A Dart collection framework

In general, a collection is an object that holds a group of objects. Each item in a collection is called an element. A Dart collection framework has the following benefits:

- It is a set of interfaces that forces developers to adopt some design principles
- It can improve the performance of applications significantly

A framework provides a unified interface to store and manipulate the elements of a collection and hide the actual implementation. The Dart implementation of collections is highly optimized for execution in Dart and JavaScript VMs and is far more efficient than what you could create yourself.

# Ordering of elements

Several collections implicitly support ordering of elements and help in sorting them without any effort. We can find any element with or without the filter predicate or perform a binary search within a sorted array to improve the performance of large collections. We can sort collections by providing a collection-compare function via a comparator or an object-compare method via the **Comparable** interface.

# The Comparable interface

There are many core classes in Dart that support a native comparison via the implementation of the Comparable interface. You can implement the Comparable interface in classes that you have created to use them in collections to prevent unusual results of the sorting operation. Here, we will modify the `Entity` class to implement the Comparable interface. All we have to do is implement the `compareTo` method as shown in the following code:

```
class Entity implements Comparable {
   final int index;

   Entity(this.index);

   int compareTo(Entity other) {
      return this.index.compareTo(other.index);
   }

   @override
   String toString() => index != null? index.toString() : null;
}
```

The `compareTo` method of the Comparable interface compares this `Entity` class to another one. It returns:

- A negative integer if the class is ordered before another element
- A positive integer if the class is ordered after another element
- A zero if the class and another element are ordered together

Now, we can safely order instances of the `Entity` class in our code with the `sort` method of the `List` class, as shown in the following code:

```
void main() {
   var first = new Entity(1),
       second = new Entity(2);
```

```
    var list = [second, first];
    print(list);
    // => [2, 1]
    list.sort();
    print(list);
    // => [1, 2]
}
```

# The Comparator type

So how can you sort a class that doesn't implement a Comparable interface? Here is an `Entity2` class where implementing a Comparable interface is either impossible or not desired:

```
class Entity2 {
    final int index;

    Entity2(this.index);

    @override
    String toString() => index != null ? index.toString() : null;
}
```

In order to compare this class, you must use the **Comparator** type definition as follows:

```
typedef int Comparator<T>(T a, T b);
```

The `sort` method of all the collection classes accepts a function that matches the signature of the Comparator. Here, we pass an anonymous function to sort the comparison of our `Entity2` classes as follows:

```
void main() {
    var list = [new Entity2(2), new Entity2(1)];
    print(list);
    // => [2, 1]
    list.sort((Entity2 a, Entity2 b) {
        return a.index.compareTo(b.index);
    });
    print(list);
    // => [1, 2]
}
```

As you can see, the anonymous function takes two arguments of the same type and returns an integer. This exactly matches the signature of the Comparator type definition.

If the arguments of the `sort` method are omitted, it uses the static `compare` method of the Comparable interface.

# Collections and generics

All the collection classes that are implemented use generics very heavily. As discussed in *Chapter 2*, *Advanced Techniques and Reflection*, generics provide the type of object that a collection contains. Every attempt to add another type of element generates a static analysis warning. Generics in collections have the following advantages:

- They help avoid class cast errors at runtime since we get the warnings during the static analysis time

- They make the code cleaner, as there is no need to use casting operators and conditions to check types

- They add to the runtime benefit only because the execution is done in the production mode. The code that is compiled to JavaScript does not check types and generics

# The collection class hierarchy

The Dart collection framework has a usable set of collection classes that exists in the `dart:core` and `dart:collection` libraries, as shown in the following diagram:

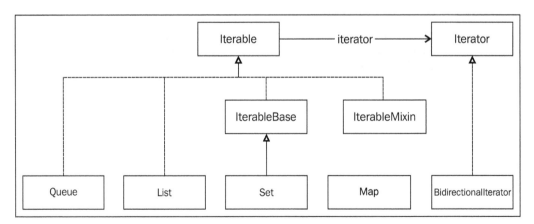

The standard collection interfaces simplify the passing and returning of collections to and from the class methods and allows the methods to work on a wide variety of collections. Using the common collection implementations makes the code shorter and quicker. By adhering to these implementations, you can make your code more standardized and easier to understand for yourself and others.

# The Iterable interface

The **Iterable** interface can be defined as the common behavior of all classes in the collection framework that supports a mechanism to iterate through all the elements of a collection. It is an object that uses an Iterator interface to iterate over all the elements in a collection. There are two abstract classes, `IterableBase` and `IterableMixin`, that implement the Iterator interface. The `IterableMixin` class is perfectly suited to be extended in the mixin solutions. If you plan to create your own implementation of the Iterable interface, you need to extend one of them. There are many different methods in the Iterable interface to help you manipulate the elements in a collection.

 The Iterable interface doesn't support adding or removing elements from a collection.

# Properties of the Iterable collection

Here is a list of the read-only properties that are common for all collections:

- `length`: This property returns the number of elements in a collection
- `isEmpty`: This property returns `true` if there are no elements in a collection
- `isNotEmpty`: This property returns `true` if there is at least one element in a collection
- `first`: This property returns the first element of a collection or throws `StateError` if the collection is empty
- `last`: This property returns the last element of a collection or throws `StateError` if the collection is empty
- `single`: This property returns a single element in a collection. It throws `StateError` if the collection is empty or has more than one element
- `iterator`: This property returns a reference on instance of the Iterator class that iterates over the elements of the collection

# Checking the items of a collection on a condition

Sometimes, you want to know if all or any of the objects in a collection comply with a specific condition. The following methods check whether the collection conforms to specific conditions:

- `every`: This method returns `true` if every element in the collection satisfies the specified condition. This can be seen in the following code:

```
List colors = ['red', 'green', 'blue'];
print(colors.every((color) => color != null || color != ''));
// => true
```

- `any`: This method returns `true` if one element in the collection satisfies the specified condition. This is illustrated in the following code:

```
List colors = ['red', 'green', 'blue'];
print(colors.any((color) => color == 'red'));
// => true
```

## The iterate over collection

The following method helps you iterate through elements of the collection:

- `forEach`: This method applies the specified function to each element of the collection. This can be seen in the following code:

```
List colors = ['red', 'green', 'blue'];
colors.forEach((color) => print(color));
// => red
// => green
// => blue
```

## The search over collection

The search over collection list includes the following methods that are used to search for an element in a collection:

- `contains`: This method returns `true` if the collection contains an element that is equal to the requested one. This is shown in the following code:

```
List colors = ['red', 'green', 'blue'];
print(colors.contains('red'));
// => true
```

- `elementAt`: This method returns the `index`th element. Exactly which object is returned depends on the sorting algorithm implemented by the specific collection class that you're using, as shown in the following code:

```
List colors = ['red', 'green', 'blue'];
print(colors.elementAt(0));
// => red
```

 If the collection does not support ordering, then the result of calling `elementAt` may be any element.

- `firstWhere`: This method returns the first element in the collection that satisfies the given predicate test or the result of the `orElse` function. It throws `StateError` if `orElse` was not specified, as illustrated in the following code:

```
List colors = ['red', 'green', 'blue'];
print(colors.firstWhere((color) => color == 'orange',
orElse:() => 'orange'));
// => orange
```

- `lastWhere`: This method returns the last element in the collection that satisfies the given predicate test or the result of the `orElse` function. It throws `StateError` if `orElse` was not specified, as shown in the following code:

```
List colors = ['red', 'green', 'blue'];
print(colors.lastWhere((color) => color != 'orange',
    orElse:() => ''));
// => blue
```

- `singleWhere`: This method returns a single element of the collection that satisfies the test. If the collection is empty or more than one element matches, then it throws `StateError`. The code is as follows:

```
List colors = ['red', 'green', 'blue'];
print(colors.singleWhere((color) => color == 'red'));
// => red
```

# Creating a new collection

The following list includes methods to create a new collection from the original one; all of them return Lazy Iterable results:

- `expand`: This method returns new collections by expanding each element of the original one to zero or more elements. This can be seen in the following code:

```
List colors = ['red', 'green', 'blue'];
print(colors.expand((color) {
  return color == 'red'
      ? ['orange', 'red', 'yellow']
      : [color];
}));
// => [orange, red, yellow, green, blue]
```

- `map`: This method creates a new collection of elements based on the elements from the original collection that are transformed with specified function. The code is as follows:

```
List colors = ['red', 'green', 'blue'];
print(colors.map((color) {
  if (color == 'green') return 'orange';
  if (color == 'blue') return 'yellow';
  return color;
}));
// => ['red', 'orange', 'yellow']
```

- `take`: This method returns an Iterable collection with a specified number of elements from the original collection. The value of these elements must not be negative. If the number of requested elements is more than the actual number of elements, then it returns all the elements from the collection:

```
List nums = [1, 2, 3, 4, 5, 6];
print(nums.take(7));
// => [1, 2, 3, 4, 5, 6]
```

- `takeWhile`: This method returns an Iterable collection that stops once the test is not satisfied anymore. This is illustrated in the following code:

```
List nums = [1, 2, 3, 4, 5, 6];
print(nums.takeWhile((element) => element < 5));
// => [1, 2, 3, 4]
```

- `skip`: This method returns an Iterable collection that skips the specified number of initial elements. If it has fewer elements than the specified number, then the resulting Iterable collection is empty. Also, the specified number must not be negative. The code is as follows:

```
List nums = [1, 2, 3, 4, 5, 6];
print(nums.skip(4));
// => [5, 6]
```

- `skipWhile`: This method returns an Iterable collection that skips the elements while the test is satisfied. This is shown in the following code:

```
List nums = [1, 2, 3, 4, 5, 6];
print(nums.skipWhile((element) => element <= 4));
// => [5, 6]
```

- `where`: This method returns a Lazy Iterable collection with all the elements that satisfy the predicate test. This is illustrated in the following code:

```
List nums = [1, 2, 3, 4, 5, 6];
print(nums.where((element) => element > 1 && element < 5));
// => [2, 3, 4]
```

- `toList`: This method creates a list that contains the elements of the original collection. It creates a fixed length `List` if the `growable` attribute is `false`:

```
List nums = [1, 2, 3];
print(nums.toList(growable:false));
// => [1, 2, 3]
```

- `toSet`: This method creates a set that contains the elements of the original collection. It ignores the duplicate elements. The code is as follows:

```
List nums = [1, 2, 1];
print(nums.toSet());
// => {1, 2}
```

# Reducing a collection

The following list includes methods to reduce the number of elements in a collection:

- `reduce`: This method reduces the collection to a single value by iteratively combining the elements of the collection using the provided function. If the collection is empty, this results in `StateError`. In the following example, we will calculate the sum of all elements in the collection:

```
List nums = [1, 2, 3];
print(nums.reduce((sum, element) => sum + element));
// => 6
```

- `fold`: This method reduces the collection to a single value by iteratively combining each element of the collection with an existing value using the specified function. Here, we have to specify the initial value and aggregation function:

```
List nums = [1, 2, 3];
print(nums.fold(0, (acc, element) => acc + element));
// => 6
```

## Converting a collection

The following method is used to convert all the elements of a collection:

- `join`: This method converts each element of the collection into a string and returns the concatenated result separated with an optional separator. If the collection is empty, it doesn't actually modify the type of the elements in the collection, but just returns an empty string:

```
List nums = [1, 2, 3];
print(nums.join(' - '));
// => 1 - 2 - 3
```

## Generating a collection

The Iterable interface has a factory method that helps to create a new Iterable interface and is filled with a specified number of values generated by a generator function, as shown in the following code:

```
Iterable generated = new Iterable.generate(4,
        (count) => "Is $count");
print(generated);
// => [Is 0, Is 1, Is 2, Is 3]
```

If the generator function is absent, this method generates a collection with only the integer values:

```
Iterable generated = new Iterable.generate(4);
print(generated);
// => [0, 1, 2, 3]
```

## The Lazy Iterable

The Lazy Iterable term is used plenty of times in Iterable interfaces. It is an iteration strategy that delays the iteration of a collection until its value is needed and avoids repeated iterations. In the following example, our code iterates over the list of numbers.

The `where` method prints the information about the current fetched element. This function calls the object only when we actually fetch the element in the `forEach` method of the Iterable interface, as shown in the following code:

```
lazyIterable() {
  List nums = [1, 2, 3];
  print('Get Iterable for $nums');
  Iterable iterable = nums.where((int i) {
    print('Fetched $i');
    return i.isOdd;
  });
  print('Start fetching');
  iterable.forEach((int i) {
    print("Received $i");
  });
}
```

Here is the output of the preceding function:

```
Get Iterable for [1, 2, 3]
Start fetching
Fetched 1
Received 1
Fetched 2
Fetched 3
Received 3
```

The following are the benefits of the Lazy Iterable:

- The performance increases because unnecessary iterations are avoided
- The memory usage footprint decreases because the values are iterated when needed
- It helps to create infinite data structures

Bear in mind that iteration over the Lazy Iterable could be much slower than a normal iteration because the code incurs the cost of an invocation to fetch the next item from the Iterable source.

# The Iterable interface

The Iterable interface has a strong relation to the Iterator. The Iterator is an interface used to get items from a collection, one at a time. It follows the fail-fast principles to immediately report whether the iterating collection was modified. The Iterator has a property called `current`, which is used to return a currently pointed element. The Iterator is initially positioned before the first element in a collection. The `moveNext` method returns `true` if there is a next element in the collection and `false` if not. Before using the Iterator, it must be initialized with the `moveNext` method to point it to the first element. In the following code, we don't initialize the Iterator with the `moveNext` method:

```
void main() {
  List<String> colors = ['red', 'green', 'blue'];

  Iterator<String> iter = colors.iterator;
  do  {
    print(iter.current);
  } while (iter.moveNext());
}
```

The result of this code is unspecified, but it can return `null` or generate an exception, as shown in the following code:

```
null
red
green
blue
```

 Always initialize the Iterator with the `moveNext` method to prevent unpredictable results.

Here is an example that shows you how to use the Iterator properly:

```
void main() {
  List<String> colors = ['red', 'green', 'blue'];

  Iterator<String> iter = colors.iterator;
  while (iter.moveNext()) {
    print(iter.current);
  }
}
```

The result is as expected:

```
red
green
blue
```

Invocation of the moveNext method returns false after the collection ends, and the current pointer always returns the last element.

The for loop statement uses the Iterator transparently to iterate through the collection:

```
void main() {
  List<String> colors = ['red', 'green', 'blue'];

  for (String color in colors) {
    print(color);
  }
}
```

The result is similar to that of the preceding example.

# BidirectionalIterator

Sometimes, we need to iterate over a collection of elements in both directions. To help in such cases, Dart provides BidirectionalIterator. In the following code, BiListIterator is the implementation of BidirectionalIterator:

```
class BiListIterator<E> implements BidirectionalIterator<E> {
  final Iterable<E> _iterable;
  final int _length;
  int _index;
  E _current;
```

The constructor has an extra optional back parameter that defines the direction of the iteration:

```
BiListIterator(Iterable<E> iterable, {bool back:false}) :
  _iterable = iterable, _length = iterable.length,
  _index = back ? iterable.length - 1 : 0;

E get current => _current;
```

The following code shows the `moveNext` method of the Iterator to move forward. This and the next method compare the length of the Iterable and the actual length of the collection to check concurrent modifications. The code is as follows:

```
bool moveNext() {
  int length = _iterable.length;
  if (_length != length) {
    throw new ConcurrentModificationError(_iterable);
  }
  if (_index >= length) {
    _current = null;
    return false;
  }
  _current = _iterable.elementAt(_index);
  _index++;
  return true;
}
```

The following `movePrevious` method of `BidirectionalIterator` is used to move backwards:

```
bool movePrevious() {
  int length = _iterable.length;
  if (_length != length) {
    throw new ConcurrentModificationError(_iterable);
  }
  if (_index < 0) {
    _current = null;
    return false;
  }
  _current = _iterable.elementAt(_index);
  _index--;
  return true;
  }
}
```

I have created a small example to prove that we can move in both directions:

```
main() {
  var list = new List.from([1, 2, 3, 4]);
  // Forward Iteration
  BiListIterator iter = new BiListIterator(list);
  while(iter.moveNext()) {
    print(iter.current);
  }
  // => 1, 2, 3, 4
```

```
  // Backward Iteration
  iter = new BiListIterator(list, back:true);
  while(iter.movePrevious()) {
    print(iter.current);
  }
  // => 4, 3, 2, 1
}
```

First, I created an instance of `List`, but it might be `Set` or `Queue` or any other collection that implements the Iterable interface. Then, I instantiated `BiListIterator` and pointed it to my Iterable collection so that we are ready to traverse via elements of the collection in the forward direction. Later, I created another instance of `BiListIterator` but specified the backward direction of the iteration. Finally, I could call `movePrevious` to move in the backward direction.

# The collection classes

The collection framework has the following classes for all occasions:

- `List`: This is an ordered collection that supports indexed access to elements and allows duplicate elements
- `Set`: This is a collection of elements in which each element can occur only once
- `Queue`: This is a collection that can be manipulated at both ends
- `Map`: This is a collection of key-value pairs where each element is accessible by a unique key

All of them define their own specific way to add or remove elements from collections. Let's discuss each of them.

# List

The `List` class implements the Iterable interface and intensively uses the indexed order to iterate over elements in the collection. The `List` class can be of a fixed or variable length. A fixed-length list can only be created by a constructor with a specific number of elements: `new List(5)`. The fixed-length type has restrictions on all operations changing the length of the list and finishing with `UnsupportedError`. The features of the fixed-length type are as follows:

- The length cannot be changed
- Any value can be assigned to the list but by the index operator only

- The elements cannot be removed from the list
- The list cannot be cleaned

The variable list returns as a result of the `new List()` or `[]` operations. It has an internal buffer and dynamically changes its size when needed. Any attempt to change the length of the `List` class during iteration will result in `ConcurrentModificationError`. The following diagram shows the hierarchy of the list-based classes:

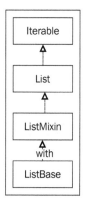

Dart always creates an instance of the `List` class as a result of instantiation. If the standard implementation of the `List` class is not enough, you can create your own implementation; just extend the `ListBase` class to align with your needs, as shown in the following code:

```
import "dart:collection";

class NewList<E> extends ListBase {
  final List<E> _elements;

  NewList() :_elements = new List<E>();

  @override
  operator [](int index) {
    return _elements[index];
  }

  @override
  void operator []=(int index, value) {
    _elements[index] = value;
  }
```

```
  @override
  int get length => _elements.length;

  @override
  void set length(int newLength) {
    _elements.length = newLength;
  }
}
```

You might be surprised to know that you need to implement only four methods to have a fully functional list-based class. This is because the other methods of the `ListBase` class use those four main methods to manage the internal buffer and iterate over elements. If you do not desire to extend the `ListBase` class, you can use `ListMixin` as follows:

```
class OtherList<E> extends MainList with ListMixin<E> {
  // ...
}
```

The `List` class interface supports ordering via a `sort` method.

 The asMap method of the `List` class returns a `Map` view that cannot be modified.

Sometimes, we need to randomly rearrange the elements in the `List` class. The `shuffle` method of the `List` class can come in handy while doing that:

```
import 'dart:math';

main() {
  var list = new List.from([1, 2, 3, 4, 5]);
  print(list);
  // => [1, 2, 3, 4, 5]
  // Crete seed to initialize internal state of
  // random-number generator
  var seed = new DateTime.now().millisecondsSinceEpoch;
  // Create instance of generator
  var random = new Random(seed);
  // Re-arrange elements in list
  list.shuffle(random);
  print(list);
  // => [4, 5, 1, 3, 2]
}
```

Run the preceding code snippet a couple of times and see the different results of the shuffle operation.

# LinkedList

The LinkedList class is a double-linked list. A LinkList class is a collection of elements of the same data type, and it is efficient when it comes to the insertion and deletion of elements of a complex structure. Despite the name, it has nothing in common with the List class.

[  The LinkedList class does not extend or implement the List class. ]

Let's take a look at the class hierarchy of the LinkedList class:

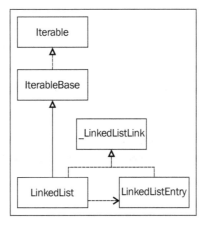

All the elements in LinkedList are based on LinkedListEntry and connected through pointers. Each LinkedListEntry class has a pointer field pointing to the next and previous elements in the list. It contains the link of the LinkedList instance it belongs to. Before adding the element to another LinkedList class, it must be removed from the current one. If it is not, StateError is thrown. Each element of the LinkedList class knows its own position, so we can use methods such as addBefore, addAfter, or unlink of LinkedListEntry to manipulate them:

```
import "dart:collection";
```

We must create a wrapper class `Element` based on `LinkedListEntry` to keep our elements, as shown in the following code:

```
class Element<E> extends LinkedListEntry {
  final E value;
  Element(this.value);
  @override
  String toString() => value != null ? value.toString() : null;
}
```

Here, we create the `LinkedList` instance and use the `Element` wrapper:

```
main() {
  LinkedList<Element> list = new LinkedList<Element>();
  Element b = new Element("B");
  list.add(b);
  //
  b.insertAfter(new Element("A"));
  b.insertBefore(new Element("C"));
  print(list);
  // => (C, B, A)
  b.unlink();
  print(list);
  // => (C, A)
}
```

Finally, we use `insertAfter`, `insertBefore`, and `unlink` of the `Element` methods to manipulate these elements. The advantages of `LinkedList` are as follows:

- It is not necessary to know the number of elements in advance, and it does not allocate more memory than necessary
- Operations such as insertion and deletion have a constant time and handle memory efficiently, especially when the element is inserted in the middle of a list
- It uses the exact amount of memory needed for an underlying element and wrapper

The disadvantages of `LinkedList` are as follows:

- It doesn't support random access to any element
- The element search can be done only via iteration
- It uses more memory to store pointers on linked elements than the list uses

# Set

The `Set` class is a collection that cannot contain identical elements. It does not allow indexed access to an element in the collection, so only the `iterator` and `for-each` loop methods can traverse elements of a `Set` class:

```
void main() {
    var aset = new Set.from([3, 2, 3, 1]);
    print(aset);
    // => {3, 2, 1}
}
```

A `Set` class can contain at most one null element.

 The `Set` factory creates the instance of `LinkedHashSet`.

The `Set` class can return a new set as a result of the execution of the intersection method between its internal collection and the other one:

```
main() {
    var aset = new Set.from([3, 2, 3, 1]);
    print(aset);
    // => {3, 2, 1}
    var other = new Set.from([2, 1, 5, 6]);
    print(other);
    // => {2, 1, 5, 6}
    var intersect = aset.intersection(other);
    print(intersect);
    // => {2, 1}
}
```

The `union` method returns a new `Set` class that contains all the elements in its internal collection and the other one:

```
main() {
    var aset = new Set.from([3, 2, 3, 1]);
    print(aset);
    // => {3, 2, 1}
    var other = new Set.from([2, 1, 5, 6]);
    print(other);
    // => {2, 1, 5, 6}
    var union = aset.union(other);
    print(union);
    // => {3, 2, 1, 5, 6}
}
```

If you need to find the difference between the elements of a certain collection and other collections, use the difference method of the Set class as follows:

```
main() {
  var aset = new Set.from([3, 2, 3, 1]);
  print(aset);
  // => {3, 2, 1}
  var other = new Set.from([2, 1, 5, 6]);
  print(other);
  // => {2, 1, 5, 6}
  var difference = aset.difference(other);
  print(difference);
  // => {3}
}
```

Here is the class hierarchy of the set-based classes:

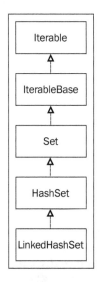

# HashSet

The HashSet class is a hash-table implementation of Set, providing fast lookup and updates. There are operations such as add, contains, remove, and length that have a constant time of execution:

```
import 'dart:collection';

void main() {
  var hset = new HashSet.from([3, 2, 3, 1]);
  print(hset);
  // => {1, 2, 3}
}
```

With `HashSet`, we can control the consistent equality via the constructor arguments:

```
import 'dart:collection';

void main() {
  var hset = new HashSet(equals:(e1, e2) {
    return e1 == e2;
  }, hashCode:(e) {
    return e.hashCode;
  });
  hset.addAll([3, 2, 3, 1]);
  print(hset);
  // => {1, 2, 3}
  hset.add(1);
  print(hset);
  //  => {1, 2, 3}
}
```

The constructor's named argument, `equals`, must be a function to compare the equality of two elements in the collection. Another constructor's named argument, `hashCode`, must be a function that calculates the hash code of the specified element. If both the elements are deemed equal, then they should return the same hash code. If both named arguments are omitted, the `Set` class uses the internal `equals` and `hashCode` methods of the element.

# LinkedHashSet

The `LinkedHasSet` class is an ordered hash-table-based `Set` implementation that maintains the insertion order of elements for iteration and runs nearly as fast as `HashSet`. The order of adding items to a collection determines the order of iteration via elements of the collection. The consistent equality in `LinkedHasList` is defined by the `equals` operator and mostly based on the value of the `hashCode` method. Adding an element that is already in `Set` does not change its position in the iteration order, but removing an element and adding it again will make it the last element of iteration:

```
import 'dart:collection';

void main() {
  var hset = new LinkedHashSet();
  hset.addAll([3, 2, 3, 1]);
  print(hset);
  // => {3, 2, 1}
  hset.add(1);
  print(hset);
  //  => {3, 2, 1}
}
```

# SplayTreeSet

Last but not least, `SplayTreeSet` is a class that maintains the collection in a sorted order, but is slow when it comes to lookups and updates. It extends a `_SplayTree` class. `Class_SplayTree` is a self-balancing **binary search tree** (**BST**). The time taken by most operations in BST is proportional to the height of the tree, and it is better to keep it small. Self-balancing BST reduces the height by performing tree transformation at logarithmic time, `O(log(n))`, where `n` is the height of the tree. The following diagram shows the hierarchy of classes:

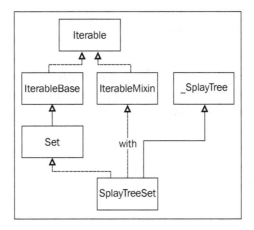

By default, a `SplayTreeSet` class assumes that all elements are comparable and uses an object-compare method to order them. In my example, I have added an array of strings to `SplayTreeSet`:

```
import 'dart:collection';

main() {
  var sset = new SplayTreeSet();
  sset.addAll(['33', '2', '33', '10']);
  print(sset);
  // => (10, 2, 33)
}
```

The order of the result is correct from the perspective of comparing the strings, but we have to order them with respect to the integer values to represent them as strings. To fix this problem, we can pass the compare function as an argument of the constructor:

```
import 'dart:collection';

main() {
  var sset = new SplayTreeSet((e1, e2) {
```

```
      return int.parse(e1).compareTo(int.parse(e2));
    });
    sset.addAll(['33', '2', '33', '10']);
    print(sset);
    // => (2, 10, 33)
  }
```

Now the result looks exactly the way we want it to be.

# Queue

A `Queue` class is a collection of elements that are added and removed in a specific order at both ends. It generally accepts null elements. A `ListQueue` class is the implementation of the general purpose `Queue` class. It uses a `List` instance to keep the collection elements and uses head and tail pointers to manipulate them. The `ListQueue` class implementation is a very efficient solution for any queue or stack usage with a small memory footprint, as shown in the following code:

```
import 'dart:collection';

void main() {
  var queue = new Queue();
  queue.add(2);
  queue.add(3);
  queue.addFirst(1);
  print(queue);
  // => {1, 2, 3}
  queue.removeLast();
  print(queue);
  // => {1, 2}
}
```

Here is the class hierarchy of `Queue`:

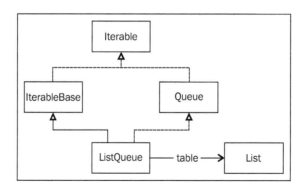

The initial capacity of `ListQueue` is eight elements, and can be changed by passing another number as an argument of the constructor. Actually, this value will be rounded up to the nearest power of two. It always checks the number of elements in queue and grows an internal collection automatically via the creation of a new `List` instance and copying elements from the old one to the new one. The removal of elements is performed by moving elements one by one to fill the hole. The `Queue` class does not reduce the size of an internal collection when it removes elements. Elements in a `Queue` class can be traversed via a `for-each` loop or within an Iterator.

# Map

The `Map` class is a collection of key-value pairs. Each key has a reference to only one value. It does not allow duplicate keys, but allows duplicate values. The `Map` class is not a subtype of the Iterator, `IteratorBase`, or even `IteratorMixin`. The `Map` class provides separate iterators for keys and values:

```
void main() {
    var map = new Map.fromIterables([3, 2, 1], ['3', '2', '1']);
    print(map);
    // => {3: 3, 2: 2, 1: 1}
}
```

The `Map` class allows you to use the `null` value as a key. Each of the `Map` class implementations behave a little differently with respect to the order of elements when iterating the map. A key of the `Map` class must implement the `equals` operator and the `hashCode` method.

 The Map factory creates the instance of `LinkedHashMap`.

The `Map` class doesn't support duplicate keys. It has a `putIfAbsent` method to look up the value of the key or add a new value if it is not present, as shown in the following code:

```
void main() {
    var map = new Map.fromIterables([3, 2, 1], ['3', '2', '1']);
    print(map);
    // => {3: 3, 2: 2, 1: 1}
    map.putIfAbsent(3, () => '33');
    map.putIfAbsent(4, () => '4');
    print(map);
    // => {3: 3, 2: 2, 1: 1, 4: 4}
}
```

This method adds key-value pairs only if the key is absent. The `containsKey` and `containsValue` methods return the search result:

```
void main() {
    var map = new Map.fromIterables([3, 2, 1], ['3', '2', '1']);
    print(map);
    // => {3: 3, 2: 2, 1: 1}
    print(map.containsKey(1));
    // => true
    print(map.containsKey(5));
    // => false
    print(map.containsValue('2'));
    // => true
    print(map.containsValue('55'));
    // => false
}
```

Here is the hierarchy of the `Map` class:

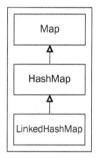

## HashMap

The `HashMap` class is a hash-table-based implementation of `Map`, providing fast lookup and updates. It maps the keys and values without guaranteeing the order of elements. In the following code, the `print` function result might be in a different order:

```
import 'dart:collection';

void main() {
    var map = new HashMap.fromIterables([2, 3, 1], ['2', '3', '1']);
    print(map);
    // => {2: 2, 1: 1, 3: 3}
}
```

Iteration of keys and values happens in parallel to reduce the time to search elements:

# LinkedHashMap

The `LinkedHashMap` class is a hash-table-based implementation of `Map` with the link list of keys to facilitate `insert` and `delete` operations, and it runs nearly as fast as `HashMap`. It remembers the key insertion order and uses it when it iterates via keys. The change in the values doesn't affect the keys' order:

```
import 'dart:collection';

void main() {
  var map = new LinkedHashMap.
      fromIterables([3, 2, 1], ['3', '2', '1']);
  print(map);
  // => {3: 3, 2: 2, 1: 1}
  map.remove(3);
  map[3] = '3';
  print(map);
  // => {2: 2, 1: 1, 3: 3}
}
```

You can provide the custom `equals` and `hashCode` functions as arguments of the constructor. The `equals` function is used to compare the keys in the table with the new keys. The following `hashCode` function is used to provide a hash value of the key:

```
import 'dart:collection';

void main() {
  var map = new LinkedHashMap(equals: (e1, e2) {
    return e1 == e2;
  }, hashCode: (e) {
    return e.hashCode;
  });
  map.addAll({3: '3', 2: '2', 1: '1'});
  print(map);
  // => {3: 3, 2: 2, 1: 1}
  map.remove(3);
  map[3] = '3';
  print(map);
  // => {2: 2, 1: 1, 3: 3}
}
```

If the `equals` attribute in a constructor is provided, it is used to compare the keys in the hash table with the new keys, else the comparison of the keys will happen with the `==` operator. Similarly, if the `hashCode` attribute of a constructor is provided, it is used to produce a hash value for the keys in order to place them in the hash table or else use the keys' own `hashCode` method.

# SplayTreeMap

The `SplayTreeMap` class is an ordered map that maintains a collection in a sorted order, but is slower when it comes to lookups and updates. This class is based on the `_SplayTree` class and also on `SplayTreeSet`. The `SplayTreeMap` class is a self-balancing binary search tree, as shown in the following diagram:

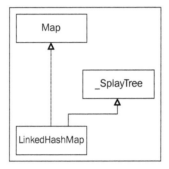

In the following code, the keys of the map are compared with the compare function passed in the constructor:

```dart
import 'dart:collection';

void main() {
  var map = new SplayTreeMap((e1, e2) {
    return e1 > e2 ? 1 : e1 < e2 ? -1 : 0;
  });
  map.addAll({3: '3', 2: '2', 1: '1'});
  print(map);
  // => {1: 1, 2: 2, 3: 3}
  map.remove(3);
  map[3] = '3';
  print(map);
  // => {1: 1, 2: 2, 3: 3}
}
```

By default, a `SplayTreeMap` function assumes that all the keys are comparable and uses an object-compare method to compare the keys of elements.

# Unmodifiable collections

The collection framework has unmodifiable versions of the existing collections with the following advantages:

- To make a collection immutable once it has been built and not modify the original collection to guarantee absolute immutability, although the elements in that collection are still mutable

- To allow read-only access to your data structure from the client code and the client code can look into it without modifying it while you have full access to the original collection

# The unmodifiable list

The unmodifiable collection based on the `List` class is `UnmodifiableListView`. It creates an unmodifiable list backed by the source provided via the argument of the constructor:

```
import 'dart:collection';

void main() {
  var list = new List.from([1, 2, 3, 4]);
  list.add(5);
  var unmodifiable = new UnmodifiableListView(list);
  unmodifiable.add(6);
}
```

The execution fails when we try adding a new element to an unmodifiable collection, as shown in the following code:

```
Unsupported operation: Cannot add to an unmodifiable list
#0 ListBase&&UnmodifiableListMixin.add (…)
#1 main (file:///…/bin/unmodifiable.dart:7:19)
…
```

The following diagram shows the class hierarchy of `UnmodifiableListView`:

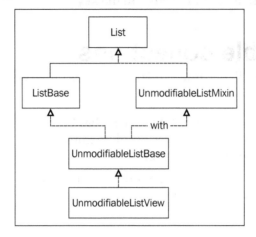

# The unmodifiable map

Another unmodifiable collection is `UnmodifiableMapView`, which is based on the `Map` class. It disallows modifying the original map via the view wrapper:

```
import 'dart:collection';

void main() {
  var map = new Map.fromIterables(
    [1, 2, 3, 4], ['1', '2', '3', '4']);
  map[5] = '5';
  var unmodifiable = new UnmodifiableMapView(map);
  unmodifiable[6] = '6';
}
```

Any attempt to modify the collection throws a runtime exception as follows:

```
Unsupported operation: Cannot modify unmodifiable map
#0      MapView&&_UnmodifiableMapMixin.[]= (…)
#1      main (file:///…/bin/unmodifiable_map.dart:7:15)
…
```

The following diagram shows the class hierarchy of `UnmodifiableMapView`:

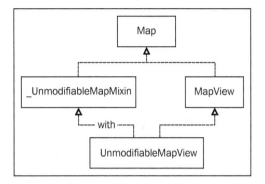

# Choosing the right collection

How do you choose the right collection for specific cases? I'm sure many of us have asked that question at least once. Let me try to help you to make the right choice:

- The `List`, `Set` (such as `LinkedHasSet`), and `Map` (such as `LinkedHashMap`) classes are perfect choices for general purposes. They have enough functionality to cover all of your needs.

- Choosing a class implements the minimum functionality that you require. Don't choose a class that supports sorting if you don't actually need it.

Here is a table that combines all the classes with the supported features:

| Class | Order | Sort | Random access | Key-values | Duplicates | Null |
|---|---|---|---|---|---|---|
| List | Yes | Yes | Yes | No | Yes | Yes |
| LinkedList | Yes | No | No | No | Yes | Yes |
| Set or LinkedHashSet | Yes | No | No | No | No | No |
| HashSet | No | No | No | No | No | No |
| SplayTreeSet | Yes | Yes | No | No | No | No |
| Queue or ListQueue | Yes | Yes | No | No | Yes | Yes |
| Map or LinkedHashMap | Yes | No | Yes | Yes | No | Yes |
| HashMap | No | No | Yes | Yes | No | Yes |
| SplayTreeMap | Yes | Yes | Yes | Yes | No | Yes |

The order is supported via iteration. Sort is supported via a collection-compare function via a Comparator or an object-compare method via the Comparable interface.

# Summary

We have now discovered the collection framework, and it's time to have a look at what we have mastered.

The collection framework is set for high-performance classes to store and manipulate groups of objects. The framework provides a unified architecture to store and manipulate the elements of a collection and hide the actual implementation.

Several collections implicitly support ordering of elements and help us to sort elements without effort. We can also sort collections by providing a collection-compare function via a Comparator or an object-compare method via the Comparable interface.

The Iterable interface defines the common behavior of all the classes in a collection framework that supports a mechanism to iterate through all the elements of a collection. The Iterator follows the fail-fast principles to immediately report whether the iterating collection was modified. If you plan to create your own implementation of the Iterable interface, you need to extend `IterableBase` or `IterableMixin`. `BidirectionalIterator` helps to iterate over collections of elements in both directions.

The collection framework also has the `List`, `Map`, `Queue`, and `Set` classes for all occasions. `LinkedList` does not extend the `List` class. `HashSet`, `LinkedHashSet`, and `SplayTreeSet` are implementations of the `Set` interface. `ListQueue` is the implementation of the `Queue` interface. `HasMap`, `LinkedHasMap`, and `SplayTreeMap` are implementations of the `Map` interface.

The collection framework has a couple of unmodifiable implementations of known interfaces, such as `UnmodifiableListView` and `UnmodifiableMapView`.

Many different programs can be written in JavaScript. In the next chapter, you will learn how to communicate with them from Dart. We will shed light on how to use Dart and JavaScript together to build web applications.

# 7
# Dart and JavaScript Interoperation

A lot of web applications are written in JavaScript nowadays and in this chapter, we will focus on how to communicate with them using Dart. We will also cover the following topics:

- The dart:js library
- Type conversion
- JsObject and instantiation
- JsFunction and the this keyword
- Dart with jQuery

## Interoperation at a glance

Web applications written in Dart can be executed only in a Dart VM that is embedded in a browser called Dartium, a special build of Chromium. To be executed in other web browsers, the Dart code must be compiled to JavaScript — the language supported by all web browsers. Latest tendencies indicate that JavaScript will exist as the language for web development for a long time to come, as it is popular among people and has a lot of tools and frameworks. This means that Dart must have the ability to communicate with the JavaScript code in any web browser.

 The JavaScript libraries need to be included in HTML before the Dart code.

# The dart:js library

The core set of Dart libraries include `dart:js` to facilitate interoperation between the Dart and JavaScript code. The Dart code can create new instances, invoke methods, and read and write properties of the code written in JavaScript. While communicating, the `dart:js` library translates the JavaScript objects to Dart objects and vice versa, or uses proxy classes. Let's take a look at the class hierarchy of the `dart:js` library:

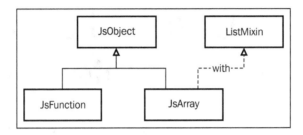

# JsObject

Similar to an `Object` class in JavaScript, `JsObject` is a main class in the `dart:js` library. It represents a proxy of a JavaScript object and provides the following advantages:

- Access to all the properties of the underlying JavaScript object by indexing the `[]` and `[] =` operators

- Access to invoke any methods of the underlying JavaScript object through `callMethod`

- Access to the global JavaScript object (usually `window`) in the web browser through the `context` property

- Usage of the `instanceOf` method to check if the underlying JavaScript object has the specified type in its prototype chain

- Checks the existence of the property of the underlying JavaScript object via the `hasProperty` method; this method is equivalent to the `in` operator in JavaScript

- Any property of the underline JavaScript object can be removed with the `deleteProperty` method; this method is equivalent to the `delete` operator in JavaScript

`JsObject` can be acquired from the JavaScript object or can be created using the following factory constructors:

- `factory JsObject(JsFunction constructor, [List arguments])`:
  This constructor creates a new JavaScript object from the JavaScript constructor function and returns a proxy on it.

- `factory JsObject.fromBrowserObject(object)`: This constructor creates a new JavaScript object from a native Dart object and returns a proxy on it. Use this factory constructor only if you wish to access the properties of the browser-hosted objects such as `Node` or `Blob`. This constructor throws an exception if the object is `null` or has the type `bool`, `num`, or `string`.

- `factory JsObject.jsify(object)`: This constructor creates a new JavaScript object or an array from the Dart Map or Iterable and returns a proxy on it. This constructor recursively converts each Dart object from the collection into a JavaScript object.

A library has a top-level context getter that provides the `JsObject` class instance, which represents the JavaScript global object in a web browser, as shown in the following code:

```
import 'dart:js' as js;

void main() {
  print('Context is ${js.context}');
}
```

The print result of the preceding code confirms that the context points to the `Window` object:

```
Context is [object Window]
```

Let's assume we need to log some information on the console from Dart. This can be done as follows:

```
import 'dart:js' as js;

void main() {
  js.JsObject console = js.context['console'];
  console.callMethod('log', ['Hello World!']);
}
```

Firstly, we used js.context to receive the proxy of the JsObject console object. Then, we used callMethod of JsObject to invoke the log function of the console. The second optional argument of callMethod delivers arguments in the underline JavaScript function. Finally, we get the **Hello World!** message on the web browser's console.

 The context returns null if the requested object does not exist.

## JsFunction

The next important piece of JavaScript is the Function type. The dart:js library has the JsFunction class that extends JsObject to represent a proxy to the JavaScript function. To call the alert JavaScript function from the Dart code, you can use the following code:

```
import 'dart:js' as js;

void main() {
    js.JsFunction alert = js.context['alert'];
    alert.apply(['Hello World!']);
}
```

When we get a proxy of the alert function, we invoke the apply method with a list of parameters and get the following result:

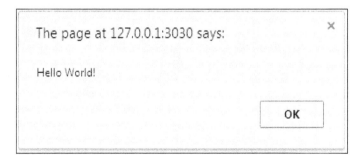

# JsArray

An array in JavaScript is the object used to store multiple values in a single variable. JsArray extends the JsObject class by representing a JavaScript array and proxy underlying instance to be available in the Dart code. I created a JavaScript code with the colors array, as shown in the following code:

```
var colors = ['red', 'green', 'white'];
```

To get all the colors and print them in Dart, we use the following code:

```
import 'dart:js' as js;

void main() {
    js.JsArray colorsArray = js.context['colors'];
    print(colorsArray);
}
```

Now, we assign a proxy to the array from the colors in JavaScript and finally print them all, as shown in the following screenshot:

```
<js_array.html>
[red, green, white]
```

If you select the colorsArray property in the variable inspector of Dart Editor when it reaches the breakpoint, you might see a set of items from the JavaScript array:

| Name | Value |
| --- | --- |
| colorsArray | [red, green, white] [id=5] |
| class | JsArray [id=6] |
| [[JavaScript View]] | Array[3] [id=1] |
| 0 | "red" |
| 1 | "green" |
| 2 | "white" |

# Type conversion

All the code we've seen so far was based on the automatic type conversion that happens inside the `dart:js` library. This conversion always happens in both directions. Once you know how this happens, you will have a better understanding of the limits of that solution and it will help you avoid mistakes.

## Direct type conversion

Dart supports the following small subset of types by directly converting them from the JavaScript types:

- `null`, `bool`, `num`, `String`, and `DateTime` (basic types)
- `Blob`
- `Event`
- `HtmlCollection`
- `ImageData`
- `KeyRange`
- `Node`
- `NodeList`
- `TypedData` (including its subclasses such as `Int32List`, but not `ByteBuffer`)
- `Window`

Here is set of different types of JavaScript variables that we prepared in the JavaScript file:

```
var v_null = null;
var v_bool = true;
var v_num = 1.2;
var v_str = "Hello";
var v_date = new Date();
var v_blob = new Blob(
  ['<a id="a"><b id="b">hey!</b></a>'],
  {type : 'text/html'});
var v_evt = new Event('click');
var v_nodes = document.createElement("form").children;
var v_img_data = document.createElement("canvas").
  getContext("2d").createImageData(10, 10);
var v_key_range = IDBKeyRange.only(100);
var v_node = document.createElement('div');
var v_node_list = document.createElement('div').childNodes;
var v_typed = new Int32Array(new ArrayBuffer(8));
var v_global = window;
```

Now, we'll use reflection to investigate how conversion happens in Dart in the following code:

```
import 'dart:js' as js;
import 'dart:mirrors';

void main() {
  print(getFromJSContext('v_null'));
  print(getFromJSContext('v_bool'));
  print(getFromJSContext('v_num'));
  print(getFromJSContext('v_str'));
  print(getFromJSContext('v_date'));
  print(getFromJSContext('v_blob'));
  print(getFromJSContext('v_evt'));
  print(getFromJSContext('v_nodes'));
  print(getFromJSContext('v_img_data'));
  print(getFromJSContext('v_key_range'));
  print(getFromJSContext('v_node'));
  print(getFromJSContext('v_node_list'));
  print(getFromJSContext('v_typed'));
  print(getFromJSContext('v_byte_data'));
  print(getFromJSContext('v_global'));
}

getFromJSContext(name) {
  var obj = js.context[name];
  if (obj == null) {
    return name + ' = null';
  } else {
    return name + ' = ' + obj.toString() + ' is ' + getType(obj);
  }
}

getType(obj) {
  Symbol symbol = reflect(obj).type.qualifiedName;
  return MirrorSystem.getName(symbol);
}
```

In the preceding code, the `getFromJSContext` method returned the name, value, and type of the converted JavaScript object. Here is the result printed on the web browser's console:

```
v_null = null
v_bool = true is dart.core.bool
v_num = 1.2 is dart.core._Double
v_str = Hello is dart.core._OneByteString
v_date = 2014-06-21 18:09:03.145 is dart.core.DateTime
v_blob = Instance of 'Blob' is dart.dom.html.Blob
v_evt = Instance of 'Event' is dart.dom.html.Event
v_nodes = [object HTMLCollection] is dart.js.JsObject
v_img_data = Instance of 'ImageData' is dart.dom.html.ImageData
v_key_range = Instance of 'KeyRange' is dart.dom.indexed_db.KeyRange
v_node = div is dart.dom.html.DivElement
v_node_list = [object NodeList] is dart.js.JsObject
v_typed = [0, 0] is dart.typed_data._ExternalInt32Array
v_byte_data = null
v_global = <window> is dart.dom.html.Window
```

You can check which Dart type will be converted from the JavaScript object with the preceding technique.

## Proxy type conversion

All the other JavaScript types are converted to Dart types with the help of a proxy. Let's take a look at the following JavaScript code:

```
var Engine = function(type) {
  this.type = type;
  this.start = function() {
    alert('Started ' + type + ' engine');
  };
};

var v_engine = new Engine('test');
```

In the preceding code, we instantiated the `Engine` class and assigned it to the `v_engine` variable. The following code helps to investigate the conversion of the `Engine` class to Dart:

```
import 'dart:js' as js;
import 'dart:mirrors';

void main() {
```

```
    print(getFromJSContext('v_engine'));
  }

getFromJSContext(name) {
  var obj = js.context[name];
  if (obj == null) {
    return name + ' = null';
  } else {
    return name + ' = ' + obj.toString() + ' is ' + getType(obj);
  }
}

getType(obj) {
  Symbol symbol = reflect(obj).type.qualifiedName;
  return MirrorSystem.getName(symbol);
}
```

In the preceding code, we copied getFromJSContext and getType from the previous code. Here is the result that is displayed in the web browser console:

```
v_engine = [object Object] is dart.js.JsObject
```

This result confirms that any ordinary object can be converted to Dart with the JsObject proxy.

# Collection conversion

Dart collections can be converted into JavaScript collections with the jsify constructor of JsObject. This constructor converts Dart Maps and Iterables into JavaScript objects and arrays recursively, and returns a JsObject proxy to it. It supports internal collections as well. The following JavaScript code has the variable data and the toType and log methods:

```
function toType(obj) {
  return ({}).toString.call(obj).
    match(/\s([a-zA-Z]+)/)[1].toLowerCase()
};

var data;

function log() {
  console.log(toType(data));
  for (i in data) {
    console.log('- ' + i.toString() + ': ' +
      data[i].toString() + ' (' + toType(data[i]) + ')');
  }
};
```

Let's take a look at the Dart code that has references to the `log` function of JavaScript:

```dart
import 'dart:js' as js;

void main() {
  js.JsFunction log = js.context['log'];

  js.JsArray array = new js.JsObject.jsify([1, 'a', true]);
  js.context['data'] = array;
  log.apply([]);

  js.JsObject map = new js.JsObject.jsify(
    {'n':1, 't':'a', 'b':true, 'array':array}
  );
  js.context['data'] = map;
  log.apply([]);
}
```

In the preceding code, we created an `array` and assigned it to a JavaScript `data` variable. We logged all the items of the JavaScript `array` via the `apply` method of log. We send empty array as argument of the apply function because the corresponding JavaScript function doesn't have parameters. Later, we created a `map` object, filled it, and then call a `log` JavaScript function again. To check the support of the internal collections, we inserted the `array` into the `map` object as the last item. Here is the result:

```
array
- 0: 1 (number)
- 1: a (string)
- 2: true (boolean)
object
- n: 1 (number)
- t: a (string)
- b: true (boolean)
- array: 1,a,true (array)
```

All our objects and internal collections were converted into the correct JavaScript objects.

# JsObject and instantiation

The object constructor function is a standard way to create an instance of an Object class in JavaScript. An object constructor is just a regular JavaScript function and it is robust enough to define properties, invoke other functions, and do much more. To create an instance of the object, we need to call the object constructor function via a `new` operator. Let's have a look at the next JavaScript code:

```
function Engine(type) {
  this.type = type;
  this.start = function() {
    console.log ('Started ' + type + ' engine');
  };
};
```

`Engine` is an object constructor function. It has a `type` property and a `start` method. Here is how we can create an instance of the JavaScript object from Dart:

```
import 'dart:js' as js;

void main() {
  js.JsFunction JsEngine = js.context['Engine'];
  js.JsObject engineObj = new js.JsObject(JsEngine, ['diesel']);
  assert(engineObj.instanceof(JsEngine));
  engineObj.callMethod('start');
}
```

We created a `JsFunction` variable, `JsEngine`, as a reference to the JavaScript object constructor function `Engine`. To create an object type `engineObj`, we used an object constructor created via the `JsObject` proxy. The function arguments must be sent via a second parameter, so we specified `diesel` as the engine type. Later, we check whether `engineObj` is an instance of the `JsEngine` type. Finally, we call the `start` method from `engineObj` and it prints the following message on the console:

```
Started diesel engine
```

If you select the JsEngine property in the variable inspector of the Dart Editor when the breakpoint is reached, you will see the source code of the JavaScript function, as shown in the following screenshot:

```
Name                    Value
 ▷  ● JsEngine            function Engine(type) { this.type ...
function Engine(type) {|
  this.type = type;
  this.start = function() {
    console.log('Started ' + type + ' engine');
  };
}
```

# JsFunction and the this keyword

The this keyword refers to the current instance of a class in Dart and never changes once the class object is instantiated. Generally, we should omit the this keyword and use it only if we have name conflicts between the class members and function arguments or variables. In JavaScript, the this keyword refers to the object that owns the function and behaves differently compared to Dart. It mostly depends on how a function is called. We can't change the value of this during function execution and it can be different every time the function is called. The call and apply methods of Function.prototype were introduced in ECMAScript 3 to bind any particular object on the value of this in the call of these methods:

```
fun.call(thisArg[, arg1[, arg2[, ...]]])
fun.apply(thisArgs[, argsArray])
```

While the syntax of both these functions looks similar, the fundamental difference is that the call method accepts an argument list while the apply method accepts a single array of arguments.

All the functions in JavaScript inherit the call and apply methods from Function.prototype, so both the methods invoke the original function and assign the first argument to the value of the this keyword permanently so it cannot be overridden.

The following bind method of Function.prototype was introduced in ECMAScript 5:

```
fun.bind(thisArg[, arg1[, arg2[, ...]]])
```

This method creates a new function with the same body and scope as the original function, but the `this` keyword is permanently bound to the first argument of the `bind` function, regardless how the function is being used. The `call` and `bind` methods can solve the issues we face while changing the `this` keyword. Let's take a look at how we can do this with the following JavaScript code:

```
this.name = 'Unknown';

function sendMessage(message) {
   console.log('Send message: ' + this.name + ' ' + message);
}

function DieselEngine() {
   this.name = 'Diesel';
}

sendMessage('engine started');

var engine = new DieselEngine()

var dieselLog = sendMessage.bind(engine);
dieselLog('engine started');
```

The invocation of the `sendMessage` function results in the following console log:

```
Send message: Unknown engine started
```

The `sendMessage` function prints a message on the console with the `Unknown` name because `this` references the global object in the web browser. Then, we create an instance of `Engine` and bind the `sendMessage` function to `engine`. The `bind` method creates a new function `dieselLog` with the same body, but the `this` keyword is permanently bound to `engine`. So, when you call the `dieselLog` function, it uses the name from `DieselEngine` and prints the following message:

```
Send message: Diesel engine started
```

If we need to use the Dart version of `sendMessage` instead of the original one, we can use `JsFunction` instantiated with the `withThis` constructor of the `JsObject` class to call the function with the value of `this` passed as the first argument:

```
import 'dart:js' as js;

void main() {
   js.context['sendMessage'] = new
     js.JsFunction.withThis(otherSendMessage);
```

```
    js.JsFunction DieselEngine = js.context['DieselEngine'];
    js.JsObject engine = new js.JsObject(DieselEngine);

    js.JsFunction sendMessage = js.context['sendMessage'];
    sendMessage.apply(['engine started'], thisArg: engine);
}

otherSendMessage(self, String message) {
    print('Message sent: ' + self['name'] + ' ' + message);
}
```

First, we assigned Dart's `otherSendMessage` function to JavaScript's `sendMessage` function. The named constructor `withThis` creates a JavaScript function pattern and uses the reference on `otherSendMessage` instead of `func` in all the future calls:

```
function () {
    return func(this, Array.prototype.slice.apply(arguments));
}
```

So, when we call the `apply` method of `sendMessage`, the JavaScript function calls the original `otherSendMessage` function. It passes the `engine` object to the `self` parameter of the `otherSendMessage` function and passes the `engine started` string in the `message` parameter. The result is printed to the web console:

```
Send message: Unknown engine started
Send message: Diesel engine started
Message sent: Diesel engine started
```

Bear in mind that the type of parameter `self` of the `otherSendMessage` function depends on the value passed as the second argument of the `apply` method of `sendMessage` instance.

# Dart with jQuery

There is no doubt that jQuery has become very popular among developers because of its simplicity. Let's try to combine the simplicity of jQuery and the power of Dart in a real example. For demonstration purposes, we created the `js_proxy` package to help the Dart code to communicate with jQuery. It is available on the pub manager at `https://pub.dartlang.org/packages/js_proxy`. This package is layered on `dart:js` and has a library of the same name and sole class `JProxy`. An instance of the `JProxy` class can be created via the generative constructor where we can specify the optional reference on the proxied `JsObject`:

```
JProxy([this._object]);
```

We can create an instance of `JProxy` with a named constructor and provide the name of the JavaScript object accessible through the `dart:js` context as follows:

```
JProxy.fromContext(String name) {
  _object = js.context[name];
  }
```

The `JProxy` instance keeps the reference on the proxied `JsObject` class and makes all the manipulation on it, as shown in the following code:

```
js.JsObject _object;
js.JsObject get object => _object;
```

# How to create a shortcut to jQuery

We can use `JProxy` to create a reference to jQuery via the context from the `dart:js` library as follows:

```
var jquery = new JProxy.fromContext('jQuery');
```

Another very popular way is to use the dollar sign as a shortcut to the jQuery variable as shown in the following code:

```
var $ = new JProxy.fromContext('jQuery');
```

Bear in mind that the original `jQuery` and `$` variables from JavaScript are functions, so our variables reference to the `JsFunction` class. From now, jQuery lovers who moved to Dart have a chance to use both the syntax to work with selectors via parentheses.

# Why does JProxy need a method call?

Usually, jQuery sends a request to select HTML elements based on IDs, classes, types, attributes, and values of their attributes or their combination, and then performs some action on the results. We can use the basic syntax to pass the search criteria in the `jQuery` or `$` function to select the HTML elements:

```
$(selector)
```

As mentioned in *Chapter 3, Object Creation,* Dart has a syntactic sugar method, `call`, that helps us to emulate a function and we can use the `call` method in the jQuery syntax. Dart knows nothing about the number of arguments passing through the function, so we use the fixed number of optional arguments in the `call` method. Through this method, we invoke the proxied function (because `jquery` and `$` are functions) and returns results within `JProxy`:

```
dynamic call([arg0 = null, arg1 = null, arg2 = null,
    arg3 = null, arg4 = null, arg5 = null, arg6 = null,
    arg7 = null, arg8 = null, arg9 = null]) {
  var args = [];
  if (arg0 != null) args.add(arg0);
  if (arg1 != null) args.add(arg1);
  if (arg2 != null) args.add(arg2);
  if (arg3 != null) args.add(arg3);
  if (arg4 != null) args.add(arg4);
  if (arg5 != null) args.add(arg5);
  if (arg6 != null) args.add(arg6);
  if (arg7 != null) args.add(arg7);
  if (arg8 != null) args.add(arg8);
  if (arg9 != null) args.add(arg9);
  return _proxify((_object as js.JsFunction).apply(args));
}
```

# How does JProxy invoke jQuery?

The `JProxy` class is a proxy to other classes, so it marks with the `@proxy` annotation. We override `noSuchMethod` intentionally to call the proxied methods and properties of jQuery when the methods or properties of the proxy are invoked. The logic flow in `noSuchMethod` is pretty straightforward. It invokes `callMethod` of the proxied `JsObject` when we invoke the method on proxy, or returns a value of property of the proxied object if we call the corresponding operation on proxy. The code is as follows:

```
@override
dynamic noSuchMethod(Invocation invocation) {
  if (invocation.isMethod) {
    return _proxify(_object.callMethod(
      symbolAsString(invocation.memberName),
      _jsify(invocation.positionalArguments)));
  } else if (invocation.isGetter) {
    return
      _proxify(_object[symbolAsString(invocation.memberName)]);
  } else if (invocation.isSetter) {
```

```
      throw new Exception('The setter feature was not implemented
        yet.');
    }
    return super.noSuchMethod(invocation);
  }
```

As you might remember, all Map or Iterable arguments must be converted to
JsObject with the help of the jsify method. In our case, we call the _jsify method
to check and convert passed arguments aligned with a called function, as shown in
the following code:

```
List _jsify(List params) {
  List res = [];
  params.forEach((item) {
    if (item is Map || item is List) {
      res.add(new js.JsObject.jsify(item));
    } else {
      res.add(item);
    }
  });
  return res;
  }
```

Before return, the result must be passed through the _proxify function as follows:

```
dynamic _proxify(value) {
    return value is js.JsObject ? new JProxy(value) : value;
}
```

This function wraps all JsObject classes within a JProxy class and passes other
values as it is.

# An example project

Now create the jquery project, open the pubspec.yaml file, and add js_proxy to
the dependencies. Open the jquery.html file and make the following changes:

```
<!DOCTYPE html>

<html>
  <head>
    <meta charset="utf-8">
    <meta name="viewport"
      content="width=device-width, initial-scale=1">
    <title>jQuery</title>
```

```
     <link rel="stylesheet" href="jquery.css">
   </head>
   <body>
     <h1>Jquery</h1>

     <p>I'm a paragraph</p>
     <p>Click on me to hide</p>
     <button>Click me</button>
     <div class="container">
           <div class="box"></div>
     </div>

   </body>

   <script src="//code.jquery.com/jquery-1.11.0.min.js"></script>

   <script type="application/dart" src="jquery.dart"></script>
   <script src="packages/browser/dart.js"></script>
</html>
```

This project aims to demonstrate that:

- Communication is easy between Dart and JavaScript
- The syntax of the Dart code could be similar to the jQuery code

In general, you can copy the JavaScript code, paste it in the Dart code, and probably make slightly small changes.

# How to get the jQuery version

It's time to add js_proxy in our code. Open jquery.dart and make the following changes:

```
import 'dart:html';
import 'package:js_proxy/js_proxy.dart';

/**
 * Shortcut for jQuery.
 */
var $ = new JProxy.fromContext('jQuery');

/**
 * Shortcut for browser console object.
 */
```

```
var console = window.console;

main() {
  printVersion();
}

/**
 * jQuery code:
 *
 *    var ver = $().jquery;
 *    console.log("jQuery version is " + ver);
 *
 * JS_Proxy based analog:
 */
printVersion() {
  var ver = $().jquery;
  console.log("jQuery version is " + ver);
}
```

You should be familiar with jQuery and console shortcuts by now. The call to jQuery with empty parentheses returns JProxy and contains JsObject with reference to jQuery from JavaScript. The jQuery object has a jquery property that contains the current version number, so we reach this one via noSuchMethod of JProxy. Run the application, and you will see the following result in the console:

```
jQuery version is 1.11.1
```

Let's move on and perform some actions on the selected HTML elements.

# How to perform actions in jQuery

The syntax of jQuery is based on selecting the HTML elements and it also performs some actions on them:

```
$(selector).action();
```

Let's select a button on the HTML page and fire the click event as shown in the following code:

```
/**
 * jQuery code:
 *
 *    $("button").click(function(){
 *      alert('You click on button');
 *    });
 *
```

```
 * JS_Proxy based analog:
 */
events() {
  // We remove 'function' and add 'event' here
  $("button").click((event) {
    // Call method 'alert' of 'window'
    window.alert('You click on button');
  });
}
```

All we need to do here is just remove the `function` keyword, because anonymous functions on Dart do not use it, and then add the `event` parameter. This is because this argument is required in the Dart version of the event listener. The code calls jQuery to find all the HTML button elements to add the `click` event listener to each of them. So when we click on any button, a specified alert message will be displayed. On running the application, you will see the following message:

## How to use effects in jQuery

The jQuery supports animation out of the box, so it sounds very tempting to use it in Dart. Let's take a look at the following code snippet:

```
/**
 * jQuery code:
 *
 *   $("p").click(function() {
 *     this.hide("slow",function(){
 *       alert("The paragraph is now hidden");
 *     });
 *   });
 *   $(".box").click(function(){
 *     var box = this;
```

```
 *        startAnimation();
 *        function startAnimation(){
 *          box.animate({height:300},"slow");
 *          box.animate({width:300},"slow");
 *          box.css("background-color","blue");
 *          box.animate({height:100},"slow");
 *          box.animate({width:100},"slow",startAnimation);
 *        }
 *      });
 *
 * JS_Proxy based analog:
 */
effects() {
  $("p").click((event) {
    $(event['target']).hide("slow", (){
      window.alert("The paragraph is now hidden");
    });
  });
  $(".box").click((event) {
    var box = $(event['target']);
    startAnimation() {
      box.animate({'height':300},"slow");
      box.animate({'width':300},"slow");
      box.css("background-color","blue");
      box.animate({'height':100},"slow");
      box.animate({'width':100},"slow",startAnimation);
    };
    startAnimation();
  });
}
```

This code finds all the paragraphs on the web page to add a `click` event listener to each one. The JavaScript code uses the `this` keyword as a reference to the selected paragraph to start the hiding animation. The `this` keyword has a different notion on JavaScript and Dart, so we cannot use it directly in anonymous functions on Dart. The `target` property of `event` keeps the reference to the clicked element and presents `JsObject` in Dart. We wrap the clicked element to return a `JProxy` instance and use it to call the `hide` method.

The jQuery is big enough and we have no space in this book to discover all its features, but you can find more examples at `https://github.com/akserg/js_proxy`.

# What is the impact on performance?

Now we should talk about the performance impact of using different approaches across several modern web browsers. The algorithm must perform all the following actions:

- It should create 10000 DIV elements
- Each element should be added into the same DIV container
- Each element should be updated with one style
- All elements must be removed one by one

This algorithm must be implemented in the following solutions:

- The clear jQuery solution on JavaScript
- The jQuery solution calling via `JProxy` and `dart:js` from Dart
- The clear Dart solution based on `dart:html`

We implemented this algorithm on all of them, so we have a chance to compare the results and choose the champion. The following HTML code has three buttons to run independent tests, three paragraph elements to show the results of the tests, and one DIV element used as a container. The code is as follows:

```html
<div>
    <button id="run_js" onclick="run_js_test()">Run JS</button>
    <button id="run_jproxy">Run JProxy</button>
    <button id="run_dart">Run Dart</button>
</div>

<p id="result_js"></p>
<p id="result_jproxy"></p>
<p id="result_dart"></p>

<div id="container"></div>
```

The JavaScript code based on jQuery is as follows:

```javascript
function run_js_test() {
  var startTime = new Date();
  process_js();
  var diff = new Date(new Date().getTime() -
    startTime.getTime()).getTime();
  $('#result_js').text('jQuery tooks ' + diff +
    ' ms to process 10000 HTML elements.');
}
```

```
function process_js() {
  var container = $('#container');
  // Create 10000 DIV elements
  for (var i = 0; i < 10000; i++) {
    $('<div>Test</div>').appendTo(container);
  }
  // Find and update classes of all DIV elements
  $('#container > div').css("color","red");
  // Remove all DIV elements
  $('#container > div').remove();
}
```

The main code registers the `click` event listeners and the call function
`run_dart_js_test`. The first parameter of the `run_dart_js_test` function
must be a function which we will investigate. The second and third parameters
are used to pass the selector of the result element and test the title:

```
void main() {
  querySelector('#run_jproxy').onClick.listen((event) {
    run_dart_js_test(process_jproxy, '#result_jproxy', 'JProxy');
  });
  querySelector('#run_dart').onClick.listen((event) {
    run_dart_js_test(process_dart, '#result_dart', 'Dart');
  });
}

run_dart_js_test(Function fun, String el, String title) {
  var startTime = new DateTime.now();
  fun();
  var  diff = new DateTime.now().difference(startTime);
  querySelector(el).text = '$title tooks ${diff.inMilliseconds} ms
    to process 10000 HTML elements.';
}
```

Here is the Dart solution based on `JProxy` and `dart:js`:

```
process_jproxy() {
  var container = $('#container');
  // Create 10000 DIV elements
  for (var i = 0; i < 10000; i++) {
    $('<div>Test</div>').appendTo(container.object);
  }
  // Find and update classes of all DIV elements
  $('#container > div').css("color","red");
  // Remove all DIV elements
  $('#container > div').remove();
}
```

Finally, a clear Dart solution based on `dart:html` is as follows:

```
process_dart() {
  // Create 10000 DIV elements
  var container = querySelector('#container');
  for (var i = 0; i < 10000; i++) {
    container.appendHtml('<div>Test</div>');
  }
  // Find and update classes of all DIV elements
  querySelectorAll('#container > div').forEach((Element el) {
    el.style.color = 'red';
  });
  // Remove all DIV elements
  querySelectorAll('#container > div').forEach((Element el) {
    el.remove();
  });
}
```

All the results are in milliseconds. Run the application and wait until the web page is fully loaded. Run each test by clicking on the appropriate button. My result of the tests on Dartium, Chrome, Firefox, and Internet Explorer are shown in the following table:

| Web browser | jQuery framework | jQuery via JProxy | Library dart:html |
|---|---|---|---|
| Dartium | 2173 | 3156 | 714 |
| Chrome | 2935 | 6512 | 795 |
| Firefox | 2485 | 5787 | 582 |
| Internet Explorer | 12262 | 17748 | 2956 |

Now, we have the absolute champion—the Dart-based solution. Even the Dart code compiled in the JavaScript code to be executed in Chrome, Firefox, and Internet Explorer works quicker than jQuery (four to five times) and much quicker than `dart:js` and `JProxy` class-based solutions (four to ten times).

# Summary

Let me finish the story of Dart to JavaScript interoperation to highlight our expertise.

The core set of Dart libraries include `dart:js` to help you interoperate between the Dart and JavaScript code. The `dart:js` library converts the original JavaScript objects, functions, and collections with the help of `JsObject`, `JsFunction`, and `JsArray`. It supports automatic type of conversion in both directions. Dart supports a small subset of types, transferring directly from JavaScript types. All other JavaScript types are converted to Dart types with the help of a proxy. Dart Map and Iterable collections could be translated into JavaScript collections with the `jsify` constructor of `JsObject`.

We compared `jQuery`, `JProxy`, and `dart:js` and cleared the Dart code based on the `dart:html` solutions to identify who is quicker than the others. The `dart:html` library-based solution is the unbeatable champion and hero of this chapter.

In the next chapter, we will talk about how i18n and l10n accesses can be embedded into our code to help design and develop web applications that enable easy localization for different cultures, regions, and languages.

# 8

# Internalization and Localization

If you are planning to work with multiple languages, you need to add internalization support to your web applications. We will see how the i18n and l10n access can be embedded in our code to help design and develop web applications that enable easy localization for different cultures, regions, and languages. The topics that will be covered in this chapter are as follows:

- The key principles
- The Intl library
- How to internationalize a web application
- How to extract messages
- How to use Google Translator Toolkit
- How to use translated messages

## The key principles

The development of globalized software is not a simple task. In general, the standard development process to create globalized software includes the following steps:

- Internalization that covers designing and developing web applications
- Localization that covers translating and customizing web applications for a specific locale

We will start designing and developing globalized software with the Intl library from the intl package available on the pub manager and follow some rules that will help us to easily translate and customize our application.

# Executable code versus User Interface

All executable code must be separated from the programming code that implements the **User Interface (UI)**. Also, code that describes the UI elements and the layout of the UI elements must be kept separated from the code that implements and manages them.

# Numbers and dates

Various cultures have different ways to represent numbers and dates. You must avoid converting numbers and dates into strings directly.

 Converting numbers and dates must be done with special formatters.

# Messages

Often, messages that contain individual pieces of text are used together to create complete sentences. In the process of localization, these pieces of text might go together in a different order. Using the message method of the Intl class allows you to display messages as simple expressions.

# Measuring units and currencies

Measuring units such as meters and miles and currencies such as USD and Euro are ubiquitous and depend on the locale. The NumberFormat class contains special constructors for the quick creation of frequently used patterns that can be very handy to measure units and currencies.

# Text input and layout

The size of the text on the screen is one of the biggest problems that affect programmers who develop globalized software. The main reason for this is that any assumption about the width of the text, the direction of its flow, and its position on the screen, if incorrect, can hamper well-structured layouts in a flash. Using the BidiFormatter class helps manage messages that contain text in both the text directionalities.

# Formatting date and time

The locale determines how the date and time must be displayed. The DateFormat class has a big set of naming patterns that is useful to avoid mistakes and display data in the correct format.

# The Intl library

The Intl library can help you design and develop globalized server and web client applications. It supports all major locales and sublanguage pairs. As all information on the screen represents a set of strings, we must translate the other types of objects into the string format with special formatters provided by the Intl library. Translated versions of displayed strings are bundled in separate text files. The Intl library contains a class of the same name that is used to work with messages. The Intl library considers numbers, dates, and messages in different internalization areas. Each area is intentionally initialized separately to reduce the application size and avoid loading unnecessary resources. The internalization of numbers and dates is implemented via formatters. Messages are internalized through special functions and can be externalized into files in the **Application Resource Bundle (ARB)** format.

# Changing a locale

By default, the current locale is set to the English language of USA (en_US). A new value assigned to defaultLocale can affect all the methods of the Intl library using the following code:

```
Intl.defaultLocale = "fr_FR";
```

There are several ways to use a different locale on a temporary basis than using the current one. They are as follows:

- Specify the locale directly when you call the methods of the Intl class
- Provide the locale when you create an instance of the formatter class
- Use the following special withLocale method of the Intl class:

```
static withLocale(String locale, Function message_function)
```

The main purpose of the withLocale method is to delay calling the message_function function until the proper locale has been set. The message_function function can be a simple message function, a wrapper around the message function, or a complex wrapper that manipulates multiple message functions. As the locale string is not known at the static analysis time, this method silently performs the following steps:

1. It swaps the specified locale string with the current one.
2. Then, it executes the message_function function and saves the result.
3. It swaps the locales back.
4. Finally, it returns the result of the message_function function.

**International Components for Unicode** (ICU) is an open source project created for the Unicode support via the implementation of the Unicode standard. The `Intl` library uses the ICU patterns for internalization and localization.

# Formatting numbers

The `NumberFormat` class provides the ability to format a number in a locale-specific manner. To create `NumberFormat`, we must specify the pattern in the ICU format, as shown in the following code:

```
var f = new NumberFormat("###.0#");
print(f.format(12.345));
// Result: 12.35
```

The second optional parameter of the `NumberFormat` factory constructor is the locale. If the locale parameter is not specified, the constructor uses a default value in the current locale. The `NumberFormat` class contains the following named constructors for the quick creation of frequently used patterns in a specific locale:

- The decimal format uses the decimal pattern, that is, `#,##0.###`:

```
var d = new NumberFormat.decimalPattern("de_DE");
print(d.format(12.345));
// Result: 12,345
```

- The percent format uses the percent pattern, that is, `#,##0%`:

```
var p = new NumberFormat.percentPattern("de_DE");
print(p.format(12.345));
// Result: 1.235%
```

- The scientific format prints only the terms equivalent to `#E0` and does not take into account the significant digits:

```
var s = new NumberFormat.scientificPattern("de_DE");
print(s.format(12.345));
// ==> 1E1
```

- The currency format always uses the name of the currency passed as the second parameter:

```
var c = new NumberFormat.currencyPattern("de_DE", 'EUR');
print(c.format(12.345));
// ==> 12,35EUR
```

# Formatting dates

The DateFormat class can format and parse the date in a locale-sensitive manner. We can choose the format-parse pattern from a set of standard date and time formats, or we can create a customized one under certain locales. The DateFormat class formats the date in the default en_US locale without any initialization. For other locales, the formatting data must be obtained and the global initializeDateFormatting function must be called to return Future that is complete once the locale data is available. Depending on the type of the application you develop, you can choose one of the following libraries that provide this function implementation and enables you to access to the formatting data:

- date_symbol_data_local: For a small application, the data to be formatted can be embedded in the code that is available locally so that you can choose the date_symbol_data_local library. In the following code, we initialize the date formatting for all the locales at once. Both the parameters of the initializeDateFormatting method are ignored because the data for all the locales is directly available, as shown in the following code:

```
import 'package:intl/date_symbol_data_local.dart';
import 'package:intl/intl.dart';

void main() {
  initializeDateFormatting(null, null)
  .then((_) {
    Intl.defaultLocale = "de_DE";
    DateFormat df = new DateFormat("EEE, MMM d, yyyy");
    print(df.format(new DateTime.now()));
  }).catchError((err) {
    print(err);
  });
  // Result: Sa., Sep. 20, 2014
}
```

- date_symbol_data_http_request: For the client side, you need an application that runs inside the web browser and possibly compiles into the JavaScript code. You need to read the data from the server using the XmlHttpRequest mechanism so that you can choose the date_symbol_data_http_request library. We need set up the lookup for the date symbols using URL as a second parameter of the initializeDateFormatting method. We use the path package that provides common operations to manipulate paths in our example:

```
import 'package:intl/date_symbol_data_http_request.dart';
import 'package:intl/intl.dart';
import 'package:path/path.dart' as path;
```

```
void main() {
  String datesPath = path.join(path.current,
      path.fromUri("packages/intl/src/data/dates/"));
  initializeDateFormatting("pt_BR", datesPath)
  .then((_) {
    Intl.defaultLocale = "pt_BR";
    DateFormat df = new DateFormat("EEE, MMM d, yyyy");
    print(df.format(new DateTime.now()));
  }).catchError((err) {
    print(err);
  });
}
// Result: sáb, set 20, 2014
```

In the preceding code, we requested the date formats for `Portuguese -` `BRAZIL` locale and then set them as a default locale. After that, we used `DateFormat` to format current date and time.

- `date_symbol_data_file`: For the server side, you need an application that executes inside the Dart VM so that you can choose the `date_symbol_data_` `file` library that helps you to read the data from the files in the filesystem. We use the second parameter of the `initializeDateFormatting` method to pass the path to those files. The `path` parameter will end with a directory separator that is appropriate for the platform. We use the path package for the following example again:

```
import 'package:intl/date_symbol_data_local.dart';
import 'package:intl/Intl.dart';
import 'package:path/path.dart' as path;

void main() {
  String datesPath = path.join(path.current,
      path.fromUri("packages/intl/src/data/dates/"));
  initializeDateFormatting("fr", datesPath)
  .then((_) {
    DateFormat df = new DateFormat("EEE, MMM d, yyyy",
      "fr_FR");
    print(df.format(new DateTime.now()));
  }).catchError((err) {
    print(err);
  });
  // Result: sam., sept. 20, 2014
}
```

When the locale data is ready to use, we need to specify the ICU date/time patterns, which should be used either in full names or preferably their compact skeleton forms as shown in the following code:

```
new DateFormat.yMd(); // Skeleton form
new DateFormat(DateFormat.YEAR_NUM_MONTH_DAY); // ICU full name
// Result: 7/10/2005
```

We can create compound formats with a set of the add_* methods as follows:

```
new DateFormat.yMd().add_Hm();
// Result: 7/10/2005 09:10 PM
```

The DateFormat class accepts custom formats that follow the explicit pattern syntax. The constructor resolves a custom pattern and adapts it in different locales, as shown in the following code:

```
new DateFormat("EEE, MMM d, yyyy");
// Result: Fri, October 7, 2005
```

The locale is the second optional parameter of the DateFormat constructor that helps to create the formatter in a specific locale. The constructor generates ArgumentError if a specified locale does not exist in the set of supported locales.

# Internalizing messages

The internalization of messages is based on a lookup via a named localized version of messages and returning the translated message, possibly interpolated with a list of specified arguments. So, to localize any message, such as Hello $name from Dart!, we will create a lookup message function that returns the result of the Intl.message method call, as shown in the following code:

```
String hello(name) => Intl.message(
    "Hello $name from Dart!",
    name:"hello",
    args: [name],
    examples: {"name":"World"},
    desc: "Greet the user with specified name");
```

We will use the hello message function as a wrapper due to the following reasons:

- The function scope can encapsulate an implementation
- The function parameters can be passed as parameters in the Intl.message method

The message string that is passed as the first parameter must be a simple expression where only function parameters and curly brackets are allowed. Other parameters must be literal and should not contain any interpolation expressions.

 The name and args arguments of the message function are required and the name argument must match the name of the caller function.

Now, instead of assigning the message to our code, we will call the hello function to return the translated message for us, as shown in the following code:

```
querySelector("#dart_greating")
    ..text = hello('John');
```

In other cases that are similar to our example, the hello function can interpolate the results of the translated message with a list of arguments that is passed in. The examples and desc parameters are not used at runtime and are only made available to the translators. Now, we ready to start using the message functions without any localization and will finally have the correct translation in the current locale.

# Adding parentheses

We can use parentheses to combine the singular and the plural forms into one string with the plural method of the Intl class, as shown in the following code:

```
String replace(int num, String str) => Intl.plural(
    num,
    zero: "No one occurrence replaced for $str",
    one: "$num occurrence replaced for $str",
    other: "$num occurrences replaced for $str",
    name: "replace",
    args: [num, str],
    desc:"How many occurrences replaced for string",
    examples: {'num':2, 'str':'hello'});
```

The plural method translates and interpolates the contents of the zero, one, and other parameters into a localized message. We missed the two, few, and many parameters because a method can only combine the one and other methods but you can specify them if necessary. The plural method when represented as a String expression can be used as part of Intl.message, which specifies only the plural attributes as shown in the following code:

```
String replace(int num, String str) =>  Intl.message(
    """${Intl.plural(
        num,
```

```
        zero: "No one occurrence replaced for $str",
        one: "$num occurrence replaced for $str",
        two: "$num occurrence replaced for $str",
        few: "$num occurrences replaced for $str",
        other: "$num occurrences replaced for $str")}""",
    name: "replace",
    args: [num, str],
    desc:"How many occurrences replaced for string",
    examples: {'num':2, 'str':'hello'});
 );
```

# Adding gender

The gender method of the Intl class provides out-of-the-box support for gender-based selection, as shown in the following code:

```
String usage(String name, String gender, String car) =>
  Intl.gender(
    gender,
    male: "$name uses his $car",
    female: "$name uses her $car",
    other: "$name uses its car",
    name: "usage","",
    args: [name, gender, car],
    desc: "A person uses the car.");
```

The gender parameter must equal to one of the literal values: male, female, or other. This method can be used as a part of the Intl.message method:

```
String usage(String name, String gender, String car) =>
  Intl.message(
    """${Intl.gender(
        gender,
        male: "$name uses his $car",
        female: "$name uses her $car",
        other: "$name uses its car")}""",
    name: "usage",
    args: [name, gender, car],
    desc: "A person uses the car.");
```

# Adding select

Last but not least, a `select` method from the `Intl` class is used to format messages differently, depending on the available choice:

```
String currencySelector(currency, amount) => Intl.select(currency,
    {
        "USD": "$amount United States dollars",
        "CDN" : "$amount Canadian dollars",
        "other" : "$amount some currency or other."
    },
    name: "currencySelector",
    args: [currency, amount],
    examples: {'currency': 'USD', 'amount':'20'},
    desc: "Translate abbreviation into full name of currency");
```

The `select` method looks up the value of the currency in a map of cases and returns the results that are found or returns an empty string. It can be a part of the `Intl.message` method, as shown in the following code:

```
String currencySelector(currency, amount) => Intl.message(
    """${Intl.select(currency,
        {
            "USD": "$amount United  States dollars",
            "CDN" : "$amount Canadian dollars",
            "other" : "$amount some currency or other."
        })}""",
    name: "currencySelector",
    args: [currency, amount],
    examples: {'currency': 'USD', 'amount':'20'},
    desc: "Translate abbreviation into full name of currency");
```

# Creating complex message translations

The `message`, `plural`, `gender`, and `select` methods can be combined with each other to create complex message translations as shown in the following code:

```
String currencySelector(currency, amount) => Intl.select(currency,
    {
        "USD": """${Intl.plural(amount,
                one: '$amount United States dollar',
                other: '$amount United States dollars')}""",
        "CDN": """${Intl.plural(amount,
                one: '$amount Canadian dollar',
                other: '$amount Canadian dollars')}""",
```

```
        "other": "$amount some currency or other.",
    },
    name: "currencySelector",
    args: [currency, amount],
    examples: {'currency': 'USD', 'amount':'20'},
    desc: "Translate abbreviation into full name of currency");
```

In the preceding code, we translated the abbreviation into a full currency name depending on the amount of money and use them to create the available choice.

# Bidirectional formatting

The Intl library supports the development of web applications localized for both **right-to-left** (RTL) and **left-to-right** (LTR) locales.

We can combine languages with locales that have different directions in only one text by easily using the HTML markup wrappers. In the following code, we use the <span> HTML tags to embed the company name in Hebrew and have the surrounding text in English:

```
<span dir="RTL">Copyright 2014 עתיד שותיףות</span>
```

In cases where the information is entered by the user or if it comes from the backend or third-party web resources, the BidiFormatter class can insert it automatically at runtime as shown in the following code:

```
copyrightLbl() => Intl.message("Copyright 2014 עתיד שותיףות",
    name: "copyrightLbl",
    desc: "Copyright label");
...
BidiFormatter bidiFormatter = new BidiFormatter.UNKNOWN();
querySelector("#copyrightLbl").text =
    bidiFormatter.wrapWithUnicode(copyrightLbl());
```

# Internationalizing your web application

Let's see an example of how we can internationalize a standard web application. To do so, we will create a simple web application in Dart Editor, designed the registration form, and embedded it inside the body of an index.html file. The code is as follows:

```
<h1>Registration Form</h1>
<form>
  <table>
    <tr>
      <td><label for="firstName">First Name:</label></td>
```

```
            <td><input type="text" id="firstName" name="firstName"></td>
        </tr>
        <tr>
          <td><label for="lastName">Last Name:</label></td>
          <td><input type="text" id="lastName" name="lastName"></td>
        </tr>
        <tr>
          <td><label>Gender:</label></td>
          <td>
            <input type="radio" name="sex" value="male">
            <span>Male</span>
            <input type="radio" name="sex" value="female">
            <span>Female</span>
          </td>
        </tr>
        <tr>
          <td colspan="2"><input type="submit" value="Register"></td>
        </tr>
        <tr>
          <td colspan="2">
            <span dir="RTL">Copyright 2014 עתיד ושיתוף</span>
          </td>
        </tr>
      </table>
    </form>
```

The following screenshot shows the result of the preceding code in a web browser:

First of all, we add the `intl` package in the dependency section of our `pubspec.yaml` file. Then, we decide to try out a combination of naming conventions and internationalization methods to offer the utmost flexibility in setting up the display names, because meaningful display names are very important here. To create a display name of a component, we will perform the following actions:

- Make all the levels of the header tag end with the `Head` suffix
- End all the labels with the `Lbl` suffix
- End the input elements to be submitted with the `Btn` suffix

Each referencing element must use the identifier name of the references element in combination with the previously mentioned suffix. So, now we are ready to internationalize the registration form.

All elements in the form that contains the string messages must have unique identifiers. We will remove all the text messages from the registration form, using the following code:

```
<h1 id="formHead"></h1>
<form>
  <table>
    <tr>
      <td><label for="firstName" id="firstNameLbl"></label></td>
      <td><input type="text" id="firstName" name="firstName"></td>
    </tr>
    <tr>
      <td><label for="lastName" id="lastNameLbl"></label></td>
      <td><input type="text" id="lastName" name="lastName"></td>
    </tr>
    <tr>
      <td><label id="genderLbl"></label></td>
      <td>
        <input type="radio" name="sex" value="male">
        <span id="maleLbl"></span>
        <input type="radio" name="sex" value="female">
        <span id="femaleLbl"></span>
      </td>
    </tr>
    <tr>
      <td colspan="2"><input type="submit" id="registerBtn"></td>
    </tr>
    <tr>
      <td colspan="2"><span id="copyrightLbl"></span></td>
    </tr>
  </table>
</form>
```

We need to create one function per message that is getting translated in the Dart code. In such cases, you must choose the naming convention for the following code:

```
formHead() => "Registration Form";
firstNameLbl() => "First name:";
lastNameLbl() => "Last name:";
genderLbl() => "Gender:";
maleLbl() => "Male";
femaleLbl() => "Female";
registerBtn() => "Register";
copyrightLbl() => "Copyright 2014 עתיד ושיתופֿ";
```

We will use the `querySelector` function to find all the elements that are translated by the unique identifier and assign the translated messages to their appropriate property, as shown in the following code:

```
querySelector("#formHead").text = formHead();
querySelector("#firstNameLbl").text = firstNameLbl();
querySelector("#lastNameLbl").text = lastNameLbl();
querySelector("#genderLbl").text = genderLbl();
querySelector("#maleLbl").text = maleLbl();
querySelector("#femaleLbl").text = femaleLbl();
(querySelector("#registerBtn") as InputElement)
  .value = registerBtn();
BidiFormatter bidiFormatter = new BidiFormatter.UNKNOWN();
querySelector("#copyrightLbl").text =
  bidiFormatter.wrapWithUnicode(copyrightLbl());
```

Now, apply the `Intl.message` method to every function that's created, as shown in the following code:

```
formHead() => Intl.message("Registration Form",
    name:"formHead",
    desc: "Registration Form title");
firstNameLbl() => Intl.message("First name:",
    name: "firstNameLbl",
    desc: "First Name label");
lastNameLbl() => Intl.message("Last name:",
    name: "lastNameLbl",
    desc: "Last Name label");
genderLbl() => Intl.message("Gender:",
    name: "genderLbl",
    desc: "Gender label");
maleLbl() => Intl.message("Male",
    name: "maleLbl",
    desc: "Male label");
```

```
femaleLbl() => Intl.message("Female",
    name: "femaleLbl",
    desc: "Female label");
registerBtn() => Intl.message("Register",
    name: "registerBtn",
    desc: "Registration Button name");
copyrightLbl() => Intl.message("Copyright 2014 דיתע ושיתוף",
    name: "copyrightLbl",
    desc: "Copyright label");
```

If you open your page in a web browser, it will now look like the original one. Now that you know how messages can be translated with the Intl class, it's time to discuss localization.

# Extracting messages

Now, we have all the messages separated from the UI and we are ready for translation. We need to extract them from the source code into the external file with a special program called extract_to_arb.dart from the intl package, as shown in the following code:

```
pub run intl:extract_to_arb --output-dir=web web/registration_form.
dart
```

The preceding program generates the intl_messages.arb file inside the specified web directory. This file contains all the messages in the ARB format. ARB is a localization resource format based on JSON. This format provides the following benefits:

- **Simplicity**: This format is simple and human-readable because it is based on JSON
- **Extensibility**: In this format, vocabulary can be added without affecting the existing tools and usage
- **Direct usability**: Applications can access the resource directly from this format without converting them to another form

You can find more about the ARB format in the specification available at https://code.google.com/p/arb/wiki/ApplicationResourceBundleSpecification.

After this, you can send the files in the ARB format to the human translator. This is done as the form in our case is quite simple and we can translate the files into other languages ourselves by using Google Translator Toolkit.

# Using Google Translator Toolkit

The following steps will show you how to use Google Translator Toolkit:

1.  Open your web browser and navigate to `https://translate.google.com/toolkit`. Click on the **UPLOAD** button to upload a file as shown in the following screenshot:

2.  You will be taken to another web page where you can add the content that you want to translate. You can choose the `intl_messages.arb` file to be translated:

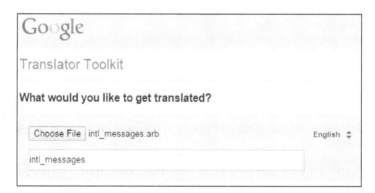

3.  Select the appropriate translating language that you want the message to be translated into, and then click on the **Next** button:

4. On the next page, you can choose any one of the vendors that are ready for translation or click on the **No, thanks** button to translate the messages yourselves. The resulting new file will appear in the list of files ready for translation, as shown in the following screenshot:

5. Now click on the filename in the list of files and Google Translator Toolkit will open it in the editor:

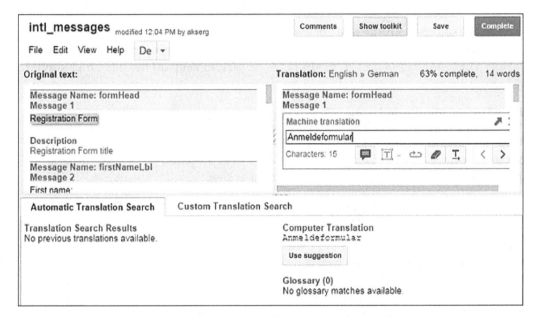

6. Google Translator Toolkit helps you translate your messages easily, giving you suggestions. You can just choose all of them and click on the **Complete** button, but you can play with the translation options to properly translate your messages if you want. Finally, choose **Save** and close the menu item in the **File** menu to return to the main page of Google Translator Toolkit:

7. We selected our file and clicked on the **Download** button to save it with the name `translate_de.arb`. We also changed the name of the file from `intl_messages.arb` to `translate_en.arb` to keep all the filenames similar.

# Using translated messages

Now, it's time to generate a set of Dart libraries that contain translated versions of our messages – one per locale from the ARB files prepared before. We use the `generate_from_arb` program from the `intl` package:

```
pub run intl:generate_from_arb --output-dir=web web/registration_form.
dart web/translate_en.arb web/translate_de.arb
```

The program generates the `message_de.dart`, `message_en.dart`, and `messages_all.dart` files in the specified web directory. Each `message_<locale_tag>.dart` file contains the `MessageLookup` class that implements `MessageLookupByLibrary`. The `MessageLookup` class has a getter method `localeName`, a set of static functions that are returned translated on the specific locale text messages, and final constant `messages` that contain the name of all the static methods. The `messages_all.dart` file combines all the lookups in one place to make them available for the localization code from the `Intl` library. The single available public method of the `message_all` library is `initializeMessages`, as shown in the following code:

```
Future initializeMessages(String localeName)
```

This method should be called first before using the specified `localeName` method. Let's change our code to make the German locale available by default. All we need to do is import the `messages_all.dart` file to our project and add `initializeMessages` in the `main` method, as shown in the following code:

```
import 'messages_all.dart';
...
void main() {
  initializeMessages('de').then((_) {
    Intl.defaultLocale = 'de';
    querySelector("#formHead").text = formHead();
    querySelector("#firstNameLbl").text = firstNameLbl();
    querySelector("#lastNameLbl").text = lastNameLbl();
    querySelector("#genderLbl").text = genderLbl();
    querySelector("#maleLbl").text = maleLbl();
    querySelector("#femaleLbl").text = femaleLbl();
    (querySelector("#registerBtn") as InputElement)
      .value = registerBtn();
    BidiFormatter bidiFormatter = new BidiFormatter.UNKNOWN();
    querySelector("#copyrightLbl").text =
      bidiFormatter.wrapWithUnicode(copyrightLbl());
  });
}
```

In the preceding code, we specified the German locale when we initialized the messages as default. Now, open the `index.html` file in the browser to see the correct translation of our form in the German locale:

# Summary

In this chapter, we discussed some important aspects of internalization and localization of projects based on the Dart language. The development of globalized software includes internationalization and covers designing and developing web applications, and localization that includes translating and customizing web applications for a specific locale.

The `intl` package from the pub manager helps you design and develop applications for the server side and client side in a pretty straightforward manner. All the executable code must be separated from the programming code that implements the UI. You must avoid converting numbers and dates into strings directly because various cultures have different ways of presenting numbers and dates.

The `NumberFormat` class contains special constructors to quickly create the frequently used patterns, which can be very handy to measure units and currencies. The `BidiFormatter` class helps manage messages that contain text in both directions with the `BiDi` wrapping, automatic directionality estimation, and character escaping. The `DateFormat` class has a huge set of naming patterns that are useful to avoid mistakes and display data in the correct format. The internalization of messages is based on the lookup via the named localized version of messages and returns the translated messages, possibly those interpolated with a list of specified arguments.

The `plural` method of the `Intl` class can help use parentheses to combine the singular and the plural forms to one string. The `gender` method of the `Intl` class provides out-of-the-box support for gender-based selection. The `select` method from the `Intl` class helps format the message differently based on the available choice. The `message` method of the `Intl` class can represent messages as simple expressions with possibilities of interpolating them with attributes.

In the next chapter, we will show you how to properly organize client to server communication. You will find answers on presumably important questions about the right choice of Dart classes using the client-to-server communication.

# 9
# Client-to-server Communication

In this chapter, we will discuss how to organize client-to-server communication. We will find answers to presumably the important questions, such as the right choice of Dart classes using the client-to-server communication. In this chapter, we will cover the following topics:

- Communication at a glance
- Hypertext Transfer Protocol
- AJAX polling request
- AJAX long polling request
- Server-Sent Events
- WebSocket

## Communication at a glance

Some of us can't imagine the modern world without the Internet, cell phones, or computers. Each device connected to the Internet can either be a client, a server, or both of these simultaneously. Communication between a client and a server is the basis of modern digital world. Communication based on a system of special rules and format of messages is known as a communication protocol that enables data exchange between clients and servers.

# The Internet protocol stack

Any device connected to the Internet has an **Internet Protocol (IP)** address. An IP address can be permanent or temporary when it is obtained from the **Dynamic Host Configuration Protocol (DHCP)** server. In any case, any device that is connected to the Internet has a unique IP address. Many programs working in scope of a single unique IP address use different port numbers to have access to the Internet simultaneously. A message transmitted from one device to another over the Internet is delivered through a long route via the protocol stack, which is represented as a set of layers that lie on top of one another as shown in the following diagram:

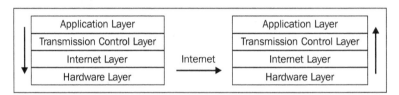

Let's see what actually happens with a message:

1. A message arrives at the application protocol layer present on the top of the protocol stack, and then moves down. Usually, the application layer formats the message in one of the standard ways that is applicable to applications such as HTTP, SMTP, FTP, or others.

2. The formatted message is then forwarded to the **transmission control protocol (TCP)** layer. It splits the message into small, manageable chunks of data known as packets and assigns a number to each of them. This number specifies the order of the packets and allows the recipient's TCP layer to reconstruct the original message from the packets. It assigns a port number to each packet, depending on the protocol being used at the application level.

3. Then, these packets proceed to the IP layer. It attaches the IP address of the sender and recipient to each packet. A combination of the IP address and port number is called a socket address.

4. Finally, a hardware layer attaches the **Media Access Control (MAC)** address of the sender and recipient to the packets. It allows the packets to be directed to a specific network interface on the IP address of the destination device. On the hardware layer, all packets are converted to electronic signals one by one, transmitted over the wire, and connected to the **Internet Service Provider (ISP)** modem.

5. From here, it is the ISP's task to deliver packets of message to the specified IP address on the Internet via routers and ISP backbones.

6.  Packets delivered by the ISP start at the bottom of the protocol stack of the destination device. Any extra information stripped from the packets goes upwards.

7.  Eventually, data reaches the top of the stack where it is decoded into the original message.

# Hypertext Transfer Protocol

The **World Wide Web (WWW)** is one of the most commonly used services on the Internet. The **Hypertext Transfer Protocol (HTTP)** is a text-based application layer protocol that makes it work. All web browsers and web service applications use HTTP to communicate with each other over the Internet. A web browser or standalone application opens a connection and sends a request to the web server. The web server services the request and closes the connection to the web client.

 HTTP is a stateless protocol.

You cannot find any information about persistent connections in the HTTP 1.0 specification. However, in essence, it was unofficially added to an existing protocol via the following additional header to the request:

```
Connection: Keep-Alive
```

So, if a client supports `Keep-Alive`, it adds the preceding header to his request. A server receives this request and generates a response includes this header.

Starting from HTTP 1.1, all the connections are considered persistent unless declared otherwise. A HTTP persistent connection does not use external `Keep-Alive` messages. Multiple requests could be sent to use a single opened connection.

We can use the HTTP protocol for communication purposes via the following different libraries:

*   The `dart:io` library from the Dart SDK contains the `HttpClient` class, which communicates with the server over the HTTP protocol.

*   The `dart:html` library from the Dart SDK has the `HttpRequest` class uses a client-side `XMLHttpRequest` to obtaining data from the URL. It also helps in obtaining data from HTTP or FTP, or updating page content via AJAX.

- The http package from the pub server written by the Google development team contains a future-based library to create HTTP requests. It is platform independent, so we can use the `http.dart` library to generate HTTP requests from standalone applications or the `browser_client.dart` library for web browser-based applications.

Let's see how we can organize communication between the web browser or standalone application on one side and the web server on the other side.

# Web server

In this chapter, we will create a simple web server that can be used for all examples as follows:

```
import 'dart:io';
import 'package:route/server.dart';

import 'urls.dart' as urls;
import 'files.dart';
main() {
  final allUrls = new RegExp('/(.*)');

  HttpServer.bind(urls.serverAddress, urls.serverPort)
  .then((server) {
    print("Server runs on ${server.address.host}:${server.port}");
    new Router(server)
      ..serve(urls.dataUrl, method:'GET').listen(processParams)
      ..serve(urls.dataUrl, method:'DELETE').listen(processParams)
      ..serve(urls.dataUrl, method:'POST').listen(processBody)
      ..serve(urls.dataUrl, method:'PUT').listen(processBody)
      ..serve(allUrls).listen(serveDirectory('', as: '/'))
      ..defaultStream.listen(send404);
  });
}
```

In the preceding code, we intentionally used the `route` package from the pub server to reduce the number of code wraps around the `main` functionality. Our code serves the client's request to match `dataUrl`. Depending on the method of request, the code invokes the `processParams` or `processBody` functions. We keep `serverAddress`, `serverPort`, and `dataUrl` inside the `urls.dart` file. We especially move them away to the external file to share this data with client code. We set the shared headers in the `setHeaders` method as shown in following code:

```
setHeaders(HttpRequest request) {
  request.response.headers.contentType =
    new ContentType("text", "plain", charset: "utf-8");
}
```

The following method processes the query parameters:

```
processParams(HttpRequest request) {
  setHeaders(request);
  request.response.write(
    "${request.method}: ${request.uri.path}");
  if (request.uri.queryParameters.length > 0) {
    request.response.write(", Params:" +
        request.uri.queryParameters.toString());
  }
  request.response.close();
}
```

The following method processes the requested message body. Depending on the amount of the content, we write the content in the output stream or just return the message with the method name and path, as follows:

```
processBody(HttpRequest request) {
  setHeaders(request);
  if (request.contentLength > 0) {
    request.listen((List<int> buffer) {
      request.response.write(
          "${request.method}: ${request.uri.path}");
      request.response.write(", Data:" +
          new String.fromCharCodes(buffer));
      request.response.close();
    });
  } else {
    request.response.write(
        "${request.method}: ${request.uri.path}");
    request.response.close();
  }
}
```

Our server doesn't do anything special. It responds with the method's name, query parameters, or the message body, which is represented as a string per request. The server must always be online to handle our requests. Dart Editor can run different Dart programs simultaneously. To do this, just right-click on the `server.dart` file and run it as shown in the following screenshot:

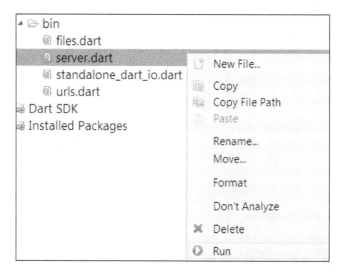

# Standalone HTTP communication via the dart:io library

Let's start from the standard `dart:io` library and the `HttpClient` class to organize communication from the standalone client to the web server. Any method of the `HttpClient` class that is used for communication is a two-step process. The first time we call the original method, it returns `Future` with `HttpClientRequest`. From now, the underlying network communication is opened but no data is sent yet. You can set the HTTP headers or body on the request and finally return the results of the request's `close` method. Take a look at the following code based on the `HttpClient` class from the `dart:io` library:

```
import 'dart:io';
import 'dart:convert';
import 'urls.dart' as urls;

var url = "http://${urls.serverAddress}:${urls.serverPort}${urls.
    dataUrl}";
var name = "HttpClient Standalone";
// The following method processes all responses:
responseHandler(response) {
```

```
    if (response is HttpClientResponse) {
      response.transform(UTF8.decoder).listen((contents) {
        print("${response.statusCode}: ${contents}");
      });
    } else {
      print("Readed: " + response.toString());
    }
}
// We send data to a server via this method:
sendData(HttpClientRequest request, data) {
  request.headers.contentType =
        new ContentType("application", "json", charset: "utf-8");
  List<int> buffer = JSON.encode(data).codeUnits;
  request.contentLength = buffer.length;
  request.add(buffer);
}

main() {
  // We need to encode name before sending it:
  String query = "name=" + Uri.encodeQueryComponent(name);
  // We create the client instance to send multiple requests:
  HttpClient client = new HttpClient();
  // Make a GET request with query:
  client.getUrl(Uri.parse("$url?$query"))
  .then((HttpClientRequest request) {
    return request.close();
  }).then(responseHandler);
  // Here we send a map with data via the POST request:
  client.postUrl(Uri.parse(url))
  .then((HttpClientRequest request) {
    sendData(request, {'post name': name});
    return request.close();
  }).then(responseHandler);
  // The PUT request is very similar to the POST one:
  client.putUrl(Uri.parse(url))
  .then((HttpClientRequest request) {
    sendData(request, {'put name': name});
    return request.close();
  }).then(responseHandler);
  // Here is the DELETE request:
  client.deleteUrl(Uri.parse("$url?$query"))
  .then((HttpClientRequest request) {
    return request.close();
  }).then(responseHandler);
}
```

Run the server code as explained in the *Web server* section and then run the code in
standalone_dart_io.dart via the context-sensitive menu. Refer to the following
client output:

```
200: GET: /data, Params:{name: HttpClient Standalone}
200: DELETE: /data, Params:{name: HttpClient Standalone}
200: POST: /data, Data:{"post name":"HttpClient Standalone"}
200: PUT: /data, Data:{"put name":"HttpClient Standalone"}
```

The HttpClient class provides a set of methods to create HTTP requests but a two-
step process is a real disadvantage.

# Standalone HTTP communication via the http package

Let's see how the http library from the http package can improve the client-side
development experience. Before using the http library, we should add the http
package in a group of dependencies in the pubspec.yaml file of our project.
We create a standalone_http.dart file with the help of the following code:

```
import 'package:http/http.dart' as http;
import 'dart:async';
import 'urls.dart' as urls

var url = "http://${urls.serverAddress}:${urls.serverPort}${urls.
    dataUrl}";
var name = "Http Standalone";
// We process all responses in this method:
responseHandler(response) {
  if (response is http.Response) {
    print("${response.statusCode}: ${response.body}");
  } else {
    print("Readed: " + response.toString());
  }
}

main() {
  // We need to encode name before sending it:
  String query = "name=" + Uri.encodeQueryComponent(name);
  // Static functions such as GET, POST, and so on create new
instances of the Client interface per request:
  // All static functions such as get from the http library always
create
  // new instance of the Client class
  http.get("$url?$query").then(responseHandler);
```

```
   var client = new http.Client();
   Future.wait([
   client.get("$url?$query").then(responseHandler),
   client.post(url, body: {"name": name}).then(responseHandler),
   client.put(url, body: {"name": name}).then(responseHandler),
   client.delete("$url?$query").then(responseHandler)])
 .then((list) {
   client.close();
 });
 }
```

A huge advantage of using the `Client` class from the `http` library over `HttpClient` from the `dart:io` library is less verbose code with a similar result:

```
200: GET: /data, Params:{name: Http Standalone}
200: GET: /data, Params:{name: Http Standalone}
200: POST: /data, Data:name=Http+Standalone
200: PUT: /data, Data:name=Http+Standalone
200: DELETE: /data, Params:{name: Http Standalone}
```

# Web browser HTTP communication via the dart:html library

You cannot use the `dart:io` library to write a web browser-based application because this library was written especially for standalone and server applications. Instead, we will use the `HttpRequest` class from the `dart:html` library to achieve the same result. This class can be used to obtain data from the HTTP or FTP application protocols as well as AJAX polling requests, as shown in the following code:

```
import 'dart:html';
import 'dart:convert';
import 'urls.dart' as urls;

var url = "http://${urls.serverAddress}:${urls.serverPort}${urls.dataUrl}";
var name = "HttpClient Browser";
// We save the response text in a DIV element and append it to the
// DIV container:
responseHandler(DivElement log, responseText) {
  DivElement item = new DivElement()
  ..text = responseText.toString();
  log.append(item);
}

void main() {
  DivElement log = querySelector("#log");
  // Here we prepare query to send:
  String query = "name=" + Uri.encodeQueryComponent(name);
  String data = JSON.encode({"name": name});
```

```
HttpRequest request = new HttpRequest();
// We open a connection to the server via HttpRequest:
request.open("GET", "$url?$query");

request.onLoad.listen((ProgressEvent event) {
  responseHandler(log, request.response);
});
// Now send data via call the send method:
request.send();

request.open("POST", url);
request.onLoad.listen((ProgressEvent event) {
  responseHandler(log, request.response);
});
request.send(data);

request.open("PUT", url);
request.onLoad.listen((ProgressEvent event) {
  responseHandler(log, request.response);
});
request.send(data);

request.open("DELETE", "$url?$query");
request.onLoad.listen((ProgressEvent event) {
  responseHandler(log, request.response);
});
request.send();
// HttpRequest supports less verbose code:
HttpRequest.request("$url?$query")
.then((HttpRequest request)
  => responseHandler(log, request.response));

HttpRequest.request(url, method: "POST", sendData: data)
.then((HttpRequest request)
  => responseHandler(log, request.response));

HttpRequest.request(url, method: "PUT", sendData: data)
.then((HttpRequest request)
  => responseHandler(log, request.response));

HttpRequest.request("$url?$query", method: "DELETE")
.then((HttpRequest request)
```

```
       => responseHandler(log, request.response));

   // The getString method is the absolute champion of size
   // if you need a simple GET request:
   HttpRequest.getString("$url?$query")
   .then((response) => responseHandler(log, response));
```

We now create a launch target to run the index.html file via the **Manage Launches** item from the **Run** menu, as shown in the following screenshot:

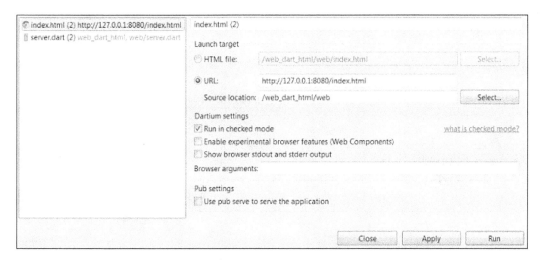

This Dartium launch configuration opens the index.html file in the default web browser. Take into account the fact that the **Use pub service to serve the application** option is unchecked because we are using our own server to serve all the browser requests. You could set breakpoints and debug code if necessary. Run the server code as mentioned in the *Web server* section and index.html through the launcher. The following is the result of our requests when printed on the web page:

```
DELETE: /data, Params:{name: HttpClient Browser}
DELETE: /data, Params:{name: HttpClient Browser}
DELETE: /data, Params:{name: HttpClient Browser}
DELETE: /data, Params:{name: HttpClient Browser}
DELETE: /data, Params:{name: HttpClient Browser}
GET: /data, Params:{name: HttpClient Browser}
POST: /data, Data:{"name":"HttpClient Browser"}
DELETE: /data, Params:{name: HttpClient Browser}
PUT: /data, Data:{"name":"HttpClient Browser"}
GET: /data, Params:{name: HttpClient Browser}
```

# Web browser HTTP communication via the http package

As mentioned earlier, the http package combines two sorts of libraries to help in client-to-server communication. Let's see how the BrowserClient class from the http package can help us achieve the same result with less effort:

```dart
import 'dart:html' as dom;
import 'package:http/browser_client.dart';
import 'package:http/src/request.dart';
import 'package:http/src/streamed_response.dart';
import 'dart:convert';
import 'urls.dart' as urls;

var url = "http://${urls.serverAddress}:${urls.serverPort}${urls.
   dataUrl}";
var name = "HttpClient Browser";
// The response handler is as follows:
responseHandler(dom.DivElement log, StreamedResponse response) {
  dom.DivElement item = new dom.DivElement();
  response.stream.transform(UTF8.decoder).listen((contents) {
    item.text = contents;
  });
  log.append(item);
}

void main() {
  dom.DivElement log = dom.querySelector("#log");
  String query = "name=" + Uri.encodeQueryComponent(name);
  String data = JSON.encode({"name": name});

  BrowserClient client = new BrowserClient();
  Request request = new Request("GET", Uri.parse("$url?$query"));
  // We organize request via call the send method of BrowserClient
  // class:
  client.send(request).then((StreamedResponse response)
      => responseHandler(log, response));

  request = new Request("POST", Uri.parse(url));
  request.body = data;
  client.send(request).then((StreamedResponse response)
      => responseHandler(log, response));
```

```
request = new Request("PUT", Uri.parse(url));
request.body = data;
client.send(request).then((StreamedResponse response)
    => responseHandler(log, response));

request = new Request("DELETE", Uri.parse("$url?$query"));
client.send(request).then((StreamedResponse response)
    => responseHandler(log, response));
}
```

Create a Dartium launch configuration and open the index.html file in a web browser. Run the server and launch the new configuration to see the following expected result:

```
GET: /data, Params:{name: HttpClient Browser}
POST: /data, Data:{"name":"HttpClient Browser"}
DELETE: /data, Params:{name: HttpClient Browser}
PUT: /data, Data:{"name":"HttpClient Browser"}
```

You now know how to easily create client-to-server communication via the BrowserClient and Request classes from the http and html packages.

# AJAX polling request

Usually, a web browser sends requests and immediately receives responses. Every new portion of data requested from the server starts to reload a whole web page. **Asynchronous JavaScript and XML (AJAX)** is a technology that allows the client-side JavaScript code to request data from a server without the need to reload the current page in the web browser. An important advantage of using AJAX compared to traditional flow of web pages is its ability to bring usability and behavior of desktop applications into a web application. HttpRequest is a client-side XHR request to get data from a URL, formally known as XMLHttpRequest, and has an important role in the AJAX web development technique.

 All the requests created within HttpRequest must be in the server from the same origin as the requested resource.

The state of many web applications is inherently volatile. Changes can come from numerous sources, such as other users, external news and data, results of complex calculations, and triggers based on the current time and date. The solution is to periodically issue a request to gain new information. For this purpose, we can use the AJAX polling request technique. Let's take a look at the client side of our web application:

```dart
import 'dart:html';
import 'dart:async';
import 'urls.dart' as urls;

var url = "http://${urls.serverAddress}:${urls.serverPort}${urls.
    dataUrl}";
```

To print the timestamp, use the following code:

```dart
timeStamp() {
  DateTime dt = new DateTime.now();
  return " (${dt.minute}:${dt.second})";
}
```

The response keeps a request number as follows:

```dart
responseHandler(DivElement log, responseText) {
  DivElement item = new DivElement()
  ..text = responseText.toString() + timeStamp;
  // We insert a new element at the top of the log:
  log.insertAdjacentElement('beforebegin', item);
}

void main() {
  DivElement log = querySelector("#log");
  int num = 0;
  // A timer in 2 seconds interval calls the callback function:
  new Timer.periodic(new Duration(seconds: 2), (Timer timer) {
    // We generate the query parameter with number:
    String query = "number=${num++}";
    HttpRequest.getString("$url?$query")
      .then((response) => responseHandler(log, response));
  });
}
```

This is a simple implementation that creates new requests in every 2 seconds. Each request has a unique number; when the server returns it, this helps us check the order of responses. We'll make small changes to the server code to add some random generated data to the response. The `readyChecker` variable is a random generator whose values determine whether the data is ready to be fetched. The `dataGenerator` variable is a random generator of integer numbers in a range between `0` and `100`, as shown in the following code:

```
import 'dart:math';
Random readyChecker = new Random(
  new DateTime.now().millisecondsSinceEpoch);
Random dataGenerator = new Random(
  new DateTime.now().millisecondsSinceEpoch);
//…
In the fetchData function, we check whether the data is ready to be
fetched or returns an empty string:
String fetchData() {
  if (ready.nextBool()) {
    return data.nextInt(100).toString();
  } else {
    return "";
  }
}
```

In the following code, we add the fetched data to the response:

```
processQueryParams(HttpRequest request) {
  setHeaders(request);
  request.response.write(
      "${request.method}: ${request.uri.path}");
  request.response.write(", Data:" + fetchData());
  if (request.uri.queryParameters.length > 0) {
    request.response.write(", Params:" +
        request.uri.queryParameters.toString());
  }
  request.response.close();
}
```

Create a Dartium launch configuration and open the `index.html` file in the web browser. Run the server and launch a new configuration to see the following result:

```
GET: /data, Data:4, Params:{number: 0} (31:28)
GET: /data, Data:26, Params:{number: 1} (31:30)
GET: /data, Data: , Params:{number: 2} (31:32)
GET: /data, Data: , Params:{number: 3} (31:34)
GET: /data, Data:47, Params:{number: 4} (31:36)
GET: /data, Data:69, Params:{number: 5} (31:38)
GET: /data, Data: , Params:{number: 6} (31:40)
GET: /data, Data: , Params:{number: 7} (31:42)
GET: /data, Data:98, Params:{number: 8} (31:44)
```

The polling requests have the following disadvantages:

- Periodical requests consume bandwidth and server resources
- The server must always respond with or without data; as a result, the client receives a lot empty strings

Let's try to use the AJAX long polling request to fix them.

# AJAX long polling request

From a client perspective, the AJAX long polling request looks similar to normal one. An important difference between them on the server side is that if the server doesn't have any information available or the client, it holds the request and waits for information to become available or for a suitable timeout, after which a completed response is sent to the client. The long polling requests reduces the amount of data that needs to be sent because the server only sends data when it is really available.

The long pooling request is useful in the following cases:

- When your solution must work in old web browsers
- When the data traffic between the client and server is low
- When the implementation is very simple

The advantages of using the long pooling request are as follows:

- It works across all browsers
- It is easy to develop and perfectly fits in the legacy code without significant changes and effort
- It can detect a connection failure quickly and resume a session to avoid data loss

- It has a strong immunity against IP address changes for free, because requests are short-lived and their state is stored independently

- It performs well for most real-time applications and reduces bandwidth consumption and server resources utilization

The disadvantages of using this request are as follows:

- The client constantly has to establish connections; if the server sends the information back to the client and the connection is closed, it must wait until the client sends the next request to open a new connection

- The client needs to create an extra connection to send data to the server

- There are problems with parallel requests

- The volume of data can make the next update from the server quite excessive if the data comes to the server until then it waits for the new connection from the client

The following browsers are supported by the long pooling request:

- Chrome 1.0+

- Firefox 0.6+

- Opera 8.0+

- Safari 1.2+

- Internet Explorer 5.0+

To implement a long-lasting HTTP connection, you need to make changes on the client side and the server side. We introduce the `longLasting` method to manage requests and register it instead of using `processParams`:

```
//...
main() {
  final allUrls = new RegExp('/(.*)');

  HttpServer.bind(urls.serverAddress, urls.serverPort)
  .then((server) {
    print("Server runs on ${server.address.host}:${server.port}");
    new Router(server)
        ..serve(urls.dataUrl, method: 'GET').listen(longLasting)
        ..serve(allUrls).listen(serveDirectory('', as: '/'))
        ..defaultStream.listen(send404);
  });
}
```

```
// Next function was changed to return data only:
String fetchData() {
  return dataGenerator.nextInt(100).toString();
}
```

The new `longLasting` function is shown in the following code. It runs two periodic timers. The first one emulates the process based on the request timeout. If no data was collected every 30 seconds, it resets the second timer and response with an empty string. The second one is managing the data availability. If the data is available in a second's interval, it resets the first timer and responds with the collected data:

```
longLasting(HttpRequest request) {
  Timer reqTimer, dataReadyTimer;

  reqTimer = new Timer.periodic(
    new Duration(seconds:30), (Timer t) {
    dataReadyTimer.cancel();
    processParams(request);
  });

  dataReadyTimer = new Timer.periodic(
    new Duration(seconds:1), (Timer t) {
    if (ready.nextBool()) {
      reqTimer.cancel();
      processQueryParams(request, ready:true);
    }
  });
}
```

The updated version of the `processQueryParams` function is illustrated in the following code. This function returns data from `fetchData` or returns an empty string depending on the value of the `ready` attribute. The code is as follows:

```
processQueryParams(HttpRequest request, {bool ready:false}) {
  request.response.write(
      "${request.method}: ${request.uri.path}");
  if (ready) {
    request.response.write(", Data:" + fetchData());
  } else {
    request.response.write(", Data:");
  }
  if (request.uri.queryParameters.length > 0) {
```

```
        request.response.write(", Params:" +
            request.uri.queryParameters.toString());
    }
    request.response.close();
}
```

Let's take a look at how we change the AJAX polling request example to organize
the long polling request at the client side. You can initiate the long polling request
by calling the `longPolling` function as follows:

```
void main() {
    DivElement log = querySelector("#log");
    int num = 0;
    longPolling(log, num);
}
```

In this function, we send the AJAX request and wait for the response from the server.
When the response is available, we call the `responseHandler` function and start the
new request immediately:

```
longPolling(DivElement log, int num) {
    String query = "number=${num++}";
    HttpRequest.getString("$url?$query")
        .then((response) {
        responseHandler(log, response);
        longPolling(log, num);
    });
}
```

Create a Dartium launch configuration, run the server, and open the `index.html` file
in the web browser to see the following result:

```
GET: /data, Data:12, Params:{number: 0} (51:0)
GET: /data, Data:9, Params:{number: 1} (51:2)
GET: /data, Data:60, Params:{number: 2} (51:3)
GET: /data, Data:41, Params:{number: 3} (51:5)
GET: /data, Data:15, Params:{number: 4} (51:7)
GET: /data, Data:0, Params:{number: 5} (51:8)
```

For now, we reduced the consumption of bandwidth and server utilization;
hence, the clients will mostly receive only valid data.

# Server-Sent Events

Another AJAX-based technique is **Server-Sent Events (SSE)**, which is also known as **Server Push** or **HTTP Streaming**. In this, the client opens a connection to the server via an initial HTTP request, and the server sends events to the client when there is new information available. So, if the usual functions of your clients are similar to stock tickers or news feeds and they need updates from the server with time, then the SSE technique is the ideal solution for you. By the way, if a client has new information to send to the server, it can send it through a new HTTP request.

SSE is useful in the following cases:

- The client is oriented towards receiving large volume of data
- The solution must work in old web browsers

The advantages of SSE are as follows:

- The server implementation is simple enough
- A web browser can automatically reconnect to the server
- The format of exchanging messages is flexible enough
- The solution is based on one permanent connection to the server
- The solution well enough for a real-time application
- Clients don't need to establish a new connection after every response
- Server solutions can be based on the event loop

The disadvantages of SSE are as follows:

- It works only from a server to client
- Internet Explorer doesn't support it
- It can be blocked by proxy servers
- It is impossible to connect to the server from another domain

The following browsers are supported:

- Chrome 6.0+
- Firefox 6.0+
- Opera 9.0+
- Safari 5.0+

The `EventSource` class is used to receive SSE. This class connects via a specified URL to a server over HTTP and receives server events without closing the connection. The events come in a `text/event-stream` format. To open a connection to a server and start receiving events, we create a new instance of the `EventSource` class via a factory constructor and pass the URL of the resource that generates the events through it. Once the connection is established, we wait for the messages.

 The URL of the resource that generates the events must match the origin of the calling page.

On the server side, each message is sent as a block of text terminated by a pair of new lines. The text data is encoded with UTF-8. Each message consists of one or more lines of text listing the fields for that message. Each field is represented by the field name, followed by a colon and the text data for that field's value. Here is an example of data-only messages:

```
; this is a comment
data: some text

data: another text
```

In the preceding code, the first line is just a comment. All the text messages starting with a colon character are comments. A comment could be useful as `Keep-Alive` if the messages are not sent regularly. The second and the third line contains just a data field with a text value. The third line contains an extra new line character terminating a message. Several events could be sent via a message. Each event has a name specified in the `event` field and `data` field whose values are any string. Data could also be in a JSON format as shown in the following code:

```
event: userLogon
data: {"username": "John", "time": "01:22:45", "text": "Hello World"}

event: userMessage
data: "Any data"
```

You can use unnamed events in messages without the `event` field. The SSE implementation uses message as a name for unnamed events. Each event might have an id. In this scenario, data can be combined as follows:

```
id: 123
data: some text
data: {"text": "Another text}
```

Let's take a look at the server side of our example:

```
      //...
main() {
  final allUrls = new RegExp('/(.*)');

  HttpServer.bind(urls.serverAddress, urls.serverPort)
  .then((server) {
    print("Server runs on ${server.address.host}:${server.port}");
    new Router(server)
        ..serve(urls.dataUrl, method: 'GET').listen(processSSE)
        ..serve(allUrls).listen(serveDirectory('', as: '/'))
        ..defaultStream.listen(send404);
  });
}


String fetchData() {
  return dataGenerator.nextInt(100).toString();
}
```

The EventSource class instance, which is created on the client side, opens a connection that submits the HTTP request with the text/event-stream value in the accept header. This is a signal for the server to start the SSE communication. In our example, we send the logon event first. The server connection remains open to the client so we can send message events periodically, as shown in the following code:

```
processSSE(HttpRequest request) {
  if (request.headers.value(HttpHeaders.ACCEPT) == EVENT_STREAM) {
    writeHead(request.response);
    int num = 0;

    new Timer.periodic(new Duration(seconds:5), (Timer t) {
      sendMessageEvent(request.response, num++);
    });

    sendLogonEvent(request.response);
  }
}
```

To allow you to send the push events, the output buffering in `HttpResponse` must be disabled. In addition to this, you need to specify content type, cache control, and the type of connection via the header attributes, as follows:

```
writeHead(HttpResponse response) {
  response.bufferOutput = false;
  response.headers.set(HttpHeaders.CONTENT_TYPE, EVENT_STREAM);
  response.headers.set(HttpHeaders.CACHE_CONTROL, 'no-cache');
  response.headers.set(HttpHeaders.CONNECTION, "keep-alive");
}
```

To send a message, you can use the `writeln` method of response. It automatically assigns to a newline character to each string, so you need to add only one newline character at the end of your event. Finally, the `flush` method of the response pushes the event to the client, as shown here:

```
sendMessageEvent(HttpResponse response, int num) {
  print("Send Message event $num");
  response.writeln('id: 123');
  response.writeln('data: {"msg": "hello world", "num": $num, "value":
${fetchData()}}\n');
  response.flush();
}
```

For the `logon` message, we create a custom-defined `userLogon` event type. If the connection opened via the `EventSource` terminates, the web browser will automatically re-establish the connection to the server after three seconds. You can change this value via the `retry` property of the event. This value must be an integer that specifies the reconnection time in milliseconds:

```
sendLogonEvent(HttpResponse response) {
  print("Send Logon event");
  response.writeln('event: userlogon');
  response.writeln('retry: 15000');
  response.writeln('id: 123');
  response.writeln('data: {"username": "John", "role":
    "admin"}\n');
  response.flush();
}
```

The SSE code implementation at the client side is as follows:

```
import 'dart:html';
import 'urls.dart' as urls;

var url = "http://${urls.serverAddress}:${urls.serverPort}${urls.
  dataUrl}";
String get timeStamp {
  DateTime dt = new DateTime.now();
  return " (${dt.minute}:${dt.second})";
}

responseHandler(DivElement log, String data) {
  DivElement item = new DivElement();
  item.text = data + timeStamp;
  log.insertAdjacentElement('beforebegin', item);
}
```

In the preceding code, we created an instance of EventSource with the specified URL. From now, we will start listening to the events from the server. We add the open and error event listeners. The EventSource class informs the code about the closed connection from the server side via changes in the readyState property. The message listener handles all the unknown events. A special event listener for the userlogon event handles the sort of events that could be added via the addEventListener method of the EventSource class. The event keeps the message information in the data property. An event identifier assigned on the server side is available via the lastEventId property, as shown in the following code:

```
main() {
  DivElement log = querySelector("#log");
  EventSource sse = new EventSource(url);
  sse.onOpen.listen((Event e) {
    responseHandler(log, "Connected to server: ${url}");
  });

  sse.onError.listen((Event e) {
    if (sse.readyState == EventSource.CLOSED) {
      responseHandler(log, "Connection closed");
    } else {
      responseHandler(log, "Error: ${e}");
    }
  });
  sse.onMessage.listen((MessageEvent e) {
    responseHandler(log,
      "Event ${e.lastEventId}: ${e.data}");
```

```
});
sse.addEventListener("userlogon", (Event e) {
  responseHandler(log,
    "User Logon: ${(e as MessageEvent).data}");
}, false);
}
```

Now, create a Dartium launcher, run the server, and open `index.html` in the web browser to see the following result:

```
Connected to server: http://localhost:8080/data (43:33)
User Logon: {"username": "John", "role": "admin"} (43:33)
Event 123: {"msg": "hello world", "num": 0, "value": 45} (43:38)
Event 123: {"msg": "hello world", "num": 1, "value": 1} (43:43)
Event 123: {"msg": "hello world", "num": 2, "value": 65} (43:48)
Event 123: {"msg": "hello world", "num": 3, "value": 10} (43:53)
//...
```

Let's take a look at the server log to see the server-generated messages:

```
Server runs on 127.0.0.1:8080
Send Logon event
Send Message event 0
Send Message event 1
Send Message event 2
Send Message event 3
//...
```

# WebSocket

**WebSocket** is a bidirectional, message-oriented streaming transport between a client and a server. It is a built in TCP that uses an HTTP upgrade handshake. WebSocket is a message-based transport. Its simple and minimal API abstracts all the complexity and provides the following extra services for free:

- The same-origin policy enforcement
- Interoperability with the existing HTTP infrastructure
- Message-oriented communication
- Availability of subprotocol negotiation
- Low-cost extensibility

WebSocket is one of the most flexible transports available in the browser. The API enables the layer and delivers arbitrary application protocols between the client and server in a streaming fashion, and it can be initiated on either side at any time.

 WebSocket is a set of multiple standards: the WebSocket API and the WebSocket protocol and its extensions.

WebSocket can be useful for the following cases:

- When the relevance of data is very critical
- When the solutions very often are based on high-volume data or data transmission

The advantages of WebSocket are as follows:

- It's a full-duplex, bidirectional communications channel that operates through a single socket
- It provides a quick file exchange based on the socket protocol
- It supports the binary format

The disadvantages of WebSocket are as follows:

- It is not HTTP and can be blocked by proxy servers
- Debugging is complicated
- It is supported only by the modern version of all browsers

The following browsers are supported:

- Chrome 14.0+
- Firefox 11.0+
- Opera 8.0+
- Safari 6.0+
- Internet Explorer 10.0+

Bear in mind that the WebSocket uses a custom WS protocol instead of HTTP. The use case for the WebSocket protocol was to provide an optimized, bidirectional communication channel between applications running in the browser and the server where using the HTTP protocol is obvious. WebSocket uses a custom URL schema because the WebSocket wire protocol can be used outside the browser and could be established via a non-HTTP exchange and the BiDirectional or Server-Initiated HTTP (HyBi) working group chooses to adopt a custom URL schema. Let's take a look at the client code of our example:

```
import 'dart:html';
import 'dart:convert';
import 'dart:typed_data';
import 'urls.dart' as urls;

var url = "ws://${urls.serverAddress}:${urls.serverPort}${urls.
   dataUrl}";

String get timeStamp {
  DateTime dt = new DateTime.now();
  return " (${dt.minute}:${dt.second})";
}

responseHandler(DivElement log, String data) {
  DivElement item = new DivElement();
  item.text = data + timeStamp;
  log.insertAdjacentElement('beforebegin', item);
}
```

First, we create a WebSocket class instance to initiate a new connection with the specified URL. Then, we create listeners for the open, error, close, and message events. As you can see, the API looks very similar to the EventSource API that we saw in the last topic. This is intentional because WebSocket offers a similar functionality and could help in the transition from the SSE solution quickly. When a connection is established, we can send data to the server. As WebSocket makes no assumption and no constrains on the application payload, we can send any data types such as Map, String, and Typed:

```
void main() {
  DivElement log = querySelector("#log");
  var webSocket = new WebSocket(url);
  if (webSocket != null) {
    webSocket.onOpen.listen((Event e) {
```

```
            responseHandler(log, "Connected to server: ${url}");
            sendData(webSocket);
        });
        webSocket.onError.listen((Event e)
            => responseHandler(log, "Error: ${e}"));
        webSocket.onClose.listen((CloseEvent e)
            => responseHandler(log, "Disconnected from server"));
        webSocket.onMessage.listen((MessageEvent e)
            => responseHandler(log, "Event ${e.type}: ${e.data}"));
    }
}
sendData(WebSocket webSocket) {
    webSocket.send(JSON.encode({'name':'John', 'id':1234}));
    webSocket.sendString("Hello World");
    webSocket.sendTypedData(new Int16List.fromList([1, 2, 3]));
}
```

The browser automatically converts the received text-based data into a DOMString object and the binary data into a Blob object, and then passes them directly to the application. We can force an arrayBuffer conversion when a binary message is received via the binaryType property of the WebSocket class:

```
webSocket.binaryType = "arraybuffer";
```

This is the perfect hint to the user agents on how to handle incoming binary data depending on the value in binaryType:

- If it is equal to Blob, then save it to the disk
- If it is equal to arrayBuffer, then keep it in the memory

The data in a Blob object is immutable and represents raw data. It could be the optimal format to keep the images downloaded from the server. We can pass that data directly to an image tag. On the other hand, the arrayBuffer object is likely a better fit for additional processing on binary data. In our example, we used a UTF-8 encoded text message, a UTF-8 encoded JSON payload, and the arrayBuffer object of the binary payload. All the send methods of the WebSocket class are asynchronous, but they are delivered in the exact order in which they are queued up by the client. As a result, a large number of messages in the queue will be delayed in delivery. To solve this problem, the application can split a large message into small chunks and monitor sending data via the bufferingAmount property of the WebSocket class as follows:

```
if (webSocket.bufferingAmount == 0) {
    ws.send(nextData);
}
```

The application that uses WebSocket should pay close attention to how and when to send messages in a queued socket.

Now let's take a look at the server side:

```
import 'dart:io';
import 'package:route/server.dart';

import 'urls.dart' as urls;
import 'files.dart';

main() {
  final allUrls = new RegExp('/(.*)');

  HttpServer.bind(urls.serverAddress, urls.serverPort)
  .then((server) {
    print("Server runs on ${server.address.host}:${server.port}");
    new Router(server)
        ..serve(urls.dataUrl).listen(processWS)
        ..serve(allUrls).listen(serveDirectory('', as: '/'))
        ..defaultStream.listen(send404);
  });
}
```

WebSocket upgrades the HTTP request to start listening to the data:

```
processWS(HttpRequest request) {
  WebSocketTransformer.upgrade(request)
  .then((WebSocket webSocket) {
    webSocket.listen((data) {
      webSocket.add("Received $data");
    });
  });
}
```

Finally, create a Dartium launcher, start the server, and open the index.html file in web browser to see the result of the short communication:

```
Connected to server: ws://127.0.0.1:8080/ws (8:55)
Event message: Received {"name":"John","id":1234} (8:55)
Event message: Received Hello World (8:55)
Event message: Received [1, 0, 2, 0, 3, 0] (8:55)
```

# Summary

To summarize what has been discussed so far, I would like to highlight some of the important aspects of the client-to-server communication. Communications based on a system of special rules and formats for messages to enable data exchange between clients and servers is known as a communication protocol. Any device connected to the Internet has a unique IP address. A message transmitted from one device to other over the Internet follows a long route to be delivered via the protocol stack. HTTP is a text-based application protocol that makes the Web work. Web browsers or standalone applications send a request and open a connection to the web server. The web server complies with the request and closes the connection to the web client.

AJAX is a technology that allows client-side JavaScript code to request data from a server without reloading the current page in the web browser. `HttpRequest` (formerly XMLHttpRequest) has an important role in the AJAX web development technique. The AJAX polling request periodically issues a request to gain new information. A long polling request always keeps an open connection to the server. This connection is still alive until the server decides to submit the information back to the client where there are changes and then closes the connection. The client will again open a connection to the server to start a new long polling request.

In SSE, a client opens a connection to the server via an initial HTTP request, and the server sends events to the client when there is new information available. The response sent back via SSE is plain text served with a `text/event-stream` content type. It contains one or more lines of string that begins with a `data:` string and ends with a newline character. Finally, the whole message ends with an extra newline character.

WebSocket is a bidirectional, message-oriented streaming transport between a client and server. It is built on TCP that uses an HTTP upgrade handshake. The API enables the layer and delivers arbitrary application protocols between a client and server in a streaming fashion and is initiated on either side at any time.

In the next chapter, we will discuss the ability to store data locally on a client and break the storage limit of cookies in our web applications. We will also demonstrate how to use Web Storage and explore a more powerful and useful IndexedDB to store a large amount of data in the user's web browser.

# 10
# Advanced Storage

In this chapter, we will talk about Dart's ability to store data locally on a client, break the storage limit, and prevent security issues in our web applications. We will also take a look at the good old cookies, show you how to use Web Storage, and elaborate on the more powerful and useful IndexedDB to store large amount of data in the user's web browser. The following topics will be covered in this chapter:

- Cookies
- Web Storage
- Web SQL
- IndexedDB

## Cookies

The concept of **cookies** was introduced for the first time in 1994 in the Mosaic Netscape web browser. A year later, this concept was introduced in Internet Explorer. From that time, the idea of tracking contents of shopping cart baskets across browser sessions remains relevant until today. So, what problem do cookies solve?

An HTTP protocol is stateless and doesn't allow the server to remember the request later. Because it was not designed to be stateful, each request is distinct and individual. This simplifies contracts and minimizes the amount of data transferred between the client and the server. In order to have stateful communication between web browsers, you need to provide an area in their subdirectories where the state information can be stored and accessed. The area and the information stored in this area is called a cookie. Cookies contain the following data:

- A name-value pair with the actual data
- An expiry date after which the cookie is no longer valid
- The domain and path of the server it should be sent to

Cookies are handled transparently by the web browser. They are added to the header of each HTTP request if its URL matches the domain and the path is specified in the cookie. Cookies are accessible via the `document.cookie` property. Bear in mind that when you create a cookie, you specify the name, value, expiry date, and optionally the path and domain of cookies in a special text format. You can find a cookie by its name and fetch the value only, as all the other information that is specified while creating a cookie is used by the web browser and is not available to you. We created the `cookies.dart` file to keep small library wrappers of the original API of the cookie to avoid boilerplate and code duplication, which allow you to easily set, get, and remove cookies from any application. The cookies use the date format derived from the RFC 1123 International format, that is, Wdy, DD Mon YYYY HH:MM:SS GMT. Let's look at them in more detail:

- **Wdy**: This is a three-letter abbreviation that represents the day of the week, and is followed by a comma
- **DD**: These are two numbers that represent the day of the month
- **Mon**: These are three letters that represent the name of the month
- **YYYY**: These are four numbers that represent the year
- **HH**: These are two numbers that represent the hour
- **MM**: These are two numbers that represent the minutes
- **SS**: These are two numbers that represent the seconds

You can see the date in this example: Thu, 09 Oct 2014 17:16:29 GMT.

Let's go through the following code and see how cookies can be reached by Dart. We import the `dart:html` package especially to make `document.cookies` available in our code. The `intl.dart` package is imported because of `DateFormat` usage in the `toUTCString` function to calculate the expiry date in the UTC format of the cookie based on the value in the `days` attribute and transforms it into a string. If the value of `days` is less than one, then the `toUTCString` function returns an empty string. To create cookies with the `setCookie` function, we need to specify the name of the cookie, value, and the number of days to expire. We can provide the optional path and domain information as well. In practice, you cannot use non-ASCII characters in cookies at all. To use Unicode, control codes, or other arbitrary byte sequences, you must use the most popular UTF-8-inside-URL-encoding that is produced by different encoding methods of the `Uri` class. To return cookies via `getCookie`, we only need the name of the cookie. At the end, you will find the `removeCookie` function.

```
library cookie;

import 'dart:html';
import 'package:intl/intl.dart';
```

```dart
// Number milliseconds in one day
var theDay = 24*60*60*1000;

DateFormat get cookieFormat =>
  new DateFormat("EEE, dd MMM yyyy HH:mm:ss");

String toUTCString(int days) {
  if (days > 0) {
    var date = new DateTime.now();
    date = new DateTime.fromMillisecondsSinceEpoch(
        date.millisecondsSinceEpoch + days*24*60*60*1000);
    return " expires=${cookieFormat.format(date)} GMT";
  } else {

    return " ";
  }
}

void setCookie(String name, String value, int days,
          {String path:'/', String domain:null}) {
  StringBuffer sb = new StringBuffer(
      "${Uri.encodeQueryComponent(name)}=" +
      "${Uri.encodeQueryComponent(value)};");
  sb.write(toUTCString(days));
  sb.write("path=${Uri.encodeFull(path)}; ");
  if (domain != null) {
    sb.write("domain=${Uri.encodeFull(domain)}; ");
  }
  document.cookie = sb.toString();
}

String getCookie(String name) {
  var cName = name + "=";
    document.cookie.split("; ").forEach((String cookie) {
    if (cookie.startsWith(cName)) {
      return cookie.substring(cName.length);
    }
  });
  return null;
}

void removeCookie(String name) {
  setCookie(name, '', -1);
}
```

The domain of the cookie tells the browser the domain where the cookie should be sent, and in its absence, the domain of the cookie becomes the domain of the page. It allows cookies to cross subdomains, but it does not allow the cookies to cross domains. The path of the domain is the directory present in the root of the domain where the cookie is active.

For a better understanding of the use of cookies in the real world, you can look at the `shopping_cart_cookie` project. This project is very big, so I will show you small code snippets and point you in the right direction. This project contains the following main classes:

- `Product`: This class describes the items in a cart with the ID, description, and price. Users can specify the quantity of items they want to buy, so the amount can be calculated by multiplying the quantity with the price.

- `ShoppingModel`: This class helps you to fetch products from the `product.json` file and returns the `Future` instance with a list of products.

- `ShoppingController`: This class renders the grid of products and updates the amount per product and the total amount. We can send a reference in the body of the table. This reference on the element keeps the total amount and the instance of the `ShoppingModel` and `StorageManager` class via a constructor injection.

We will call `getProducts` from the model in the constructor especially to return data from the server and when the data is ready, we will call the `_init` method to initialize our application. The `readQuantity` method is called for the first time to check and return the quantity of the product saved in the cookie. Later in the code, we will call `calculateAmount` of the product based on the quantity and price, as shown in the following code:

```
ShoppingController(this.tBody, this.totalAmount, this.service,
  this.storage) {
  model.getProducts().then((List<Product> products) {
    _products = products;
    _init();
  });
}

_init() {
  update().then((value) {
    draw();
    drawTotal();
  });
}
```

```
Future update() {
  return Future.forEach(_products, (Product product) {
    // Read quantity of product from cookie
    return readQuantity(product);
  });
}


Future readQuantity(Product product) {
  return storage.getItem(Product.toCookieName(product))
  .then((String quantity) {
    if (quantity != null && quantity.length > 0) {
      product.quantity = int.parse(quantity);
    } else {
      product.quantity = 0;
    }
  });
}
//…
```

The `Product.toCookieName` method creates a unique string identifier with a combination of `Product.NAME` and `product.id`. Now launch the application and open the `index.html` file on the Dartium web browser to see a list of products.

| Shopping Cart | | | |
| --- | --- | --- | --- |
| Product | Quantity | Price | Amount |
| 15 inch display, Desktop Mount, Black | 0 | 150.0 | 0.0 |
| 17 inch display, Wall mount, Black | 0 | 250.0 | 0.0 |
| 19 inch display, Desktop Mount, White | 0 | 340.0 | 0.0 |
| 24 inch display, Wall mount, Silver | 0 | 470.0 | 0.0 |
| | | Total | 0.0 |
| Check Out | | | |

We can check the existence of cookies in the web browser. In Dartium, open **Developer tools** from the **Tools** menu item and choose the **Resources** tab, as shown in the following screenshot:

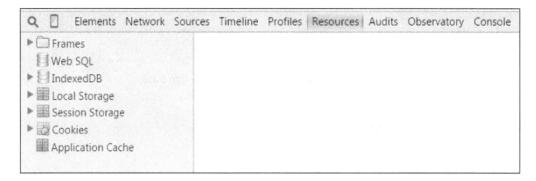

Select **Cookies** and choose **localhost** to ensure that no cookies are associated with our web server.

If the user changes the quantity of any product via the text input field, then the number of products and the total number of selected products will be recalculated. At the same time, our code calls the `saveQuantity` method of the `ShoppingController` class, as follows:

```
saveQuantity(Product product) {
    if (product.quantity == 0) {
      storage.removeItem(Product.toCookieName(product));
    } else {
      storage.setItem(Product.toCookieName(product),
        product.quantity.toString());
    }
  }
```

The product is removed from the cookie if the number in the **Quantity** field equals zero. In other cases, we will create or update the quantity value in cookies.

| Shopping Cart | | | |
|---|---|---|---|
| Product | Quantity | Price | Amount |
| 15 inch display, Desktop Mount, Black | 1 | 150.0 | 150.0 |
| 17 inch display, Wall mount, Black | 2 | 250.0 | 500.0 |
| 19 inch display, Desktop Mount, White | 0 | 340.0 | 0.0 |
| 24 inch display, Wall mount, Silver | 0 | 470.0 | 0.0 |
| | | Total | 650.0 |
| Check Out | | | |

Let's check the preceding information. Return to the **Resources** tab and navigate to the **localhost** tree item. Click on the **Refresh** icon at the bottom of the window to see the list of cookies associated with our server.

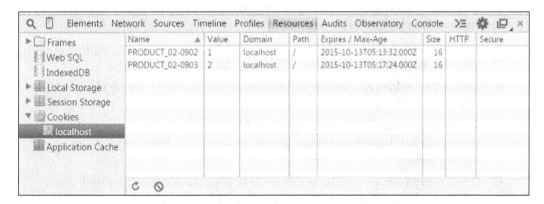

Now, close the `index.html` page and open it again. Information about the selected products along with their specified quantity and number will be available here. Click on the **Check Out** button to invoke a `cart.checkOut` method to show a message about the paid items and remove the cookies from them. The code is as follows:

```
checkOut.onClick.listen((Event event){
   cart.checkOut();
});
```

The following screenshot shows the resulting message:

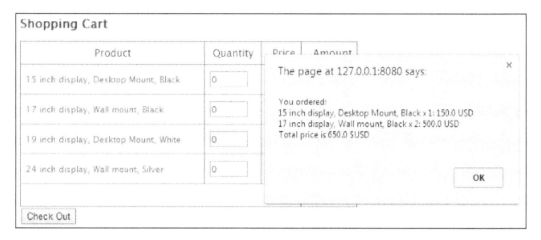

Cookies are a universal mechanism that help to persist user-specific data in the web browser. They can be very useful while essaying the following roles:

- Tracking a cookie helps compile long-term records of the browsing history.

- The authentication cookie used by the web server helps you know whether the user was logged in or not.

- Session cookies exist until the user navigates to a website and expires after a specified interval, or if the user logs in again via the server logic.

- Persistent cookies live longer than session cookies and may be used to keep vital information about the user, such as the name, surname, and so on.

- Secure cookies are only used via HTTPS with a secure attribute enabled to ensure that the cookie transmission between the client and the server is always secure.

- Third-party cookies are the opposite of first-party cookies, and they don't belong to the same domain that is displayed in the web browser. Different content presented on web pages from third-party domains can contain scripts that help track users' browser history for effective advertising.

You can combine different roles to the achieve specific requirements of your business logic. The following are the benefits of having cookies:

- **Convenience**: Cookies can remember every website you have been to and also the information in forms such as residential or business address, e-mail address, username, and so on

- **Personalization**: Cookies can store preferences, which helps every user to personalize the website content
- **Effective advertising**: Cookies can help run marketing campaigns to offer products or services relevant to a specific user
- **Ease of control**: Cookies can be cleared or disabled via the client's web browser

The following are the disadvantages of cookies:

- **Privacy**: Cookies keep a track of all the websites that you have visited
- **Security**: Implementation of cookies on different web browsers is accompanied by the detection of various security holes
- **Limitation**: Cookies have a limit of 4095 bytes per cookie
- **Data**: Cookies can overhead each request with excessive extra data

So, the main purpose of cookies is to make the client-to-server communication stateful. If you need to only save data on a client or work offline, you can use other techniques and one of them is Web Storage.

# Web Storage

**Web Storage** (or DOM storage) represents a mechanism for a better and more secured way of persisting data on the client than cookies. Web Storage is better in the following situations:

- When you need greater storage capacity (it can keep 5 - 10 MB per the available storage, depending on the web browser)
- When you don't need to communicate with the server to manage the client data
- When you don't want the stored data to expire
- When the stored data spans across different tabs or windows of the same browser

There are two Web Storage objects (Session and Local) that can be used to persist the user data in the web browser for the length of the session and indefinitely. Both of them have a similar simple API declared via the Storage interface. Web Storage has an event-driven implementation. The storage event is fired whenever a storage area changes.

# The Session storage

The **Session storage** is available through the `window.sessionStorage` attribute. It is intended to keep short-lived data opened in the same tab or window and shared only between the pages of the same domain. The browser creates a new session storage database every time a user opens a new tab or a window.

# The Local storage

As opposed to the Session storage, the **Local storage** is available via the `window.localStorage` attribute and allows you to keep data longer than a single session. The Local storage saves all data in a special local storage area and is not limited to the lifetime of the tab or a window. The local storage area is shared between different tabs and windows and can be very handy in multitransactional scenarios.

Let's see how we can change the examples from the previous *Cookies* section to use them in Web Storage. We will not delete the cookie completely so that we have chance to compare different persisting techniques. Open the `shopping_cart_web_storage` project. In the following code, we add the business logic to check whether Web Storage is supported by the web browser with the `StorageManager` class:

```
abstract class StorageManager {
  factory StorageManager() {
    if (WebStorageManager.supported) {
      return new WebStorageManager();
    } else {
      return new CookieStorageManager();
    }
  }

  Future<String> getItem(key);
  Future setItem(key, value);
  Future removeItem(key);
}
```

In the preceding code, you can see the new `WebStorageManager` class. It is quite difficult to determine whether the web browser supports Web Storage or not. You may find one of the possible solutions in the following code that uses the supported `getter` method. The `getItem` function returns the value associated with the given key. The `setItem` function sets a key-value pair in this method and the `last` method removes the item with the specified key. The code is as follows:

```
class WebStorageManager implements StorageManager {
  static bool get supported {
    if (window.localStorage != null) {
      try{
        window.localStorage["__name__"] = "__test__";
```

```
        window.localStorage.remove("__name__");
        return true;
      } catch(e) {
        return false;
      }
    } else {
      return false;
    }
  }

  Future<String> getItem(key) {
    return new Future.sync(() {
      return window.localStorage[key];
    });
  }

  Future setItem(key, value) {
    return new Future.sync(() {
      window.localStorage[key] = value;
    });
  }
  Future removeItem(key) {
    return new Future.sync(() {
      window.localStorage.remove(key);
    });
  }
}
```

The following screenshot shows the result of executing the program:

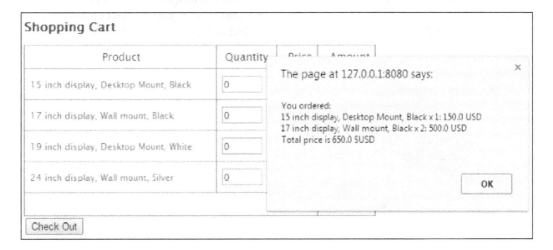

You can find information about the status of the local storage in the same place where we saw the cookies. Expand the **Local Storage** tree item and choose the **localhost** option to see the local storage data:

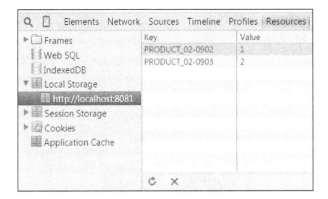

Now, we can use Web Storage and cookies to store a date for the client. We will continue our trip across advanced storages and the next target is Web SQL.

# Web SQL

**Web SQL** was introduced by Apple and is based on a free database SQLite. It will be discontinued very soon, and I intend to add it here only to show you how it could be used and how we can migrate to other advanced techniques without glitches. In the following code, we created a new `shopping_cart_web_sql` project as a copy of the project from the *Web Storage* section and added `WebSQLStorageManager` into the `StorageManager` class:

```
abstract class StorageManager {
  factory StorageManager() {
    if (WebSQLStorageManager.supported) {
      return new WebSQLStorageManager();
    } else if (WebStorageManager.supported) {
      return new WebStorageManager();
    } else {
      return new CookieStorageManager();
    }
  }

  Future<String> getItem(key);
  Future setItem(key, value);
  Future removeItem(key);
}
```

First of all, check whether the web browser supports Web SQL and instantiate it if successful. You should specify the version and initial size of the database to be used. The web browser support for Web SQL can be quickly checked with the supported property `SqlDatabase` class. Web SQL needs a big preparation before it can be used. First of all, we need to open the database. After the database is open, we can create a table if it does not exist. Web SQL has a more complex API than a cookie and Web Storage; each method increases in size exponentially. It is vital that all methods must execute very specific SQL statements. WebSQL also supports read and write transactions. When a transaction begins, you need to specify the `key` that will be assigned to the SQL parameters. The instance of `SqlResultSet` keeps a track of the transactions. The `rows.isEmpty` property of `SqlResultSet` is an important property that tells us exactly how many rows were returned, as shown in the following code:

```
class WebSQLStorageManager implements StorageManager {

    static const SHOPPING = "SHOPPING";
    static const PRODUCT = "PRODUCT";
    static const TRANS_MODE = "readwrite";
    static final String VERSION = "1";
    static const int SIZE = 1048576;

    SqlDatabase _database;
    static bool get supported => SqlDatabase.supported;
    Future<SqlDatabase> _getDatabase(
        String dbName, String storeName) {
      if (_database == null) {
        _database = window.openDatabase(dbName, VERSION,
            dbName, SIZE);
        var sql = 'CREATE TABLE IF NOT EXISTS ' +
            storeName +
            ' (id NVARCHAR(32) UNIQUE PRIMARY KEY, value TEXT)';
        var completer = new Completer();
        _database.transaction((SqlTransaction tx) {
          tx.executeSql(sql, [],
          (SqlTransaction txn, SqlResultSet result) {
            completer.complete(_database);
          }, (SqlTransaction transaction, SqlError error) {
            completer.completeError(error);
          });
        }, (error) => completer.completeError(error));
        return completer.future;
      } else {
        return new Future.sync(() => _database);
      }
```

```
      }

      Future<String> getItem(key) {
        var sql = 'SELECT value FROM $PRODUCT WHERE id = ?';
        var completer = new Completer();
        _getDatabase(SHOPPING, PRODUCT).then((SqlDatabase database) {
          database.readTransaction((SqlTransaction tx) {
            tx.executeSql(sql, [key],
            (SqlTransaction txn, SqlResultSet result) {
              if (result.rows.isEmpty) {
                return completer.complete(null);
              } else {
                Map row = result.rows.first;
                return completer.complete(row['value']);
              }
            }, (SqlTransaction transaction, SqlError error) {
              completer.completeError(error);
            });
          });
        });
        return completer.future;
      }
```

For the create and update operations, we use the following transaction and specify the special SQL statement, and we need to specify the SQL parameters `key` and `value` as well:

```
      Future setItem(key, value) {
        var sql = 'INSERT OR REPLACE INTO $PRODUCT (id, value) ' +
          'VALUES (?, ?)';
        var completer = new Completer();
        _getDatabase(SHOPPING, PRODUCT).then((SqlDatabase database) {
          database.transaction((SqlTransaction tx) {
            tx.executeSql(sql, [key, value],
            (SqlTransaction txn, SqlResultSet result) {
              return completer.complete(value);
            }, (SqlTransaction transaction, SqlError error) {
              completer.completeError(error);
            });
          }, (error) => completer.completeError(error));
        });
        return completer.future;
      }
```

To remove an item, we use the following transaction and specify the `key` parameter that will be assigned to the SQL parameters:

```
Future removeItem(key) {
    var sql = 'DELETE FROM $PRODUCT WHERE id = ?';
    var completer = new Completer();
    _getDatabase(SHOPPING, PRODUCT).then((SqlDatabase database) {
      database.transaction((SqlTransaction tx) {

        tx.executeSql(sql, [key],
        (SqlTransaction txn, SqlResultSet result) {
          return completer.complete();
        }, (SqlTransaction transaction, SqlError error) {
          completer.completeError(error);
        });
      }, (error) => completer.completeError(error));
    });
    return completer.future;
  }
}
```

Launch our application and change the number of products. Expand the **Web SQL** tree item from the **Resources** tab to see the Web SQL storage data. The following screenshot shows the **SHOPPING** database and the **PRODUCT** table with the stored data:

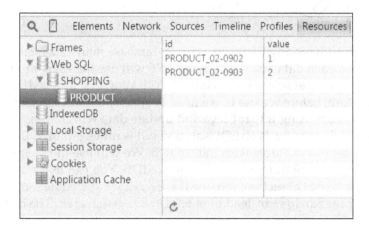

The Web SQL database API isn't actually a part of the HTML5 specification. Therefore, it's time to migrate to IndexedDB if you have a code that uses Web SQL.

# IndexedDB

**IndexedDB** was introduced by Oracle and became popular very quickly. It's a Not Only SQL (NoSQL) database. The IndexedDB API is a more capable and far more complex API. IndexedDB has the following significant benefits:

- It improves the responsiveness and speed of web programs by minimizing the number of HTTP requests
- It provides more space for data without Web Storage limits
- It provides the ability to work offline
- A NoSQL database helps you work directly with Dart and JavaScript objects
- It allows fast indexing, object searching, and granular locking per transaction
- It supports synchronous and asynchronous APIs

One of the major disadvantages can be the difficulty in understanding it if you are coming from the world of rational databases. In IndexedDB, we can store a large amount of structured data, images, arrays, and whole objects; you just need to index them with a key. It follows the same origin policy, so we cannot access data across different domains. If you still use Web SQL database with your products, it's time to migrate to IndexedDB because the Web SQL database was deprecated by **World Wide Web Consortium (W3C)** in November 2010.

 IndexedDB is an indexed table system.

IndexedDB doesn't have any limits on a single database item's size, but it may impose a limit on each database's total items. We will use the asynchronous API because it works in most scenarios, including Web Workers. IndexedDB is a real database; therefore, before we use it, we need to specify a database schema, open a connection, and start using it to retrieve and update data within transactions. In this case, it gets very close to the Web SQL solution but is much simpler. Let's take a look at how we can use our example with IndexedDB. We will use the dart:indexed_db package from the Dart SDK to work with IndexedDB. You can make a copy of the project from the *Web SQL* section, rename it shopping_cart_indexed_db, and use IndexedDBStorageManager instead of WebSQLStorageManager. The code is as follows:

```
abstract class StorageManager {
  factory StorageManager() {
    if (IndexedDBStorageManager.supported) {
      return new IndexedDBStorageManager();
```

```
    } else if (WebStorageManager.supported) {
      return new WebStorageManager();
    } else {
      return new CookieStorageManager();
    }
  }

  Future<String> getItem(key);
  Future setItem(key, value);
  Future removeItem(key);
}
```

The preceding code shows the `IndexedDBStorageManager` class. We constructed a special `_getDatabase` method to retrieve an instance of the `Database` class. As we mentioned earlier, before we use IndexedDB, we need to open the IndexedDB database. In the following code, we use the `window.indexedDB.open` method to open our database. Next, we need to check whether the store exists in an `objectStoreNames` array of the database. If it doesn't exist, we must close the database and open it again with a higher version number. Because this process is asynchronous, we create a new instance of the `store` object inside the `onUpgradeNeeded` listener. Each manipulation of the objects of the database happens inside a transaction. So, we will create a new transaction every time and return the `ObjectStore` instance in the `startTransaction` method. We will return the value of `ObjectStore` via the `getObject` method. To set an item in the database, we use the `put` method of `ObjectStore`. To remove the object from the store, just call the `delete` method, as shown in the following code:

```
class IndexedDBStorageManager implements StorageManager {

  Database _database;

  static const SHOPPING = "SHOPPING";
  static const PRODUCT = "PRODUCT";
  static const TRANS_MODE = "readwrite";
  Future _getDatabase(String dbName, String storeName) {
    if (_database == null) {

      return window.indexedDB.open(dbName).then((Database d) {
        _database = d;
        if (!_database.objectStoreNames.contains(storeName)) {
          _database.close();
          return window.indexedDB.open(dbName,
              version: (d.version as int) + 1,
              onUpgradeNeeded: (e) {
```

```
            Database d = e.target.result;
            d.createObjectStore(storeName);
          }).then((Database d) {
            _database = d;
            return _database;
          });
        }
        return _database;
      });
    } else {
      return new Future.sync(() => _database);
    }
  }
}
Future
<ObjectStore> startTransaction(String storeName) {
  return _getDatabase(SHOPPING, PRODUCT)
    .then((Database database) {
    Transaction transaction =
      _database.transactionStore(storeName, TRANS_MODE);
    return transaction.objectStore(storeName);
  });
}
Future
<String> getItem(key) {
  return new Future.sync(() {
    return startTransaction(PRODUCT).then((ObjectStore store) {
      return store.getObject(key);
    });
  });
}
Future
setItem(key, value) {
  return new Future.sync(() {
    return startTransaction(PRODUCT).then((ObjectStore store) {
      return store.put(value, key);
    });
  });
}
Future
removeItem(key) {
  return new Future.sync(() {
    return startTransaction(PRODUCT).then((ObjectStore store) {
      return store.delete(key);
    });
  });
}
}
```

That's it. We can perform all manipulations on the data within `ObjectStore`. The fact that the `ObjectStore` class instance was returned via a `Transaction` class indicates that all steps in the original one will be surrounded by a transaction. Let's expand the **IndexedDB** tree item in the **Resources** tab to see the **SHOPPING** database.

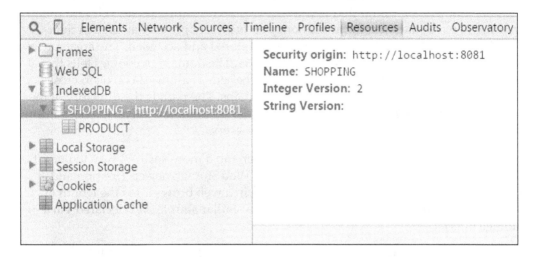

The version number of the database is **2**. Now, choose the **PRODUCT** tree item and you will see that the same name contains our data.

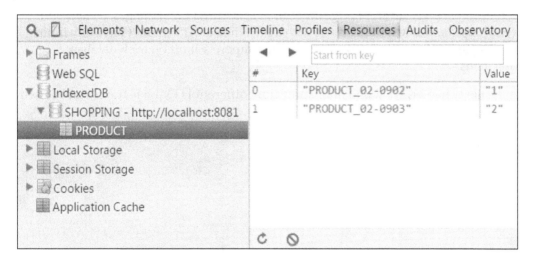

When compared to Web SQL, IndexedDB is more simple and flexible. It uses indexes to access objects in the database within transactions.

# Summary

To summarize, we will highlight some important facts about advanced storage space.

The concept of cookies was introduced for the first time on the Netscape web browser and was later migrated to Internet Explorer. It still remains relevant today. In order to have stateful communication, web browsers provide an area in their subdirectories where state information can be stored and accessed. The area and information stored in this area is called a cookie. The domain of cookies tells the browser the domain where the cookie should be sent. It allows a cookie to cross subdomains but does not allow it to cross domains. The path is the directory in the root of the domain where the cookie is active. Cookies are the universal mechanism that helps persist user-specific data in web browsers.

Web Storage represents a mechanism for better and a more secured way to persist data on the client than cookies. There are two Web Storage objects (Session and Local) that can be used to persisting user data in a web browser for the length of a session and indefinitely. Both of them have a similar simple API declared via a Storage interface.

Web SQL was introduced by Apple and is based on a free database SQLite. It will be discontinued very soon, and we used it here only to see how it could be used and how migration to other advanced technologies can be done painlessly.

In IndexedDB, we can store large amount of structured data, images, arrays, and whole objects, and just index them with a key. IndexedDB doesn't have any limits on a single database item's size, but it might impose a limit on each database's total items.

In the next chapter, we will demonstrate how different HTML5 features can be used in Dart.

# 11
# Supporting Other HTML5 Features

HTML5 was designed to deliver rich, cross-platform content without the need to use additional plugins. In this chapter, we will learn how different HTML5 features can be used in Dart. We will cover the following topics:

- The notification APIs
- The native drag-and-drop APIs
- The geolocation APIs
- Canvas

## The notification APIs

Processes that occur in web applications are asynchronous, and as time passes, they generate event messages to alert end users about the start, end, or progress of the process execution. The **web notification** API allows you to display notifications outside the context of web pages. The user agent determines the optimum presentation of the notification. This aspect depends on the device on which it is running. Usually, it can present notifications in the following areas:

- At a corner of the display
- In an area within the user agent
- On the home screen of a mobile device

The web notification API, available as part of the dart:html package, allows you to send information to a user even if the application is idle. Notifications can be useful in the following use cases:

- To notify users about new incoming messages
- To notify users about special events in game applications
- To notify users about the connection status of an application, the battery status of a device, and so on

# When to notify

When you build web applications, you can use the notification API in the event handlers or polling functions to notify the users. Event handlers are the obvious choice when it comes to responding to various happenings. Event handlers use simple, required conditions that can detect events from the DOM elements and send a notification event to the user. Sometimes, the conditions required can be a lot more complex and event handlers may not be suitable to cover them. In such cases, you can use a polling function (implemented as a combination of event handlers) to periodically check for given conditions to send notifications. Notifications can be of the following two types:

- **DOM notifications**: These come from within a web application and are very useful when detecting manipulations with the DOM structure or properties
- **System notifications**: These come from an external source (outside the application) and are used to notify users about the status of a program or system

Let's see how we can use the web notification API for our needs. You can find the source code in the notification project. In the following code, we used the standard button event handler to send notifications to the user:

```
void main() {
  var notifyBtn = querySelector("#notify_btn")
  ..onClick.listen((Event event) {
    sendNotification();
  });
}

void sendNotification() {
  Notification.requestPermission().then((String permission) {
    if (permission == "granted") {
```

```
    Notification notification =
        new Notification('My Notification', body: "Hello World");
  }
 });
}
```

Before you send any notifications to the user, the website must have permissions. You can let websites send a notification automatically or by means of a permission request first. This is a common requirement when an API tries to interact with something outside a web context, especially to avoid sending useless notifications to the user. To see the notification settings, follow these steps:

1. Open the **Settings** option in Dartium and type `notifications` in the search field, as shown in the following screenshot:

2. Open the **Content** settings pop-up dialog by clicking on the button of the same name, and then scroll down to find the **Notification** settings:

3. Choose the recommended option and open the **Notifications exceptions** dialog by clicking on the **Manage exceptions** button. For now, it will not contain our website, as shown in the following screenshot:

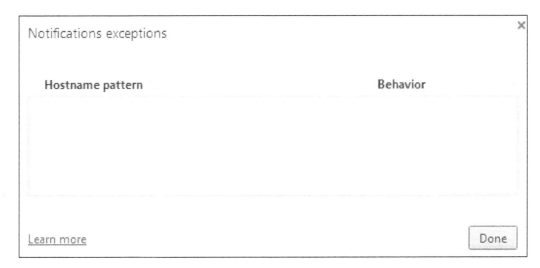

4. Now, run the application and click on the **Notify** button. As shown in the following screenshot, the `requestPermission` static method of the **Notification** class requests a permission to allow desktop notifications for the `localhost`:

5. You can allow or deny notifications for this website. Your choice will complete the future permission requests with the value of the chosen permission. The desktop notifications that are allowed are added to the list of **Notifications exceptions**. Now, open the **Notifications exceptions** dialog again to see your website, as shown in the following screenshot:

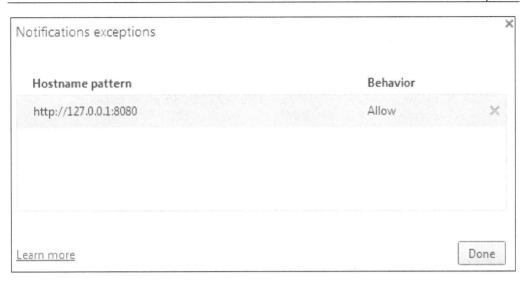

6. The next step is to create a notification. It is enough to specify only the title of the notification to create an original one. The constructor of the `Notification` class has optional properties that help us create notifications with a body and icon. A notification when instantiated is displayed as soon as possible, as shown in the following screenshot:

A notification triggers the following four events that track the current state of the notification:

- `show`: This event is triggered when the notification is displayed
- `click`: This event is triggered when the user clicks on the notification
- `close`: This event is triggered when the notification is closed
- `error`: This event is triggered when something goes wrong while displaying notifications

Notifications are still open until the user closes them, but you can use the `close` method of the `Notification` class to close them via a program, as shown in the following code:

```
void sendNotification() {
  Notification.requestPermission().then((String permission) {
    if (permission == "granted") {
      Notification notification =
        new Notification('My Notification', body: "Hello World");
      notification.onShow.listen((Event event) {
        new Timer(new Duration(seconds:2), () {
          notification.close();
        });
      });
    }
  });
}
```

# Preventing repeated notifications

Every time you click on the **Notify** button in your application, the web notification API generates new notifications and puts them on top of the previous one. Similar notifications can be marked with the following `tag` attribute to prevent crowding a user's desktop with hundreds of analogous notifications:

```
void sendNotification() {
  Notification.requestPermission().then((String permission) {
    if (permission == "granted") {
      Notification notification =
        new Notification('My Notification', body: "Hello World",
          tag: "myNotification");
      notification.onShow.listen((Event event) {
        new Timer(new Duration(seconds:2), () {
          notification.close();
        });
      });
    }
  });
}
```

Now when you generate a notification with the same tag, the web notification API removes the previous one and adds the new one instead. Web notification specifications are not stable yet, and they are supported only by the latest version of web browsers such as Chrome, Firefox, Safari, and Opera.

# The native drag-and-drop APIs

**Drag-and-drop** is a way to convert the pointing device's movements and clicks to special commands that are recognized by software to provide quick access to common functions of a program. The user grabs a virtual object, drags it to a different location or another virtual object, and drops it there. Drag-and-drop support for a native browser means faster, more responsive, and more intuitive web applications. Before you use the drag-and-drop feature, make sure you have draggable content.

# Draggable content

An abstract `Element` class has a `draggable` attribute that indicates whether the element can be dragged and dropped. As all the DOM elements emerge from the `Element` abstract class, this means all of them support the drag-and-drop operation by default. To make elements draggable, we need to set their `draggable` attribute to `true`. This can be done using the following code:

```
var dragSource = querySelector("#sample_drag_id");
dnd.draggable = true;
```

Alternatively, you can do this using the following HTML markup:

```
<p id="sample_dnd_id" draggable="true">Drag me!</p>
```

If you want to prevent the text contents of draggable elements from being selected, you can style the element, as shown in the following code:

```
[draggable] {
  -moz-user-select: none;
  -khtml-user-select: none;
  -webkit-user-select: none;
  user-select: none;
  -khtml-user-drag: element;
  -webkit-user-drag: element;
}
```

Let's open the `drag_and_drop` project and run it. In the following screenshot, you will see that you can drag the text element within the window of the browser but cannot drop it:

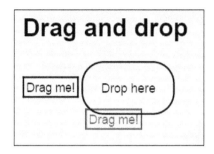

To manage the drag-and-drop operations in the example, add the drag-and-drop event listeners described in the next section.

 During a drag operation, the native drag-and-drop API is fired only by the drag events and not the mouse events.

# The drag-and-drop events

The native drag-and-drop API fires the following events:

- `dragstart`: This event is fired on an element when a drag starts. Information such as the drag data and image to be associated with the drag operation can be set in the listener.

- `dragenter`: This event is fired when the cursor is hovered over an element for the first time while a drag begins. A drop operation is not allowed by default. There are one or more listeners that perform drag-and-drop operations. Usually, the listener highlights or marks the drop element where the drop can occur.

- `dragover`: This event is fired when the cursor is hovered over an element and a drag is in process.

- `dragleave`: This event is fired when the cursor leaves an element while a drag is in process. The listener will remove highlights or markers from the element where the drop can occur.

- `drag`: This event is fired on an element where the `dragstart` event was fired.

- drop: This event is fired on an element where the drop occurred. It is fired only if the drop is allowed. Users can cancel the drag operation by pressing the *Esc* key or releasing the mouse button on an invalid drop area.

- dragend: This event is fired on an element on which the drag was started to inform that the drag operation is complete, regardless of whether it is successful or not.

We will continue to make elements draggable from our example. We need to add a listener for the dartstart event and set the drag data within the listener, as follows:

```
var dragSource = querySelector("#sample_drag_id")
..draggable = true
..onDragStart.listen((MouseEvent event) {
  //…
});
```

If an element is made draggable, you cannot select the text by clicking-and-dragging with the mouse.

 User must hold down the *Alt* key to select text with the mouse.

# Dragging data

Each drag event has a dataTransfer property that is used to hold data associated with the drag operation. If you drag the selected text, then the associated data is text. If you drag an image, then the associated data is the image itself. The drag data combines the string representation of the format of the data and the data value. We will use the format of the data in the event listeners for the dragenter and dragover events to check whether the drop operation is allowed or not. You can set multiple drag data to call the setData method multiple times with different formats. To delete them, call the clearData method of the dataTransfer property, as shown in the following code:

```
var dragSource = querySelector("#sample_dnd_id")
..draggable = true
..onDragStart.listen((MouseEvent event) {
  event.dataTransfer.setData("text/plain", "I'm draggable");
  event.dataTransfer.setData("text/data", "1234");
});
```

# Dragging the feedback image

Usually, native drag-and-drop APIs automatically create translucent images that are generated from the drag target of the `dragstart` event, which follows the mouse pointer during the drag operation. You can use the `setDragImage` method of the `dataTransfer` property to specify a custom drag image. The first argument of this function is a custom drag image, which could be a reference to a real image, canvas, or other elements. The second and third arguments are offsets where the image should appear relative to the mouse pointer. The code is as follows:

```
var dragSource = querySelector("#sample_drag_id")
..draggable = true
..onDragStart.listen((MouseEvent event) {
  event.dataTransfer.setData("text/plain", "I'm draggable");
  event.dataTransfer.setDragImage(new
    ImageElement(src:'notification.png'), 0, 0);
});
```

The following feedback image will appear instead of the standard translucent image:

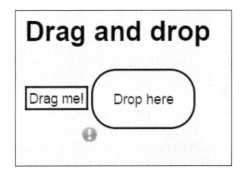

# Dragging effects

The drag-and-drop API supports operations such as copy, move, link, and their combinations that may be performed on data that is draggable. We can use the `copy` operation to indicate that the data being dragged will be copied from its present location to the drop location. Similarly, you can use the `move` operation to indicate that the data being dragged will be moved, and the `link` operation indicates that connections will be created between the source and drop locations. You should specify which operation or combinations are allowed and are performed by setting the `effectAllowed` property of the `dragstart` event within a listener, as shown in the following code:

```
var dragSource = querySelector("#sample_drag_id")
..draggable = true
```

```
..onDragStart.listen((MouseEvent event) {
  event.dataTransfer.setData("text/plain", "I'm draggable");
  event.dataTransfer.setDragImage(new
    ImageElement(src:'notification.png'), 0, 0);
  event.dataTransfer.effectAllowed = 'copy';
});
```

In the preceding example, we allowed only the `copy` operation. Let's see all the values that we can use as the name for an operation:

- `none`: This operation means that no operation is permitted
- `copy`: This operation means that the drag data can only be copied from source to drop location
- `move`: This operation means that the drag data can only be moved from source to drop location
- `link`: This operation means that the drag data can only be linked from source to drop location
- `copyMove`: This operation means that the drag data can be copied or moved from source to drop location
- `copyLink`: This operation means that the drag data can be copied or linked from source to drop location
- `all`: This operation means that the drag data can be copied, moved, or linked from source to drop location

By default, the `effectAllowed` property allows all three operations. The permitted operation can be checked in a listener for the `dragenter` or `dragover` events via the `effectAllowed` property, and it should be set in a related `dropEffect` property to specify which single operation should be performed. The valid operations for the `dropEffect` property are `none`, `move`, or `link` only, and any other combinations are prohibited. The desired operation will change the mouse pointer, so the cursor might appear with a plus for the `copy` operation. The desired effect can be modified by a user by pressing the modifier keys. The exact keys vary by platform. On Windows OS, a user typically uses the *Shift* and *Ctrl* keys to switch between the `copy`, `move`, and `link` operations. During the `dragenter` and `dragover` events, we can modify both the `effectAllowed` and `dropEffect` properties to specify the supported operations by a drop target. The effect specified in `dropEffect` must be the one that is listed within the `effectAllowed` property. The value of the `dropEffect` property can tell us exactly the result of the drag operation. If the value of the `dropEffect` property is `none`, then the drag was cancelled; otherwise, the specified effect holds the performed operation. The drag-and-drop operation is considered complete after the `dragevent` is finished.

The none value can be used for either of the property to indicate that no drop operation is allowed at the target location.

# The drop target

The drop target is a place where the dragged item may be dropped. The drop target is very important because most areas of a web page are not permitted to drop. Event listeners for the dragenter and dragover events are used to indicate a valid drop target through preventing default handling by canceling events, as shown in the following code:

```
var dropTarget = querySelector("#sample_drop_id")
  ..onDragOver.listen((MouseEvent event) {
    if (checkTarget(event.target)) {
      event.preventDefault();
      event.dataTransfer.dropEffect = 'copy';
    }
  });
```

In the preceding code, we call the checkTarget method to be sure that the target is in the right place to be dropped. In our case, the drop target must have the droppable attribute, as shown in the following code:

```
bool checkTarget(Element target) {
  return target.attributes.containsKey('droppable');
}
```

However, it is common that the drop will be accepted or rejected based on the type of drag data within the dataTransfer property. In this case, we should check the property types of the dataTransfer property to decide whether the data can be accepted to be dropped. The code is as follows:

```
var dropTarget = querySelector("#sample_drop_id")
  ..onDragOver.listen((MouseEvent event) {
    if (checkTarget(event.target) &&
        checkTypes(event.dataTransfer.types)) {
      event.preventDefault();
      event.dataTransfer.dropEffect = 'copy';
    }
  });
```

In the following code, the `checkTypes` function accepts only the `text/data` types specified through the `setData` method of `dataTransfer` inside the listener of the `dragstart` event:

```
bool checkTypes(List<String> types) {
    return types.contains("text/data");
}
```

You can now run the web application, drag your box with the `Drag me!` text, and drop it inside the box with the `Drop here` text. Let's polish our application and change the text of the drop zone.

# Finishing a drop

When a user releases the mouse, the drag-and-drop operation ends. If this happened over an element that was identified as a valid drop target, the drag-and-drop API will fire a `drop` event at the target. The `dataTransfer` property of the `drop` event holds the data that is being dragged. To retrieve the dragged data, we will use the `getData` method of the `dataTransfer` property, as follows:

```
var dropTarget = querySelector("#sample_drop_id")
..onDragOver.listen((MouseEvent event) {
    if (checkTarget(event.target) &&
        checkTypes(event.dataTransfer.types)) {
      event.preventDefault();
      event.dataTransfer.dropEffect = 'copy';
    }
})
..onDrop.listen((MouseEvent event) {
    Element dropTarget = event.target;
    dropTarget.innerHtml = event.dataTransfer.getData('text/plain');
    event.preventDefault();
});
```

The getData method will retrieve the string value that was set when the setData method was called. When an empty string is returned from getData, this means that data of the specified type does not exist. At the end of the getData method, you need to call the preventDefault method of the event if you have accepted the drop. Here is the result of the drag-and-drop operation:

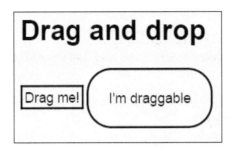

# Finishing a drag

Finally, when the drag operation is complete, the drag-and-drop API generates a dragend event at the source element that received the dragstart event. The API generates that event regardless of the result of the drag-and-drop operation. The value of the dropEffect property can tell us the exact result of the drag operation. If the value of the dropEffect property is none, then the drag was cancelled; otherwise, the specified effect holds the performed operation. The drag-and-drop operation is considered complete after dragevent is finished.

# The geolocation APIs

A **geolocation** API is a high-level interface used to locate information. It lets you find out where the user is and keep a track of his/her location when he/she moves. The geolocation API is device-agnostic of the underlying location source and doesn't care how the web browser determines the location. The following are the common sources for the location:

- GPS
- The network IP address
- RFID
- Wi-Fi
- The Bluetooth MAC address
- The GSM/CDMA cell ID
- User inputs

The API represents location by latitude and longitude coordinates.

 The geolocation APIs do not guarantee returning the actual location of the device.

The geolocation API has the following classes:

- `Geolocation`: This class is used to determine the location information associated with the hosting device
- `Geoposition`: This class is used to store the coordinates and timestamp
- `Coordinates`: This class is used to store the location information and speed of the device

# Determining the current location

Let's see how we can use the geolocation API to obtain information about the current location:

```
import 'dart:html';

void main() {
  window.navigator.geolocation.getCurrentPosition()
  .then((Geoposition geoposition) {
    querySelector("#latitude").text = geoposition.coords.latitude
      .toStringAsFixed(6);
    querySelector("#longitude").text = geoposition.coords.longitude
      .toStringAsFixed(6);
  }, onError: (PositionError error) {
    print(error.message);
  });
}
```

We can request the `geolocation` instance from the `navigator` property of the `window` object. The `getCurrentPosition` method of `geolocation` returns `Geoposition` in the `Future` object. When the Future will be resolved, we will assign the `geoposition` coordinates to the latitude and longitude HTML fields.

 Dartium doesn't support `geolocation`, so run `pub serve` and iterate with Chrome web browser.

The website must have permission before use your location information. You can let websites use your location information automatically or obtain a permission request first. This is a common requirement when an API tries to interact with something outside a web context, especially to avoid sharing user-specific information. To see the geolocation information, follow these steps:

1. Open the **Settings** option in Chrome and type `location` in the search field, as shown in the following screenshot:

2. Open the **Content settings** pop-up dialog by clicking on the button of the same name, scroll down the content, and you'll find the **Location** settings:

3.  Choose the **recommended** option and open the **Geolocation exceptions** dialog by clicking on the **Manage exceptions** button. For now, it will not contain our website, as shown in the following screenshot:

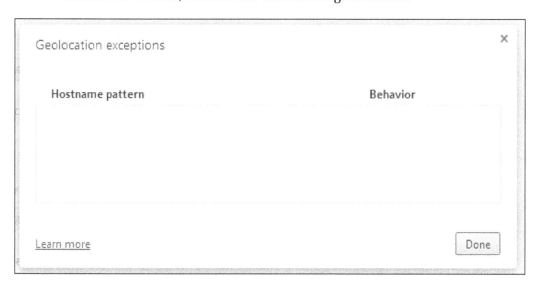

4.  Run the `geolocation` application. The Chrome web browser will ask you for permission to use your location information, as shown in the following screenshot:

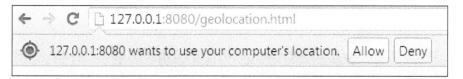

5.  You can allow or deny location requests for this website. Your choice completes the future permission requests with the value of `geoposition`. The website is then added to the list of **Geolocation exceptions**. Open the **Geolocation exceptions** dialog again to see your website:

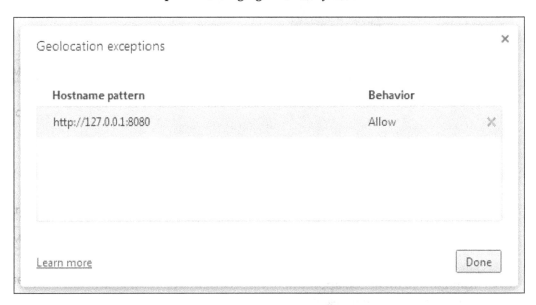

Any error that occurs in the `geolocation` service will be printed:

```
Network location provider at 'https://www.googleapis.com/'
: Returned error code 400.
```

6.  We will now run `pub serve` from the root folder of our project:

```
Loading source assets...
Serving geolocation web on http://localhost:8080
Build completed successfully
[web] GET /geolocation.html => geolocation|web/geolocation.html
[web] GET /geolocation.css => geolocation|web/geolocation.css
[web] GET /packages/browser/dart.js => browser|lib/dart.js
[Info from Dart2JS]:
Compiling geolocation|web/geolocation.dart...
[Info from Dart2JS]:
Took 0:00:27.723586 to compile geolocation|web/geolocation.dart.
Build completed successfully
[web] GET /geolocation.dart.js => geolocation|web/geolocation.
dart.js
[web] GET /geolocation.dart.js.map => geolocation|web/geolocation.
dart.js.map
```

7.  Then, open the web application in the Chrome web browser to get the following result:

# Geolocation

Latitude **54.6083**
Longitude **39.7179**

Your example will be more interesting if you add Google Maps to show your current position on a real map.

## Geolocation on maps

Add the `google_maps` package to your project and make the following changes to the code:

```
import 'dart:html';
import 'package:google_maps/google_maps.dart';

void main() {
  final mapOptions = new MapOptions()
  ..zoom = 15
  ..mapTypeId = MapTypeId.ROADMAP;
  final map = new GMap(querySelector("#map_canvas"), mapOptions);

  window.navigator.geolocation.getCurrentPosition()
  .then((Geoposition geoposition) {
    Coordinates coords = geoposition.coords;
    querySelector("#latitude").text = coords.latitude
      .toStringAsPrecision(6);
    querySelector("#longitude").text = coords.longitude
      .toStringAsPrecision(6);
    //
    map.center = new LatLng(coords.latitude, coords.longitude);
  }, onError: (PositionError error){
    print(error.message);
  });
}
```

In `mapOptions`, we specified the `zoom` and `type` of view. Maps can be presented in terms of the satellite, terrain, or hybrid view. Using the Google Maps API is very simple. Just add the `div` element with the specified ID to your HTML page. Then, execute the `pub serve` command to compile your code and run the server. When you open the **Geolocation** page in the Chrome web browser, you will get the following result:

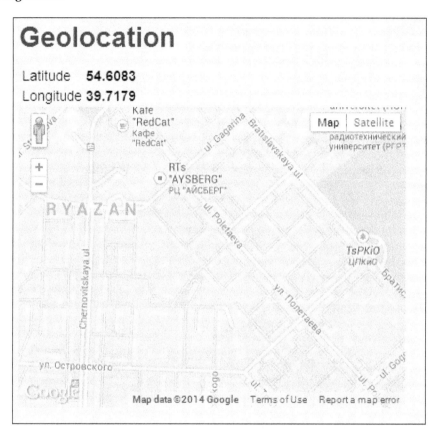

## Tracking the present location

Geolocation APIs can monitor the current location of your device using the `watchPosition` method. With the `enableHighAccuracy` parameter, the geolocation API starts to use more accurate hardware available on your device. This method returns a stream of geoposition coordinates. You only need to listen to the events to track changes in your current position. The code is as follows:

```
import 'dart:html';
import 'package:google_maps/google_maps.dart';
```

```
void main() {
  final mapOptions = new MapOptions()
  ..zoom = 25
  ..mapTypeId = MapTypeId.ROADMAP;
  final map = new GMap(querySelector("#map_canvas"), mapOptions);

  window.navigator.geolocation
  .watchPosition(enableHighAccuracy:true)
   .listen((Geoposition geoposition) {
    Coordinates coords = geoposition.coords;
    map.center = new LatLng(coords.latitude, coords.longitude);
    //
    querySelector("#location_tracker").append(new DivElement()
    ..text = coords.latitude.toStringAsPrecision(6) + " x " +
      coords.longitude.toStringAsPrecision(6));
  }, onError: (PositionError error){
      print(error.message);
  });
}
```

When you run the web application, you will receive the following result:

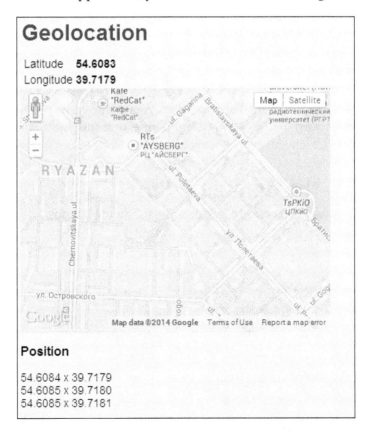

# Canvas

The HTML5 **canvas** is a fantastic feature that allows you to code programmatic drawing operations. It has become very popular because it allows you to create and manipulate imagery directly within web pages. The canvas is one of the most flexible tags in new HTML5 features. This tag is a blank state. It defines a `context` object that users can draw inside. The actual drawing operations can be split in the following ways:

- Drawing a 2D context
- Drawing a 3D context formally known as a WebGL

A 2D context is available in all modern web browsers. It is more established and stable, while the 3D context is in the early process of being defined. Let's discuss the 2D context as it is more widely supported.

The canvas API is simple and powerful at the same time. You can only draw on a 2D bitmap surface using script. In the process of drawing, you do not have any DOM nodes for the shapes you draw. All that you produce is pixels, so you can forget about the performance penalties event if the image complexity increases.

Drawing on a canvas is all about adding pixels in the appropriate coordinates on the screen. In general, the coordinates of the pixels on the screen correlate to the points in the canvas that are represented as a grid, but they can vary when we zoom in or out of the screen or when a canvas is resized with CSS. The key point on the grid is the origin located in the left-hand side corner of the canvas with coordinates (0, 0). Each shape drawn on the canvas has an offset of $x$ and $y$ axes and size by width and height.

# Example – the canvas editor

The canvas API gives you access to perform the following actions:

- Draw shapes such as rectangles, ellipses, lines, and so on
- Render text
- Pixel manipulation
- Fill colors in areas, shapes, or text
- Create gradients and patterns to fill areas, shapes, or text
- Copy images, other canvases, or video frames
- Export the content of a canvas to a file

We don't want to pass through all these features with simple examples, so let's just create a canvas painting application to discover how to use many of them practically. You can find a prepared project in the code that accompanies this book. The application is based on Bootstrap 3.2 and jQuery 1.11.1. I have made a port of `bootstrap-colorselector` (`https://github.com/flaute/bootstrap-colorselector`) to Dart specially to show you how easily it can be done. In the following screenshot, you can see it running in the web browser application:

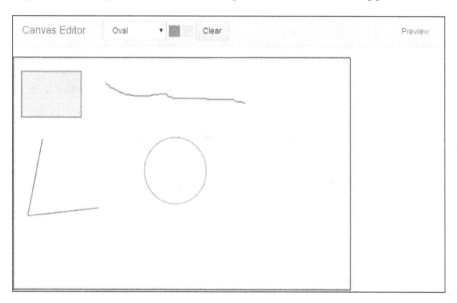

At the top of the application, we placed a **Bootstrap** navigation bar. It contains a `select` component with a drop-down option representing a list of available tools, such as **Pen**, **Rectangle**, **Line**, and **Oval**. There are two color selectors that we use to stroke and fill canvas styles. The **Clear** button helps wipe out the content of a canvas. Last but not least, the **Preview** button opens another window with the content of a canvas. Let's go deeper to discover different parts of the application and how they communicate with each other.

# Beginning with HTML

The content of the `head` tag is shown in the following code:

```
<meta charset="utf-8">
<meta name="viewport" content="width=device-width, initial-
scale=1">
<title>Canvas</title>
```

```
<link rel="stylesheet" href="https://maxcdn.bootstrapcdn.com/
bootstrap/3.2.0/css/
bootstrap.min.css">
<link rel="stylesheet" href="https://maxcdn.bootstrapcdn.com/
bootstrap/3.2.0/css/
bootstrap-theme.min.css">

<link rel="stylesheet" type="text/css" href="css/bootstrap-
colorselector.css" />
<link rel="stylesheet" type="text/css" href="css/index.css">

<!-- HTML5 Shim and Respond.js IE8 support of HTML5 elements and
media queries -->
<!-- WARNING: Respond.js doesn't work if you view the page via
file:// -->
<!--[if lt IE 9]>
  <script src="https://oss.maxcdn.com/html5shiv/3.7.2/html5shiv.min.
js"></
script>
  <script src="https://oss.maxcdn.com/respond/1.4.2/respond.min.js"></
script
>
<![endif]-->

<!-- jQuery (necessary for Bootstrap's JavaScript plugins) -->
<script src="https://ajax.googleapis.com/ajax/libs/jquery/1.11.1/
jquery.
min.js"></script>
<script src="https://maxcdn.bootstrapcdn.com/bootstrap/3.2.0/js/
bootstrap.
min.js"></script>

<script async type="application/dart" src="index.dart"></script>
<script async src="packages/browser/dart.js"></script>
```

All bootstrap style sheets and the JavaScript code included in the HTML page are downloaded from a free and public **content delivery network (CDN)**. The html5shiv and respond libraries help run HTML5 features on IE Version 8 or higher.

The body of the web page is split into two sections. The first one is the responsive navbar component that serves as a navigation header for our application. It is collapsed and toggled in a mobile view, and then becomes horizontal if the available width space increases. We split the navigation bar into two subsections. The first subsection is the primary toolbar that keeps all components related to the direct canvas manipulation. The other one is the secondary toolbar that contains components that play a supporting role in the application.

The first component of the primary toolbar is `toolSelector`, which keeps all the registered tools, as shown in the following code:

```
<div class="form-group">
<select class="form-control" id="toolSelector"
  name="toolSelector">
</select>
</div>
```

The next two components are `stroke_color_selector` and `fill_color_selector`, which contain lists of colors presented as palettes. We will include only the first one in the following code snippet because of their similarity:

```
<div class="form-group">
  <select class="stroke_color_selector">
 <option value="#000000" data-color="black">Black</option>
 <option value="#808080" data-color="gray">Gray</option>
 <option value="#C0C0C0" data-color="silver">Silver</option>
 <option value="#FFFFFF" data-color="white">White</option>
 <option value="#800000" data-color="maroon">Maroon</option>
 <option value="#FF0000" data-color="red">Red</option>
 <option value="#808000" data-color="olive">Olive</option>
 <option value="#FFFF00" data-color="yellow">Yellow</option>
 <option value="#008000" data-color="green">Green</option>
 <option value="#00FF00" data-color="lime">Lime</option>
 <option value="#008080" data-color="olive">Teal</option>
 <option value="#00FFFF" data-color="aqua">Aqua</option>
 <option value="#000080" data-color="navy">Navy</option>
 <option value="#0000FF" data-color="olive">Blue</option>
 <option value="#800080" data-color="purple ">Purple </option>
 <option value="#FF00FF" data-color="fuchsia">Fuchsia</option>
</select>
</div>
```

Both of the components, `stroke_color_selector` and `fill_color_selector`, are represented by the component ported from `bootstrap-colorselector`. The result of the color palette is shown in the following screenshot:

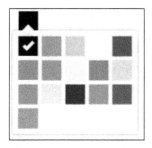

The last one in this group of components is the **Clear** button. The user can click on this button to clear the content of the canvas, as shown in the following code:

```
<div class="form-group">
  <button type="button"
    class="btn btn-default clear-btn">Clear</button>
</div>
```

The secondary toolbar is right aligned. It has only a `Preview` button component, as shown in the following code:

```
<ul class="nav navbar-nav navbar-right">
  <li><a href="#" class="previewBtn">Preview</a></li>
</ul>
```

Now, let's see our canvas components:

```
<div class="col-lg-12 text-center canvas-container">
  <canvas class="canvas view-canvas" width="600px"
    height="400px">
    <p>Unfortunately, your browser is currently unsupported by
      our web application.</p>
  </canvas>
  <canvas class="canvas draw-canvas" width="600px"
    height="400px">
    <p>Unfortunately, your browser is currently unsupported by
      our web application.</p>
  </canvas>
</div>
```

We use two canvases in our application. The first one is marked with a `view-canvas` class. It is only used to present data opposite to the second one marked with the `draw-canvas` class. The purpose of the second canvas is that all the tools must draw here. When their drawing operation ends, the pixels that they generated are then moved into the first canvas.

## Moving to the main function

The foundation of our application is the components separated in to two types: widgets and tools. Widgets are components dealing with HTML elements and include extra behavior. All tool components are based on the `Tool` class. We use the tool-based components to draw in the canvas. Here is the main function of our application:

```
// Calculate absolute value of number
num abs(num value) => value < 0 ? -value : value;
```

```
// Return offset of mouse pointer from any mouse event
Point offset(MouseEvent event) => event.offset;

void main() {
  // Create an instance of [CanvasWidget]
  CanvasWidget canvas = new CanvasWidget(
    ".view-canvas", ".draw-canvas");
  // Create an instance of [BrushSelectorWidget]
  ToolSelectorWidget tools = new ToolSelectorWidget(
    ".tool-selector")
  ..onToolSelected.pipe(canvas);
  // Create and add tools to [ShapeSelectorWidget]
  tools.addTool(new Pen());
  tools.addTool(new Rectangle(), select:true);
  tools.addTool(new Line());
  tools.addTool(new Oval());
  // Create a stroke color selector
  new ColorSelectorWidget(".stroke_color_selector",
    ColorSelectedEvent.STROKE_COLOR, 'black')
  ..onColorSelected.pipe(canvas);
  // Create a fill color selector
  new ColorSelectorWidget(".fill_color_selector",
    ColorSelectedEvent.FILL_COLOR, 'aqua')
  ..onColorSelected.pipe(canvas);
  // Register a clear button listener
  querySelector(".clear-btn").onClick.listen((MouseEvent event) {
   canvas.clear();
  });
  // Register a preview button listener
  querySelector(".preview-btn").onClick.listen((MouseEvent event)
  {
    event.preventDefault();
    window.open(canvas.viewCanvas.toDataUrl("image/png"),
      "Image Preview");
  });
}
```

Now, let's discuss each component in order to better understand how they interact with each other.

# The CanvasWidget component

As mentioned earlier, the application uses two canvas components — one on top of the other. Both of them are available via selectors. When we create an instance of the `CanvasWidget` component, we pass these selectors as arguments of the constructor. This component references the `Tool` component that is used to draw. The code is as follows:

```
/**
 * Canvas widget listens for mouse events from [CanvasElement] to draw
 * with selected tool.
 */
class CanvasWidget implements StreamConsumer {

  CanvasElement _viewCanvas, _drawCanvas;

  CanvasElement get viewCanvas => _viewCanvas;
  CanvasElement get drawCanvas => _drawCanvas;
  CanvasRenderingContext2D get context => _viewCanvas.context2D;
  CanvasRenderingContext2D get drawContext => _drawCanvas.context2D;

  Tool _tool;

  /**
   * Create an instance of CanvasWidget. The [viewCanvasSelector] and
   * [drawCanvasSelector] need to find CanvasElements.
   */
  CanvasWidget(String viewCanvasSelector, String drawCanvasSelector) {
    // Find canvas elements
    _viewCanvas = querySelector(viewCanvasSelector);
    _drawCanvas = querySelector(drawCanvasSelector);
    // Add mouse event listeners
    _drawCanvas.onMouseDown.listen((evt) =>
      _tool.beginDraw(drawContext, offset(evt)));
    _drawCanvas.onMouseMove.listen((evt) =>
      _tool.drawing(drawContext, offset(evt)));

    var _finishDraw = (evt) {
      _tool.finishDraw(drawContext, offset(evt));
      copyContext();
    };

    _drawCanvas.onMouseUp.listen(_finishDraw);
    _drawCanvas.onMouseLeave.listen(_finishDraw);
  }
```

The user holds down the mouse button when he/she begins to draw. As a result, the onMouseDown listener invokes the beginDraw method of the Tool class. The drawContext method and the offset of the mouse coordinates are passed as parameters of this method. The drawing method of the Tool class is called every time the mouse is moved. Finally, the finishDraw method is called when the user releases the mouse button, and we call the local copyContext method to copy the content of the draw canvas to the view canvas. The CanvasWidget component implements the StreamConsumer interface via the addStream method to listen to two sorts of events, that is, ColorSelectedEvent from ColorSelectorWidget and ToolSelectedEvent from ToolSelectorWidget. The addStream method processes the incoming events, as shown in the following code:

```
/**
 * Copy drawn image from draw canvas into view context.
 * After all it clears the draw canvas.
 */
copyContext() {
  context.drawImage(_drawCanvas, 0, 0);
  _drawCanvas.context2D.clearRect(0, 0,
    _drawCanvas.width, _drawCanvas.height);
}

/**
 * Clear the view canvas
 */
clear() {
  context.clearRect(0,  0, _viewCanvas.width, _viewCanvas.height);
}

/**
 * Consumes the elements of [stream].
 * Listens on [stream] and does something for each event.
 */
Future addStream(Stream stream) {
  return stream.listen((event) {
    if (event is ColorSelectedEvent) {
      if (event.type == ColorSelectedEvent.STROKE_COLOR) {
        drawContext.strokeStyle = event.value;
      } else {
        drawContext.fillStyle = event.value;
      }
    } else if (event is ToolSelectedEvent) {
```

```
      _tool = event.tool;
   }
}).asFuture();
}
```

We use the `clear` method to wipe out the content of `_viewCanvas`.

# The ToolSelector widget

This component keeps the tool-based components and presents them in `SelectElement`. A tool-based component can be added via the `addTool` method, as shown in the following code:

```
class ToolSelectorWidget {
  SelectElement _selectElement;
  Tool selectedTool;
  Map<String, Tool> _tools = new Map<String, Tool>();

  Iterable<String> get toolsNames => _tools.keys;

  StreamController<ToolSelectedEvent> _toolSelectedController =
      new StreamController<ToolSelectedEvent>();
  Stream<ToolSelectedEvent> get onToolSelected =>
      _toolSelectedController.stream;

  ToolSelectorWidget(String selector) {
    _selectElement = querySelector(selector);
    _selectElement.onChange.listen((Event event) {
      selectTool(_selectElement.value);
    });
  }

  void addTool(Tool tool, {bool select: false}) {
    _tools[tool.name] = tool;
    OptionElement item = new OptionElement(
      data: tool.name, value: tool.name);
    _selectElement.append(item);
    if (select) {
      selectTool(tool.name);
    }
  }

  Tool getTool(String name) {
    if (_tools.containsKey(name)) {
      return _tools[name];
```

```
        }
        throw new Exception("Brush with $name not found");
    }

    selectTool(String name) {
        selectedTool = getTool(name);
        _toolSelectedController.add(new ToolSelectedEvent(selectedTool));
        _selectElement.value = selectedTool.name;
    }
}
```

When the user selects a new tool, this component generates a `ToolSelectedEvent` method with the selected tool instance as the parameter. The `StreamController` method is used to broadcast `ToolSelectedEvent` to any listener, that is, `CanvasWidget`.

# The ColorSelector widget

This widget is a port of `bootstrap-colorselector` to Dart. This component creates a drop-down color palette from a predefined set of colors only. We have set predefined colors for and via the HTML markup. Every time the user chooses a new color, the `StreamController` method broadcasts a `ColorSelectedEvent` event to the `CanvasWidget` class.

# The Tool class

Our application has an abstract `Tool` class to abstract the common behavior and properties of all the tool-based components, as shown in the following code:

```
/**
 * Abstract class defines common behavior and properties
 * for all tools.
 */
abstract class Tool {
    bool isDrawing = false;
    Point startPoint;

    String get name;

    void beginDraw(CanvasRenderingContext2D context, Point point) {
        isDrawing = true;
        startPoint = point;
    }
```

```
    void drawing(CanvasRenderingContext2D context, Point point);

    void finishDraw(CanvasRenderingContext2D context, Point point) {
      if (isDrawing) {
        drawing(context, point);
        isDrawing = false;
      }
    }
}
```

The `isDrawing` property reflects the status of the drawing operation.
The `startPoint` property simply holds the cursor coordinates relative to the canvas
when the user starts drawing on the canvas. The read-only property `name` returns the
name of the tool. This name is used when the tool is added to `ToolSelectorWidget`.
Each tool has three methods, and the whole drawing process is split into the
following three phases:

- **Start the drawing phase**: The program calls the `beginDraw` method when
  a user starts holding down the mouse button. We always switch on the
  `isDrawing` property and remember the cursor coordinates in `startPoint`.

- **Drawing phase**: The `drawing` method is called every time the user moves the
  cursor. Implementation of this method strongly depends on the tool, so we
  do not implement it in the abstract class `Tool`.

- **End the drawing phase**: The program invokes the `finishDraw` method
  when the user releases the mouse button. In this method, we need to call
  the `drawing` method for the last time and switch off `isDrawing` only if the
  drawing process has happened.

Now, it's time to look at our tools implementation in detail.

## The Pen tool

As the canvas element doesn't directly support drawing a single point, we use lines
instead. Drawing in a canvas is similar to using a virtual pen. At the beginning, we
must call `beginPath` of `context` where we begin drawing. This method creates a
new drawing path, so future drawing commands will be directed to the path and
will be used to build the path. We start our path by moving to the `startPoint`
coordinates with the `moveTo` method of `context`, as shown in the following code:

```
/**
 * Simple pen tool
 */
class Pen extends Tool {
```

```dart
  String get name => "Pen";

  @override
  void beginDraw(CanvasRenderingContext2D context, Point point) {
    super.beginDraw(context, point);
    context.beginPath();
    context.moveTo(startPoint.x, startPoint.y);
  }

  @override
  void drawing(CanvasRenderingContext2D context, Point point) {
    if (isDrawing) {
      context.lineTo(point.x, point.y);
      context.stroke();
    }
  }
}
```

Every time a user moves the mouse, the program calls the `drawing` method to connect our drawn path to next line's point with the `lineTo` method of `context`. Finally, it calls the `stroke` method to draw the shape by stroking its outline.

# The Line tool

The behavior of the **Line** tool is similar to that of the **Pen** tool, but with a different drawing logic. We only implement the `drawing` method of the `Tool` class to draw our shape in a path. A path is a list of subpaths, and each of them is a list of points that are connected by straight or curved lines. Each one also contains a flag that indicates whether it is closed, so the last point of the closed subpath is connected to the first point by a straight line, as illustrated by the following code:

```dart
/**
 * Line tool is used to create lines.
 */
class Line extends Tool {

  String get name => "Line";

  @override
  void drawing(CanvasRenderingContext2D context, Point point) {
    if (isDrawing) {
      context.clearRect(0, 0,
        context.canvas.width, context.canvas.height);
      context.beginPath();
```

```
         context.moveTo(startPoint.x, startPoint.y);
         context.lineTo(point.x, point.y);

         context.stroke();
         context.closePath();
      }
    }
  }
```

We must always clear the whole drawing canvas and start a new path via the beginPath method of context. We move the first point to the startPoint position and draw the line within the current cursor coordinates. Finally, we draw the line shape by stroking its outline and close the drawing path.

# The Rectangle tool

We can draw a rectangle with individual lines, but the **Rectangle** tool makes the task much easier. The context object has the following methods to draw rectangles:

- strokeRect: This method uses the current stroke style to draw the box that outlines the given rectangle onto the canvas

- fillRect: This method uses the current fill style to draw the given rectangle onto the canvas

- clearRect: This method clears all the pixels on the canvas in the given rectangle to transparent black

The easiest way to draw a rectangle on the canvas is use the fillRect method of context. The fillRect method uses color from the fillStyle property, black by default. The Rectangle class, as shown in the following code:

```
/**
 * Rectangle tool
 */
class Rectangle extends Tool {

  String get name => "Rectangle";

  @override
  void drawing(CanvasRenderingContext2D context, Point point) {
    if (isDrawing) {
      context.clearRect(0, 0,
        context.canvas.width, context.canvas.height);

      int x = min(point.x, startPoint.x).round(),
```

```
          y = min(point.y, startPoint.y).round(),
          w = abs(point.x - startPoint.x).round(),
          h = abs(point.y - startPoint.y).round();

      context.fillRect(x, y, w, h);
      context.strokeRect(x, y, w, h);
    }
  }
}
```

In the preceding code, we drew a rectangle with `fillRect` and finally called `strokeRect` to draw the border line shape by stroking its outline.

# The Oval tool

Drawing ovals is a breeze too. The easiest way to draw ovals is using the `arc` method of `context`. The `arc` method takes the following five parameters:

```
arc(x, y, radius, startAngle, endAngle, anticlockwise)
```

The `x` and `y` parameters are the coordinates of the center of the oval on which the arc should be drawn. The `radius` parameter is the radius of the oval. The `startAngel` and `endAngel` parameters define the start and end coordinates of the arc in radians, measured from the `x` axis along with the curve of the oval. Finally, the last parameter is `anticlockwise`, which tells the canvas to draw the arc anticlockwise. The code is as follows:

```
/**
 * This tool transforms a drawing context into a rectangle
 * enclosing the oval and uses the arc method to draw it.
 */
class Oval extends Tool {

  String get name => "Oval";

  @override
  void drawing(CanvasRenderingContext2D context, Point point) {
    if (isDrawing) {
      context.save();
      context.clearRect(0, 0,
        context.canvas.width, context.canvas.height);
      context.beginPath();

      var rx = (point.x - startPoint.x) / 2;
      var ry = (point.y - startPoint.y) / 2;
```

```
context.translate(startPoint.x + rx, startPoint.y + ry);

rx = abs(rx);
ry = abs(ry);
if (rx < ry)
{
    context.scale(1, abs(ry / rx));
    context.arc(1, 1, rx, 0, 2 * PI, false);
}
else
{
    context.scale(abs(rx / ry), 1);
    context.arc(1, 1, ry, 0, 2 * PI, false);
}

context.stroke();
context.restore();
    }
  }
}
```

First, we saved the current context's settings, cleared it, and started a new path. Then, we calculated the coordinates of the center of our oval and placed the result in rx and ry. After that, we moved the origin from (0, 0) to a new place via the translate method of context. For now, we took the absolute values for rx and ry so that we can draw an oval in different directions. Depending on the drawing direction, we can draw an oval by scaling it along the *x* or *y* axis. Finally, we draw the oval shape by stroking its outline and restored the parameters of context to prepare it for further use.

## How to clear the context

Many times, we try to clear the drawing context before we actually start to draw a new shape in the drawing context. So, now it's time to look at the following self-explanatory code from the CanvasWidget class that demonstrates how the view context can be cleaned:

```
/**
 * Clear the view canvas
 */
clear() {
  context.clearRect(0,   0,
    _viewCanvas.width, _viewCanvas.height);
}
```

# How to preview the context

If you need to preview the result of what you've done in the view canvas, you can open a new window with the content of the view canvas as shown here:

```
// Register a preview button listener
querySelector(".preview-btn").onClick
.listen((MouseEvent event) {
  event.preventDefault();
  window.open(canvas.viewCanvas.toDataUrl("image/png"),
    "Image Preview");
});
```

Now if you click on the **Preview** link, you will see the next result in a new window in your web browser, as shown in the following screenshot:

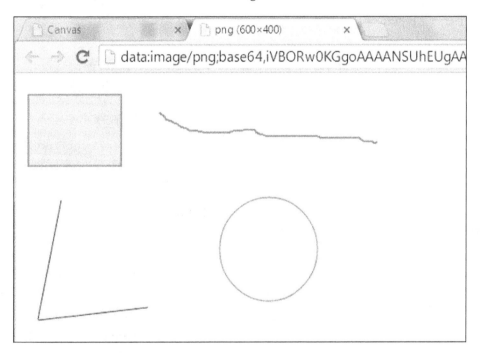

Here, we opened a new browser window with the image data URI directly and we could save it in the represented format. The data URI format shown in the address of the web browser is as follows:

```
data:[<MIME-type>][;charset=<encoding>][;base64],<data>
```

The toDataUrl method has an optional second parameter, quality. It represents the image quality in the range of 0.0 to 1.0 when the requesting type is image/jpeg or image/webp.

# Summary

To summarize, we will discuss the important facts about how to support other HTML5 features in Dart.

The web notification API allows you to display notifications outside the context of the web page. The user agent defines the best presentation of notifications, which depends on the location of the device. The web notification API is available as a part of the dart:html package and allows you to send information to a user even if the application is idle. When you build web applications, you can use the notification API in event handlers or polling functions to notify users.

Before you send any notifications to the user, the website must have permissions. Users can let websites send notifications automatically or with the permission request first. All the websites that request access to the notification API are added to the list of the notification exceptions. The constructor of the Notification class has optional properties that help you create notifications with the body and icon.

Dragging-and-dropping is a way to convert pointing device movements and clicks to special commands that are recognized by software to provide quick access to common functions of a program. Native drag-and-drop support in a browser means faster and more responsive web applications. Each drag event has a dataTransfer property that is used to hold data associated with a drag operation. The drop target is very important because most areas of the web page are not permitted to drop.

The geolocation API is a high-level interface used for location information. The API is device-agnostic of the underlying location source and is not affected by how the web browser determines a location. Using the Google Maps API with the geolocation API is very simple.

The HTML5 canvas is a fantastic feature that allows you to code programmatic drawing operations. It has become very popular because it allows you to create and manipulate imagery directly within web pages. It defines a context object that users can draw inside.

In the next chapter, we will discuss the different aspects of security. As a best practice, we will focus on validation input and escape and filter output data in our web applications.

# 12
# Security Aspects

In this chapter, we will talk about different aspects of security. You will learn about validation of user data input and security best practices in our web application. This chapter covers the following topics:

- Web security
- Securing a server
- Securing a client
- Security best practices

## Web security

Crime is a disease that plagues the minds of many individuals. Hackers are interested in everything from personal mailbox credentials to bank account details. The responsibility of maintaining security lies with web developers. Developers should use HTTPS to access web pages and resources with sensitive data.

## Transport Layer Security and Secure Socket Layer at a glance

**Secure Socket Layer (SSL)** is one of the most common protocols in use on the Internet today. SSL is capable of securing any transmission over TCP. The **Transport Layer Security (TLS)** protocol is a successor of SSL and is based on the older SSL specifications. TLS Version 1.0 was defined for the first time in January 1999 as an upgrade of SSL Version 3.0. Both of them are based on asymmetric keys to encrypt data and digital certificates for authentication through an untrusted third party. We use TLS in a client-server model, but the client usually does not provide a certificate. Instead, the server is responsible for its own authentication through signed certificates and encryption via public and private keys.

There are several versions of protocols used in web browsing, e-mail, internet faxing, instant messaging, and **Voice over IP (VoIP)**. TLS has the following benefits:

- It encrypts information
- It provides authentication
- It accepts credit card payments on websites
- It protects against phishing
- It adds power to brands and improves customer trust

Information submitted on the Internet passes through more than one node in the network before reaching the final destination, so it can be obtained by a third party. A TLS certificate inserts random characters into the original information to change it beyond recognition so that only the proper encryption key can help decrypt it. Server certification is another type of protection issued when the server's owner obtains a TLS certificate. This certificate is available to the client to validate that the TLS certificate is up to date and the client's information is being delivered to the right place. Online businesses that use credit card payments must be in compliance with the Payment Card Industry standards. This means that the server needs a TLS certificate with the proper encryption of at least 128 bits. Online businesses often offer site seals and other brand images to indicate that a trusted encryption is in use. This information gives customers an added level of assurance and creates trust between the customer and the business.

# The TLS certificate

It is really complicated to decide at which level we can address the TLS protocol in the TCP/IP stack. The TLS security protocol describes how algorithms should be used and how the TLS certificate establishes a secure connection. To get a certificate, you must create a **Certificate Signing Request (CSR)** on your server. This process creates a pair of private and public keys on your server. Then, you must send the CSR datafile that contains the public key to a **Certified Authority (CA)** in order to obtain the TLS certificate. The CA creates a data structure from the CSR file to match a private key in the future. The CA never sees the private key and it can't be compromised. Once you receive the TLS certificate, you can install it on the server. Dart uses the **Network Security Services (NSS)** library of Mozilla to handle TLS. We need to use certutil, a certificate database tool from NSS Security Tools, to manipulate the certificate database. You can obtain the source code and quickly build certutil for your platform, but I have installed the following prebuilt version of the program on my Ubuntu workstation:

```
sudo apt-get install libnss3-tools
```

The process of installation is successful and you can now check the result by running the program with the following command:

```
certutil
```

On receiving the request, the program returns information on how to use it and gives a list of available command options, as follows:

```
certutil - Utility to manipulate NSS certificate databases
Usage:  certutil <command> -d <database-directory> <options>
...
```

For now, we want to create a command-line application project with the name server in Dart Editor. Then, open the terminal and go into the bin directory of our project.

> In real life, you must obtain a real certificate from a CA such as Thawte, Entrust, and others.
>
> It is recommended to use self-signed TLS certificates for development and testing, but they are not recommended for production sites.

Follow the next steps to create a self-signed CA certificate for development and testing purposes inside the bin directory:

1. Create an NSS database in the pkcert folder. The folder name should be the name of the NSS database used on our server:

   ```
   mkdir -p pkcert
   certutil -N -d sql:/home/akserg/Project/server/bin/pkcert
   ```

   The -N command option creates a new certificate and key databases. Specify the prefix sql in front of the full path to the database folder as Dart uses the new SQLite database (cert9.db, key4.db, and pkcs11.txt) rather than a legacy security database (cert8.db, key3.db, and secmod.db). The certutil command will ask us to enter a password that will be used to encrypt our keys. Let's set the password to changeit.

2. Create a self-signed CA certificate with the following command:

   ```
   certutil -S -s "CN=CA Issuer" -n CACert -x -t "C,C,C" -v 120 -m
   1234 -d sql:/home/akserg/Project/server/bin/pkcert
   ```

The -s command option creates an individual certificate and adds it to a certificate database. The text after -s option provides a subject that identifies an owner of certificate. The -x option tells the certutil command that the created certificate is self-signed. The -v option sets the number of months for which a new certificate will be valid. The -m option sets a unique serial number to the certificate being created. When we run the certutil command, it asks us to press the keys on the keyboard to create a random seed that will be used in the creation of our key.

3. We now have a CA certificate and need to generate the key and certificate signing request. Let's do that with the following command:

```
certutil -R -s "CN=localhost, O=Mastering Dart, L=Cape Town,
ST=WC, C=CA" -p "+27 21 1234567" -o mycert.req -d sql:/home/
akserg/Project/server/bin/pkcert
```

The -R command option creates a certificate request file that can be submitted to a CA to be processed into a finished certificate. We specify the subject to identify the certificate owner; in this case, it's me. Extra information such as your telephone number can be an input as well. Output defaults to the output file marked with the -o option. When we run the certutil command, it asks for a password, and we can generate the key with a random seed again.

4. Now, we can see the list of keys in the database with the following command:

```
certutil -K -d sql:/home/akserg/Project/server/bin/pkcert
```

The result will be as follows:

```
< 0> rsa e22c881d9eb382ea69257410cf464dfedcd49354    NSS
Certificate DB:CACert
< 1> rsa b909266e0d5a14523158bfc7903ea9460fad2da6    (orphan)
```

5. We need to sign in the key with the following command:

```
certutil -C -m 2345 -i mycert.req -o mycert.crt -c CACert -
d sql:/home/akserg/Project/server/bin/pkcert
```

6. Finally, it's time to add a certificate to the database with the following command:

```
certutil -A -n localhost_cert -t "p,p,p" -i mycert.crt -d sql:/
home/akserg/Project/server/bin/pkcert
```

The name of our certificate is localhost_cert after the -n option.

7.  You can see the information about a specific certificate with the following command:

```
certutil -L -n localhost_cert -d
sql:/home/akserg/Project/server/bin/pkcert
```

The result is as follows:

```
Certificate:
    Data:
        Version: 3 (0x2)
        Serial Number: 2345 (0x929)
        Signature Algorithm: PKCS #1 SHA-1 With RSA
Encryption
        Issuer: "CN=CA Issuer"
        Validity:
            Not Before: Thu Aug 21 17:15:05 2014
            Not After : Fri Nov 21 17:15:05 2014
        Subject: "CN=Sergey Akopkokhyants,O=Mastering
Dart,L=Cape Town,ST=WC, C=CA"
        Subject Public Key Info:
            Public Key Algorithm: PKCS #1 RSA Encryption
    ...
```

8.  Alternatively, you can validate a specific certificate with the following command:

```
certutil -V -n localhost_cert -b 9803201212Z -u SR -e -l -d
sql:/home/akserg/Project/server/bin/pkcert
The result is as follows:
localhost_cert : Peer's Certificate has expired.
localhost_cert : Peer's certificate has been marked as not
trusted by the user.
```

Now that we are done with our self-signed certificate, it's time to go back to our server code and secure it.

# Securing a server

Open the `server.dart` file and type the following lines:

```
import 'dart:io';

main() {
  var pkcertDB = Platform.script.resolve('pkcert').toFilePath();
  SecureSocket.initialize(database: pkcertDB,
    password: 'changeit');

  HttpServer
    .bindSecure(InternetAddress.ANY_IP_V6, 8443,
      certificateName: 'localhost_cert')
    .then((server) {
      server.listen((HttpRequest request) {
        request.response.write('Hello, world!');
        request.response.close();
      });
    });
}
```

This is an implementation of the well-known `Hello, World!` example. I always keep the password of my certificate in the code only for demonstration purposes. Please keep your password in an external encrypted file. The code of the server is pretty straightforward. One small exception is that it references `SecureSocket` instead of the `Socket` class. By calling a static `initialize` method of this class, we initialize the NSS library. Now, we should organize binding with the static `bindSecure` method of `HttpServer` to create an HTTPS server. Let's run it and open the following URL in the Dartium web browser:

```
https://localhost:8443/index.html
```

All the magic, such as TLS handshaking, keys, and message exchange, happens behind the scenes. As our server's certificate is self-signed, a web browser informs us about that fact, as shown in the following screenshot:

Click on the **Certificate** information link to see the full certificate information, as shown in the following screenshot:

Now, close the warning message and click on the **Proceed anyway** button to see the result of the HTTP request:

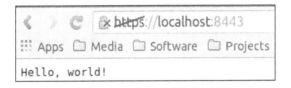

We were successful in achieving the following goals:

- We generated a self-signed certificate and registered it in the CA database
- Dart's HttpServer accepts the self-signed certificate and works with it
- The web browser shows the self-signed certificate information
- Client-to-server communication is granted

# Securing a client

We have prepared our server side to secure the communication, and now it's time to talk about the security of the client side of our web application. For all our content, we will start using secure communication with TLS and we will start updating our client side using cookies.

# Attributes of cookies

A cookie has two special attributes: Secure and HttpOnly. The Secure attribute of a cookie allows it to be sent only to the TLS connection. The other attribute, HttpOnly, marks the cookie that is accessible only via HTTP or HTTPS connections. Mark both of them as true and this small improvement in cookies prevents the web browser from sending a cookie via an insecure connection. With each request sent, the cookies are accompanied to follow the server inside headers. Let's check what we can improve in other headers.

# HTTP Strict Transport Security

The well-known SSL man-in-the-middle attacks can be safely fixed with a **HTTP Strict Transport Security (HSTS)** header sent from the server via the HTTP response header, which obliges the web browser to interact with the server through a secure HTTPS connection. The code is as follows:

```
Strict-Transport-Security: max-age=31536000; includeSubDomains
```

The server must specify the max-age option in seconds; this is the time for which the pages should be served with HTTPS. In our example, this value is equal to 365 days. The includeSubDomains option is optional and tells the web browser that all subdomains must be served with a secure connection as well. This header is supported in the following browsers:

- Firefox 4
- Chromium and Google Chrome 4.0.211.0
- Safari 7
- Opera 12
- Internet Explorer in the next major release after IE 11

# Content Security Policy

The web application security model is based on the same-origin policy principle. The origin is a combination of schema, hostname, and port number. The policy permits us to download and run scripts from the same origin. As time has shown, this policy may be broken very easily and quickly with **Cross Site Scripting (XSS)** or data injection attacks. **Content Security Policy (CSP)** is an added layer of security. It allows the web server to define the origin of each resource by securing the website and mitigates and reports on XSS attacks. Blocking all the inline scripts and styles can prevent the execution of code injected in comments or posts. CSP is backward compatible, so web browsers that don't support it still work using the standard same-origin policy.

The web browser assumes that all origins are allowed if a directive is not set. CSP can be set via an HTTP response header on a server or an HTML meta tag on a web page, as shown in the following code:

```
Content-Security-Policy: policy
```

The `policy` string is the one that contains the policy directives describing CSP with semicolon separation as source of whitelists.

 Not all web browsers support HTML meta elements to configure a policy.

The policy should include the `default-src` or `script-src` directives. This has the following advantages:

- This restricts inline scripts from running
- This blocks the use of the `eval` function
- This restricts inline styles from being applied from a `style` element or the `style` attribute of an element

The inline JavaScript code includes the `eval` function; hence, the JavaScript URLs will not be executed. You need to slightly change your mind about development with CSP. Here is an example of restricting all the content that comes only from the site's own domain and subdomains:

```
Content-Security-Policy: default-src 'self' *.mydomain.com
```

The following example shows how to restrict all the content from being loaded via a secure connection:

```
Content-Security-Policy: default-src https://ibank.mydomain.com
```

In the following example, we will allow all the assets to be loaded from our site and scripts from the Google API server:

```
Content-Security-Policy: default-src: 'self'; script-src: https://apis.
google.com;
```

We created the `csp` project to see how CSP works. The server-side code is a slightly modified version of the server code from the previous topic, and it includes the `route` library, as shown in the following code:

```
import 'dart:io';
import 'dart:async';
import 'package:route/server.dart';
import 'urls.dart';
```

```dart
import 'files.dart';

main() {
  var pkcertDB = Platform.script.resolve('pkcert').toFilePath();
  SecureSocket
  .initialize(database: pkcertDB, password: 'changeit');

  HttpServer
  .bindSecure(InternetAddress.ANY_IP_V6, 8443,
      certificateName: 'localhost_cert')
  .then((server) {
    new Router(server)
    ..filter(allUrls, filter)
    ..serve(allUrls).listen(serveDirectory('', as: '/'))
    ..defaultStream.listen(send404);
  });
}

Future<bool> filter(HttpRequest request) {
  HttpResponse response = request.response;
  response.headers.add("Content-Security-Policy",
  "default-src 'self'; style-src 'self'");
  return new Future.value(true);
}
```

We now use a `filter` method of the `Route` class to intercept each request and inject the `Content-Security-Policy` header in response, as shown in the following screenshot:

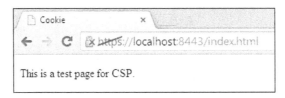

From the content of our header, it should be clear that all the scripts and styles from our website are permitted. Let's imagine a use case where you need to add a Google +1 button to your web application to allow users to recommend the content to their circles and drive traffic to your website, so simply include a +1 button on the web page via a JavaScript resource and add a +1 button tag. The script must be loaded using the HTTPS protocol. Here is the code of the changed web page:

```html
<!DOCTYPE html>
<html>
```

```html
<head>
  <meta charset="utf-8">    <meta name="viewport"
    content="width=device-width, initial-scale=1">
  <title>Cookie</title>
  <script type="text/javascript"
    src="https://apis.google.com/js/plusone.js"></script>
  <link type="text/css" href="index.css">
</head>
<body>
  <p>This is a test page for CSP. <g:plusone></g:plusone></p>
</body>
</html>
```

Let's run the server and open the modified web page in Dartium. In a moment, you will receive the following CSP violation message about loading an untrusted script:

```
Refused to load the script 'https://apis.google.com/js/plusone.js' because it
violates the following Content Security Policy directive: "default-src 'self'". Note
that 'script-src' was not explicitly set, so 'default-src' is used as a fallback.
                                                                    index.html:1
```

To make the **+1** button work, you need to add different policies to the server code to allow trusted resources on your web page, as shown in the following code:

```dart
Future<bool> filter(HttpRequest request) {
  HttpResponse response = request.response;
  response.headers.add("Content-Security-Policy",
    "default-src 'self';" +
    "style-src 'self' 'unsafe-inline';" +
    "script-src 'self' https://apis.google.com;" +
    "frame-src https://*.google.com;" +
    "img-src https://*.gstatic.com;"
  );
  return new Future.value(true);
}
```

The result of the preceding code is as follows:

CSP is very flexible and useful when it is used properly. This header is supported by the following browsers:

- Chrome 25 (from v14 with the prefix `webkit`)
- Firefox 23 (from v4 with the prefix `moz`)
- Safari 7 (from v5 with the prefix `webkit`)
- Opera 15
- Internet Explorer 10 only supports the `sandbox` directive with the prefix `ms`

# Cross Origin Resource Sharing versus JSON with padding

**JSON with padding (JSONP)** is a client-side technique used to request data from a server in a different domain. This is possible because web browsers do not enforce the same-origin policy on the HTML `script` tag. The parameters of the JSONP request are passed as arguments to a script. The format of a JSONP result is different from the format of JSON, so the server must know how to respond to it. JSONP supports only the GET request method and accepts the callback function as the recipient of data, as shown in the following code:

```
<script src="http://my.com/data?format=jsonp&callback=cb"></script>
```

A web browser will call a `cb` function at the end of the request. With this script, we will get the JavaScript code and the web browser will run it as a normal script file. This could be a big risk because the server from which we are getting this script could be compromised and easily cause an XSS attack. **Cross-origin resource sharing (CORS)** can be used as a modern alternative to JSONP, which allows cross-domain communication from the web browser. As opposed to JSONP, CORS supports all the HTTP methods and allows you to do the following tasks:

- Make an AJAX request, but in a cross-site manner
- Load web fonts for use in `@font-face` within CSS
- Load WebGL textures
- Load images drawn on a canvas with the help of the `drawImage` method

CORS headers must be returned in the header of the requested web server. To initiate a cross-origin request, we need to add new HTTP headers that allow the web browser to communicate freely with the API on another domain. The `cors` project contains two servers. The first one, located in the `server.dart` file is a web server listening to the secure connection on port `8443` from our previous topic, as shown in the following code:

```dart
import 'dart:io';
import 'dart:async';

import 'package:route/server.dart';

import 'urls.dart';
import 'files.dart';

main() {
  var pkcertDB = Platform.script.resolve('pkcert').toFilePath();
  SecureSocket
  .initialize(database: pkcertDB, password: 'changeit');

  HttpServer
  .bindSecure(InternetAddress.ANY_IP_V6, 8443,
      certificateName: 'localhost_cert')
  .then((server) {
    new Router(server)
    ..filter(allUrls, filter)
    ..serve(allUrls).listen(serveDirectory('', as: '/'))
    ..defaultStream.listen(send404);
  });
}

Future<bool> filter(HttpRequest request) {
  HttpResponse response = request.response;
  response.headers.add("Content-Security-Policy",
    "default-src 'self';" +
    "style-src 'self' 'unsafe-inline';" +
    "script-src 'self' https://apis.google.com;" +
    "frame-src https://*.google.com;" +
    "img-src https://*.gstatic.com;"
  );
  return new Future.value(true);
}
```

The second server, located in cors_server.dart, is the CORS web server listening on port 8080 and is not using HTTPS, as shown in the following code:

```dart
import 'dart:io';
import 'dart:async';

import 'package:route/server.dart';

import 'files.dart';

final allUrls = new RegExp('/(.*)');
final productUrl = new UrlPattern('/product');

main() {
  HttpServer
  .bind(InternetAddress.ANY_IP_V6, 8080)
  .then((server) {
    new Router(server)
    ..filter(allUrls, filter)
    ..serve(productUrl).listen(serverProduct)
    ..defaultStream.listen(send404);
  });
}

Future<bool> filter(HttpRequest request) {
  return new Future.value(true);
}

serverProduct(HttpRequest request) {
  return serveFile('products.json')(request);
}
```

The function filter in the second web server intends to set the header with CORS and allows any client to make cross-domain requests to this server. Our client will now look like the following code:

```dart
import 'dart:html';
import 'dart:convert';

void main() {
  onloadHandler();
}

onloadHandler() {
  var xhr = new HttpRequest();
```

```
xhr.open('GET', 'http://localhost:8080/product', async:true);
xhr.onLoad.listen((e) {
  Map repos = JSON.decode(xhr.response);
  var reposHTML = "";
  for (int i = 0; i < repos["repositories"].length; i++) {
    reposHTML += "<p>" +
        repos["repositories"][i]["name"] + "<br>" +
        repos["repositories"][i]["description"] + "</p>";
  }
  document.getElementById("allRepos").setInnerHtml(reposHTML);
}).onError((e) {
  print('error making the request. ${e.toString()}');
});
xhr.send();
}
```

The client code makes a cross-domain request and prints the markup with the result. Let's run both the servers and open our web page in Dartium on the address `https://localhost:8443/index.html`. It immediately comes with the cross-domain violation exception, as shown in the following screenshot:

```
⊗ Refused to connect to 'http://localhost:8080/product' because it violates the
  following Content Security Policy directive: "default-src 'self'". Note that
  'connect-src' was not explicitly set, so 'default-src' is used as a fallback.
                                                                  index.html:1
```

Let's add `connect-src` in the following server code for a quick fix:

```
Future<bool> filter(HttpRequest request) {
  HttpResponse response = request.response;
  response.headers.add("Content-Security-Policy",
    "default-src 'self';" +
    "style-src 'self' 'unsafe-inline';" +
    "script-src 'self' https://apis.google.com;" +
    "frame-src https://*.google.com;" +
    "img-src https://*.gstatic.com;" +
    "connect-src http:/localhost:8080/product"
  );
  return new Future.value(true);
}
```

Restart the server and refresh the web page, and you will get the following exception:

```
⊗ XMLHttpRequest cannot load http://localhost:8080/product. No 'Access-Control-
  Allow-Origin' header is present on the requested resource. Origin
  'https://localhost:8443' is therefore not allowed access.          index.html:1
```

Our request cannot pass the border of origins, so we will change the `filter` method in the CORS web server, as follows:

```
Future<bool> filter(HttpRequest request) {
  HttpResponse response = request.response;
  response.headers.add("Access-Control-Allow-Origin", "*");
  return new Future.value(true);
}
```

The preceding code will give the following result:

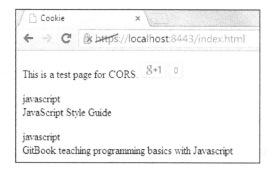

This was a simple demonstration of how we can use CORS on data provided by the web server. Dartium sends an initial request to the CORS server with an `Origin` HTTP header that matches the origin of our web page, as shown in the following screenshot:

We intend to specify `Access-Control-Allow-Origin` in the CORS server to allow all domains and a server-sent response with an asterisk symbol (*), as shown in the following screenshot:

This pattern is widely used to organize accessible resources by anyone who knows the secret. The asterisk symbol is special as it tells the web browser that it doesn't allow requests without the following credentials:

- HTTP authentication
- Client-side SSL certificates
- Cookies

In order to include the credentials from the preceding list, you can use the other CORS header as follows:

```
Future<bool> filter(HttpRequest request) {
  HttpResponse response = request.response;
  response.headers.add("Access-Control-Allow-Origin", "*");
  response.headers.add("Access-Control-Allow-Credentials",
    "true");
  return new Future.value(true);
}
```

It works in conjunction with the credentials on `HttpRequest`, as shown in the following code:

```
var xhr = new HttpRequest();
xhr.open('GET', 'http://localhost:8080/product');
xhr.withCredentials = true;
...
```

It will also include any cookies from a remote domain in the request.

> Do not set the `Access-Control-Allow-Credentials` header if you don't want to include cookies in the CORS request.

The CORS server can set any header, but the `getResponseHeader` method of the `HttpRequest` class can read only the following simple headers:

- `Cache-Control`
- `Content-Language`
- `Content-Type`
- `Expires`
- `Last-Modified`
- `Pragma`

If you need access to other headers, you must expose them via the `Access-Control-Expose-Headers` header as follows:

```
Future<bool> filter(HttpRequest request) {
  HttpResponse response = request.response;
  response.headers.add("Access-Control-Allow-Origin", "*");
  response.headers.add("Access-Control-Expose-Headers",
    "session-id");
  response.headers.add("session-id", "123456");
  return new Future.value(true);
}
```

We added a `sessionId` span element to the web page as follows:

```
<p>This is a test page for CORS. <g:plusone></g:plusone></p>
  Session ID: <span id="sessionId"></span>
<div id="allRepos"></div>
```

The following web page source code was updated as well:

```
var xhr = new HttpRequest();
xhr.open('GET', 'http://localhost:8080/product');
xhr.onLoad.listen((e) {
  var sessionId = xhr.getResponseHeader("session-id");
  document.getElementById("sessionId").text = sessionId;
```

Now, restart the CORS server and reload the web page to get the following result:

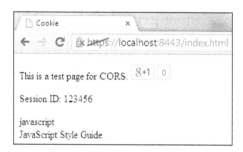

CORS is supported across the following well-known web browsers:

- Chrome 3
- Firefox 3.5
- Opera 12
- Safari 4
- Internet Explorer 8

# CAPTCHA

**Completely Automated Public Turing test to tell Computers and Humans Apart** (**CAPTCHA**) is a program whose main purpose is differentiating a human from a machine. Actually, CAPTCHA is a reverse Turing test because it is administrated by a computer. It is a barrier that prevents bots from using web services or collecting certain types of sensitive information. One of the ways of using CAPTCHA in Dart is using the free service reCAPTCHA of Google, so I decided to create a project with a sensible name, captcha, that contains one web page for user registration. We can follow several simple steps to add the reCAPTCHA solution into our project, but first we need to sign up for the API keys for our website with the following steps:

1.  Visit https://www.google.com/recaptcha and click on the **Get reCAPTCHA** button, as shown in the following screenshot:

2.  On the **Get reCAPTCHA** page, click on the **Sign up Now!** button and type your web server name in the **Domain** field, as shown in the following screenshot:

You can type as many domain names as you need; just separate them with commas. You can also use localhost or 127.0.0.1 as the name of your server, because all the API keys work on it and you can develop and test your solution on your local machine.

3.  Click on the **CREATE** button to create new API key. The server move you to the list of your domains, as shown in the following screenshot:

4.  Choose your domain to see the following details:

localhost

| | |
|---|---|
| Domain Name: | localhost |
| | reCAPTCHA will work on these domains and subdomains. |
| Public Key: | 6Lc8a_kSAAAAABk-6joEQu_wurhopTGt4xCPndnX |
| | Use this in the JavaScript code that is served to your users |
| Private Key: | 6Lc8a_kSAAAAAB49Z1belTOeM2e3SDmPG4ZvXVNL |
| | Use this when communicating between your server and our server. Be sure to keep it a secret. |
| | Delete these keys |

There are public and private keys that we will use in our solution. To integrate the reCAPTCHA solution in the captcha project, we used the small library recaptcha created by me and which is available on the https://pub.dartlang.org/ server. So, we can add it in the pubspec.yaml file under the dependencies packages. Open the captcha project in Dart Editor and navigate to index.html, which is shown in the following code:

```
<!DOCTYPE html>
<html>
  <head>
    <title>Registration</title>
    <meta charset="utf-8">
    <meta name="viewport"
      content="width=device-width, initial-scale=1">
```

```
      <link type="text/css" href="index.css">
   </head>
   <body>
     <H1>Registration form with CAPTCHA</H1>
     <form name="captcha_form" method="post" action="/register">
       <label for="username">Username:</label>
       <input type="text" name="username"><br>
       <label for="password">Password:</label>
       <input type="password" name="password">
       <script type="text/javascript"
         src="http://www.google.com/recaptcha/api/challenge?k=6Lc8a_
kSAAAAA
Bk-6joEQu_wurhopTGt4xCPndnX">
       </script>
       <noscript>
         <iframe src="http://www.google.com/recaptcha/api/
noscript?k=6Lc8a_kSAAAAAB
k-6joEQu_wurhopTGt4xCPndnX"
           height="300" width="500" frameborder="0"></iframe><br>
         <textarea name="recaptcha_challenge_field" rows="3"
           cols="40"></textarea>
         <input type="hidden" name="recaptcha_response_field"
           value="manual_challenge">
       </noscript>
       <button type="submit" value="Submit">Submit</button>
     </form>
   </body>
</html>
```

Copy and paste the public key of the domain registered on reCAPTCHA as the
parameter for JavaScript and the parameter for the source of the iframe tag. You
need to change these values for your public key. Now, let's open the server.dart
file and move to line **10** where we created an instance of the ReCaptcha class. Again,
copy and paste a pair of private and public keys of your domain here so that the
class instance can pass them via the free service reCAPTCHA on Google in order
to ensure that the sender is correct and has a registered domain, as shown in the
following code:

```
...
final ReCaptcha reCaptcha = new ReCaptcha(
  '6Lc8a_kSAAAAABk-6joEQu_wurhopTGt4xCPndnX', // public key
  '6Lc8a_kSAAAAAB49Z1belTOeM2e3SDmPG4ZvXVNL'); // private key
```

Then, create a map of the error code and human-readable text as shown in the following code:

```
final Map MESSAGES = {
    'invalid-site-private-key':'Incorrect private key',
    'invalid-request-cookie':'The challenge parameter of the verify
script was incorrect',
    'incorrect-captcha-sol':'The CAPTCHA solution was incorrect',
    'captcha-timeout':'The solution was received after the CAPTCHA
timed out',
    'recaptcha-not-reachable':"Unknown error in CAPTCHA"};
```

Then, read the POST method parameters in the serverRegister function and convert them into a map to easily access them later. All the parameters follow the reCAPTCHA verification via the checkAnswer method of ReCaptcha, as shown in the following code:

```
serveRegister(HttpRequest request) {
  HttpResponse response = request.response;
  request.listen((List<int> buffer) {
    String strBuffer = new String.fromCharCodes(buffer);
    Map data = postToMap(strBuffer);
    //
    String userName = data.containsKey('username') ?
      data['username'] : '';
    String password = data.containsKey('password') ?
      data['password'] : '';
    String cptChallenge =
      data.containsKey('recaptcha_challenge_field') ?
      data['recaptcha_challenge_field'] : '';
    String cptResponse =
      data.containsKey('recaptcha_response_field') ?
      data['recaptcha_response_field'] : '';
    reCaptcha.checkAnswer(request.uri.host, cptChallenge,
cptResponse).then((ReCaptchaResponse cptResponse) {
      response.statusCode = HttpStatus.OK;
      setCORSHeader(response);
      if (cptResponse.valid) {
        response.write("Registration success.");
      } else {
        response.write(MESSAGES[cptResponse.errorCode]);
      }
      response.close();
    });
  });
}
```

In the `setCORSHeader` function, add the CORS headers to allow the POST requests from the cross-origin web resources as follows:

```
setCORSHeader(HttpResponse response) {
  response.headers.add('Access-Control-Allow-Origin', '*');
  response.headers.add('Access-Control-Allow-Methods', 'POST,
OPTIONS');
  response.headers.add('Access-Control-Allow-Headers',
      'Origin, X-Requested-With, Content-Type, Accept');
}
```

Let's run the server and open `http://localhost:8080/index.html` in Dartium to get the following result:

Try to input a wrong CAPTCHA solution and submit the form. After submitting it, you will see the following error message:

Let's go back quickly and type the correct CAPTCHA solution. After submitting, you will see the following success message:

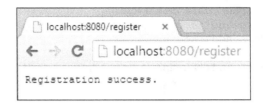

# Security best practices

It's time to discuss the best security practices, without which this story would not be complete:

- **Do not retain the password**: The HTTP basic authentication is deprecated, so use other techniques such as OAuth to make a more secure application following standards. Use safe OAuth tokens instead of passwords.

- **Perform the input validation**: You should always sanitize all input data. You need to check string length, validate file types, and check the minimum and maximum values to be sure that all the data sent to the server via the POST request is in the proper format and length.

- **Filter input and sanitize output**: You should always filter all the data that comes from the client to the web server and sanitize all the data coming back to the client.

- **Use a secure connection**: Use the TLS certificate to organize a secure connection between the web browser and server to provide all REST APIs or AJAX requests over TLS. TLS in conjunction with OAuth is a safe and suggested solution.

- **Do not expose the debug information**: Don't forget to switch off the debug logs because they can contain sensitive information.

- **Test boundaries**: Your tests must check all the possible positive and negative cases and scenarios.

- **Hide the server information**: Don't display the server information on any server-generated documents as this will allow hackers to select the right kind of hack from the hacks that are either available freely on the web or developed by hackers themselves.

# Summary

In this chapter, you learned how to create a TLS certificate with NSS tools. You saw that the certificate can be quickly embedded into a Dart web server without extra effort on the developer's part.

We discovered how to secure the client side with the `Secure` and `HttpOnly` special attributes of cookies to prevent the web browser from sending cookies via an insecure connection.

We used HSTS to prevent SSL man-in-the-middle attacks. We applied CSP to make sure that only allowed content can be loaded and used by the web browser. We also used CORS to specify what resources from our web server can be shared and why that solution is much better than JSONP. Finally, we embedded the CAPTCHA solution based on the free service reCAPTCHA from Google in our project.

# Index

effects, using 174, 175
example project 171, 172
invoking, by JProxy 170, 171
method call 170
method call, need for 169
performance, impacts 176-178
shortcut, creating with 169
version, getting 172, 173
**JsArray 159**
**JsFunction 158, 166, 167**
**JsObject**
about 156-158
and instantiation 165, 166
factory JsObject.fromBrowserObject(object)
157
factory JsObject(JsFunction constructor,
[List arguments]) constructor 157
factory JsObject.jsify(object) constructor 157
**JSONP (JSON with padding)**
versus CORS 300-306

# K

**key principles, globalized software**
about 181
executable, versus User Interface 182

# L

**last property 127**
**lastWhere method 129**
**Lazy Iterable**
about 132
benefits 133
**left-to-right (LTR) 191**
**length property 127**
**libraries**
about 9-12
private members 10
public members 10
**Line tool 283, 284**
**LinkedHashMap class 149, 150**
**LinkedHashSet class 144**
**LinkedList class**
about 140, 141
advantages 141

disadvantages 141
**link operation 261**
**List class 137-140**
**ListQueue class 146**
**locale**
changing 183
**Local storage 240-242**
**log variable 64**
**longLasting method 217**
**longPolling function 219**

# M

**main function**
moving to 276, 277
**Map class**
about 147
HashMap class 148
LinkedHashMap class 149, 150
SplayTreeMap class 150, 151
**map method 130**
**Media Access Control (MAC) 202**
**message_function function 183**
**MessageLookup class 198**
**message method 182**
**messages**
extracting 195
internalizing 187, 188
**messages_all.dart file 198**
**method call 74, 75**
**method call, JProxy**
need for 170
**methods**
and operators 26
parameter values, checking 26-28
selecting 28
well-designed methods 28, 29
**Microtask**
and Future class 83
**Mirrors**
advantages 50
URL 50
**mixins**
about 20, 21, 127
and classes 17

## Thank you for buying
# Mastering Dart

## About Packt Publishing

Packt, pronounced 'packed', published its first book "*Mastering phpMyAdmin for Effective MySQL Management*" in April 2004 and subsequently continued to specialize in publishing highly focused books on specific technologies and solutions.

Our books and publications share the experiences of your fellow IT professionals in adapting and customizing today's systems, applications, and frameworks. Our solution based books give you the knowledge and power to customize the software and technologies you're using to get the job done. Packt books are more specific and less general than the IT books you have seen in the past. Our unique business model allows us to bring you more focused information, giving you more of what you need to know, and less of what you don't.

Packt is a modern, yet unique publishing company, which focuses on producing quality, cutting-edge books for communities of developers, administrators, and newbies alike. For more information, please visit our website: www.packtpub.com.

## About Packt Open Source

In 2010, Packt launched two new brands, Packt Open Source and Packt Enterprise, in order to continue its focus on specialization. This book is part of the Packt Open Source brand, home to books published on software built around Open Source licenses, and offering information to anybody from advanced developers to budding web designers. The Open Source brand also runs Packt's Open Source Royalty Scheme, by which Packt gives a royalty to each Open Source project about whose software a book is sold.

## Writing for Packt

We welcome all inquiries from people who are interested in authoring. Book proposals should be sent to author@packtpub.com. If your book idea is still at an early stage and you would like to discuss it first before writing a formal book proposal, contact us; one of our commissioning editors will get in touch with you.

We're not just looking for published authors; if you have strong technical skills but no writing experience, our experienced editors can help you develop a writing career, or simply get some additional reward for your expertise.

## Easy Web Development with WaveMaker

ISBN: 978-1-78216-178-3        Paperback: 306 pages

A practical, hands-on guide for amateur developers to design, develop, and deploy web and mobile applications using WaveMaker

1. Develop and deploy custom, data-driven, and rich AJAX web and mobile applications with minimal coding using the drag-and-drop WaveMaker Studio.

2. Use the graphical WaveMaker Studio IDE to quickly assemble web applications and learn to understand the project's artifacts.

3. Customize the generated application and enhance it further with custom services and classes using Java and JavaScript.

## HTML5 Web Application Development By Example Beginner's Guide

ISBN: 978-1-84969-594-7        Paperback: 276 pages

Learn how to build rich, interactive web applications from the ground up using HTML5, CSS3, and jQuery

1. Packed with example applications that show you how to create rich, interactive applications and games.

2. Shows you how to use the most popular and widely supported features of HTML5.

3. Full of tips and tricks for writing more efficient and robust code while avoiding some of the pitfalls inherent to JavaScript.

Please check **www.PacktPub.com** for information on our titles

www.ingramcontent.com/pod-product-compliance
Lightning Source LLC
Chambersburg PA
CBHW062057050326
40690CB00016B/3118